Terrorism for Self-Glorification

IN FLAMMIS FAMA PARATVR

EMBLEMA. 55.

Llega el furor de la ambiciosa fama,
A tanto estremo, que el que la apetece,
No mira si se honra, o si se infama,
O si por ello gana, o desmerece:
El Ephesino templo el otro imflama,
Cuyo nombre, con gran razō merece,
Que pues le pretendio tan locamente,
Le sepulte el oluido eternamente.

Vn

Terrorism for Self-Glorification

The Herostratos Syndrome

ALBERT BOROWITZ

The Kent State University Press
Kent and London

© 2005 by The Kent State University Press, Kent, Ohio 44242
ALL RIGHTS RESERVED
Library of Congress Catalog Card Number 2004017495
ISBN 0-87338-818-6
Manufactured in the United States of America

09 08 07 06 05   5 4 3 2 1

LIBRARY OF CONGRESS CATALOGING-IN-PUBLICATION DATA
Borowitz, Albert, 1930–
    Terrorism for self-glorification : the herostratos syndrome / Albert Borowitz.
       p. cm.
    Includes bibliographical references and index.
    ISBN 0-87338-818-6 (hardcover : alk. paper) ∞
    1. Terrorism. 2. Violence—Psychological aspects. 3. Aggressiveness.
4. Herostratus. I. Title.
HV6431.B692 2004
303.6'25—dc22   2004017495

British Library Cataloging-in-Publication data are available.

In memory of Professor John Huston Finley, who,
more than half a century ago,
first told me about the crime of Herostratos.

Contents

Acknowledgments   ix

Author's Note   x

Introduction   xi

1 The Birth of the Herostratos Tradition   1

2 The Globalization of Herostratos   20

3 The Destroyers   36

4 The Killers   71

5 Herostratos at the World Trade Center   111

6 The Literature of Herostratos Since the Early Nineteenth Century   123

Afterword   159

Appendix: Herostratos in Art and Film   160

Notes   162

Index   184

Acknowledgments

FIRST AND FOREMOST my thanks go to my wife, Helen, who has contributed immeasurably to *Terrorism for Self-Glorification,* providing fresh insights into Joseph Conrad's *The Secret Agent,* guiding me through mountains of works on modern terrorism, and reviewing my manuscript at many stages. I am also grateful to Dr. Jeanne Somers, associate dean of the Kent State University Libraries, for her ingenuity and persistence in locating rare volumes from the four corners of the world.

Except as otherwise indicated in the endnotes, all translations from foreign languages are my own. When I bumped up against my linguistic barriers, Alex Cook and Markku Salmela came to my rescue, translating Japanese and Finnish sources, respectively. I am also indebted to the distinguished Turkish author, Nazli Eray, for procuring me an English version of her early Herostratos play. I also wish to thank the many authors who generously provided copies of their works relating to my themes. Among their number I cite notably the dramatists Carl Ceiss and Lutz Hübner, mystery writer Horst Bosetzky ("-ky"), and scholars Katariina Mustakallio and Kerry Sabbag.

Finally, I acknowledge with gratitude the advice of Classics professors David Lupher of the University of Puget Sound and Thomas Martin of the College of the Holy Cross on the meaning of Herostratos's name and other knotty issues.

Author's Note

IN SPELLING MY protagonist's name "Herostratos," I am transliterating the ancient Greek original. Variant spellings appear in other languages:

Latin	Herostratus
English	Herostratus (or sometimes Eratostratus)
French	Érostrate
German	Herostrat
Italian	Erostrato
Portuguese	Heróstrato
Spanish	Eróstrato

Spellings used in directly quoted passages have not been altered. In spelling other ancient names, I adopt the form most commonly encountered in my sources; e.g., Ephesus.

Introduction

AN IMPORTANT STRAND in the history of terrorism is Herostratic crime. This phenomenon, consisting of a violent act or series of violent acts motivated in whole or in part by a craving for notoriety or self-glorification, can be traced from the destruction in 356 BC of one of the Seven Wonders of the Ancient World, the Temple of Artemis at Ephesus, by the arsonist Herostratos. The man identified in ancient sources as Herostratos is a shadowy figure of whose life nothing is known before he was apprehended, tortured, and executed. The death penalty was accompanied by a postmortem sentence of the type that came to be known in Latin as *damnatio memoriae,* the damnation of the condemned man's memory through the imposition of a ban on the mention of his name. Soon after the death of the temple destroyer this prohibition was flouted by Classical authors; through the ages and around the world the terrible name of Herostratos became paradigmatic of the morbid quest for eternal fame through crimes of violence. New attacks made against lives and monuments seemed to be motivated by personal vanity, whatever high-sounding phrases the criminal might launch in justification. Writers who tried to understand these puzzling outbreaks of murder and destruction often invoked Herostratos as an archetype.

The recognizable features of these crimes for fame, and the commentaries that these acts have inspired, make it possible to attempt a definition of what can be called the "Herostratos syndrome":

1. Herostratos and his followers share a desire for fame or notoriety as long lasting and widespread as can be achieved. This desire may be appeased

by publicity for the criminal's name but often, preferring to elude detection by retaining anonymity, he is satisfied with the celebrity that arises from his act. These alternative or combined means of gratification, publicity for the name or for the crime, reflect the same underlying Herostratic impulse, that is, a drive to maximize a sense of power. The criminal feels an enhancement of power in the form of self-glorification (the achievement of name recognition) or self-aggrandizement (the demonstration of capacity for destruction through accomplishment of a flaunting act that will live in infamy). Herostratic violence may be perpetrated by a person acting alone or in conjunction with others who may or may not share his thirst for fame.

2. The aim of the crime is to cause the public to experience panic, distress, insecurity, or loss of confidence.

3. A famous person, property, or institution is often chosen as victim or target. As the Roman essayist Valerius Maximus observed in his discussion of searchers after negative fame, a killer may hope, by his attack, to absorb the celebrity of his prey—to be known, for example, as "the man who assassinated Philip of Macedon." The same mechanism operates in arsonists and other destroyers of well-known monuments, such as the Temple of Artemis.

4. A feeling of loneliness, alienation, mediocrity, and failure may trigger an envy directed against those perceived to be more successful or prestigious. Envy is exacerbated by an ambitious, competitive spirit and the conviction that avenues to success are unfairly blocked.

5. The Herostratic criminal may be afflicted by self-destructive compulsions: to confess; to taunt or to more overtly aid the police who pursue him; and to commit suicide or suffer death either in the course of the crime or by execution. Since his ultimate goal is glory, the remnant of the criminal's life becomes contemptible as a value in itself; it is a pawn to be traded for accomplishment of his motive.

6. Herostratic violence may acquire a sacrilegious dimension when the criminal strikes a religious shrine or a secular target that has iconic significance.

7. The craving for fame may combine with other motives, personal and/or ideological, in inducing a criminal act.

In November 2001, *Ego-net,* a German Web site commenting on the "age-old phenomenon of terrorism," referred to Herostratos as "the first terrorist who entered history."[1] This claim appears to be justified because the nature of the crime at Ephesus satisfies most of the criteria of the definition of terrorism espoused by a leading expert on modern terrorist activity, Walter Laqueur, who has written in the wake of the attack on the World Trade Center, "Over the centuries, terrorism has appeared in many guises. It is not an ideology or a political doctrine, but rather a method—the substate application of violence or the threat of violence to sow panic and bring about political change."[2] Laqueur's definition would fit perfectly the outrages of Herostratos and his followers, except that their need for self-glorification is satisfied by causing public panic or dismay, whether or not any of these criminals may also seek or avow a purpose to effect political change. In an earlier work, in fact, Lacqueur referred to Herostratos's motive as a common factor in the "new" terrorism: "Many terrorist acts are committed by individuals following in the footsteps of Herostrat [*sic*], the citizen of Ephesus in ancient times who burned the local temple simply so that his name would be remembered forever."[3]

In *Terrorist Lives* (1994), Maxwell Taylor and Ethel Quayle express their belief that "a core element in any account of terrorism is that it involves the use of violence to achieve political ends." Yet their analysis of terrorist groups in Ireland, Europe, and the Middle East, based on interviews with their members, reveals significant convergences of modern terrorists' motivations with those of the politically unaligned Herostratic criminal. The ideologically committed terrorists whom Taylor and Quayle have studied appear to act under the influence of a commitment even more fundamental than political allegiance—belief in the "just-world phenomenon":

> This is a widely recognised feature of our interpretation of the world as it impinges on us. We like to think that virtue is rewarded, that a hard working life should result in a comfortable retirement, that those who cheat or steal to our disadvantage are ultimately caught. . . . In one way, many terrorists and their supporters would claim that what they do is a response to an *unjust* world. . . .
>
> The sense of a "just world" seems to lie at the very heart of the social and psychological response to political violence of both terrorists and their victims.[4]

Taylor and Quayle theorize that "the individual terrorist's justification for terrorism is . . . related at a fundamental psychological level to a sense of purpose and self-worth." This association leads them to come to grips with the unjust world:

It [terrorism] is, at least initially, a means to achieve something which is intrinsically desirable and important to the person involved. That desirability may relate to nationalist or political aspirations, but as far as the person is concerned, its attainment will result in a better world, either for the individual or for his community. Seeking for " . . . *a place in the sun* . . ." or some similar phrase has occurred more than once in interviews about this subject.[5]

Although there is no evidence as to what impelled Herostratos to destroy the Temple of Artemis, speculation began even in ancient times that the instant fame that he sought through crime arose from a perceived injustice: he was deprived, through no fault of his own, of the talent and opportunity required to achieve a reputation for merit. The resentment of inadequacy or failure was increasingly emphasized as the tradition of Herostratos was elaborated over more than two millennia and his crime became regarded as setting the pattern for other attacks continually made against famous monuments and persons. Like many political terrorists, Herostratos and his successors appeared dedicated to the destruction of an unjust world.

The modern terrorist is also closely akin to Herostratos in his passion for media attention. Taylor and Quayle have observed:

Whatever else terrorism might be, it is a highly effective means of gaining attention in the media; indeed, the amount of attention is positively correlated with the severity of a terrorist attack. . . .

The former British Prime Minister, Margaret Thatcher, referred to "the oxygen of publicity" as being a vital requirement for the sustenance of a terrorist organization, and there is a clear recognition on the part of all sides that terrorism is a war largely fought in the media.[6]

Media attention does not, however, merely serve the purpose of publicizing and advancing the goals of a political cause, but also may appease the desires of individuals at the summit or base of the terrorist organization for personal stardom. The terrorist's achievement of fame carries with it an intoxicating sense of empowerment such as Herostratos felt when the temple's fire leapt up to the night sky of Ephesus. Alberto Franceschini of the Italian Red Brigades avowed the thrill of media celebrity:

My distinct feeling was that I was really making a deep mark on the reality of the country, and this sensation was given to me by the newspapers and magazines, through the mass media. When you do certain things, and these things turn into big paragraphs in the papers; and when you see that because of the things you explode, fights and chaos happens [sic] between the politicians; all this summed up gave me a sensation of great power. It gives you the feeling of being powerful.[7]

The videotape of Osama bin Laden that recorded for broadcast his rejoicing in the destruction of the World Trade Center seemed at least as much designed to satisfy the al-Qaeda leader's desire for self-aggrandizement as to spread terror or recruit killers. The elusive Osama does not seem bent on surrendering his life for the cause, but even suicide bombers may be moved, like Herostratos, by a wish to enhance and perpetuate their own sense of importance. Avishai Margalit, in her article "Suicide Bombers," argues that the Palestinian terrorists' self-sacrifice may now be encouraged less by the "idea of winning a place in paradise" than by the prospect of living on in human memory:

> If it is easy to question whether being a *shahid* [martyr] secures an immediate entrance to paradise, no one can doubt that being a *shahid* secures instant fame, spread by television stations like the Qatar-based al-Jazeera and the Lebanon-based al-Manar, which are watched throughout the Arab world. Once a suicide bomber has completed his mission he at once becomes a phantom celebrity. Visitors to the occupied territories have been struck by how well the names of the suicide bombers are known, even to small children.[8]

Even when the international media may not give them their due, the suicide bombers can count on leaving a visual and documentary record in their own communities: "The aspiring martyr is told to write last letters to his family and friends. He is photographed in a heroic pose. He makes a video explaining why he is becoming a martyr."[9] The reinforcement of ideological goals by the personal wish for fame links these bombers with such Herostratic predecessors as Luigi Lucheni; when this self-professed "anarchist" assassinated Empress Elisabeth of Austria in 1898, he gloried in his front-page prominence.

Allied as they are by perception of injustice and attraction to publicity, it is by no means certain that the ideological terrorist and the Herostratic criminal can be distinguished by psychological profiling. While acknowledging that "the psychological forces that result in the development of the terrorist are complex and obscure," Taylor and Quayle conclude that "there seems to be no discernible pathological qualities of terrorists that can identify them in any clinical sense as different from others in the community from which they come. . . . Violence and brutality may characterise the criminal, yet, as with the terrorist, we would be unlikely to place the criminal within the category of clinical abnormality."[10]

Despite Walter Laqueur's rather cursory suggestion that Herostratos and criminals in his mold belong among the "deranged,"[11] it is striking that, with the principal exception of German Expressionist Georg Heym, virtually none of the writers who have produced imagined portraits of Herostratos through the ages present him as insane. He is, instead, a man who has become a menace because he believes that life has cheated him.

It should be further noted that, under American criminal law, Herostratic criminals may be prosecuted as terrorists, for a political dimension is not a prerequisite to a finding of an act of terrorism. American criminal statutes recognize that terrorism may have the objective of intimidating the public rather than an aim to influence governmental policy. In the year following the September 11 attack, at least thirty-three states amended their criminal codes to address the enhanced threat of terrorism. Many of the legislative enactments followed federal law by defining "act of terrorism" as a violent felony intended *either* to intimidate or coerce a civilian population *or* to influence or affect governmental policy or conduct.[12]

Terrorism for Self-Glorification: The Herostratos Syndrome is the first detailed examination of the history and literature of Herostratos and his followers. This book has three principal purposes:

1. Description of the birth of the Herostratos tradition in the Hellenistic era and its spread throughout the world over more than two millennia.
2. Identification and analysis of criminal cases in which the desire for fame in the mode of Herostratos has been or can persuasively be suggested as a contributing motive. The wide-ranging cases of destruction and killing to be cited include the attempted explosion of England's Greenwich Observatory in 1894; the 1950 burning of Kyoto's Temple of the Golden Pavilion, which is the subject of Yukio Mishima's novel of the same name; the Taliban's destruction of the giant Buddhas in Afghanistan; the demolition of the Stari Most (Old Bridge) in Mostar, Bosnia-Herzegovina; the assassination of a royal, Empress Elisabeth of Austria; the celebrity killing of John Lennon; some American political assassinations; the Unabomber; and the Columbine High School Massacre. Many of these cases have inspired explicit comparisons with Herostratos, either in contemporaneous

reportage or subsequent literature. A separate chapter will be devoted to commentators who have recognized Herostratos's pertinence to the attack on the World Trade Center.

3. A critique of the principal works of literature that are either based on the life or tradition of Herostratos or contain illuminating references to his crime. Among the authors considered are Cicero, John of Salisbury, Chaucer, Montaigne, Cervantes, Sir Thomas Browne, Lord Byron, Victor Hugo, Gustave Flaubert, Jean-Paul Sartre, André Glucksmann, Alessandro Verri, Fernando Pessoa, Miguel de Unamuno, Sigmund Freud, and Mark Twain. Many genres, such as fiction, poetry, drama, philosophy, essays, and journalism, are discussed with particular emphasis on literature since the beginning of the nineteenth century, when the world's interest in Herostratos began to intensify, perhaps as a result of Romantic authors' interest in crime themes.

Like the Cain and Abel myth, the Herostratos tradition is remarkable for "the extraordinary longevity and variousness of its appeal."[13] The rich imaginative literature that has clustered around the sketchy early accounts of the Ephesian arson deepens our understanding of criminal instincts driven by a hunger for fame. New aspects of the strange compulsion are revealed as time passes and brilliant writers continue to turn to the Herostratic conundrum. The Roman essayist Valerius Maximus, for example, was the first to detect the link between the destruction of an iconic building and the assassination of a prominent leader, both crimes being intended to absorb instantly the fame of the target. The Greek satirist Lucian revealed a new facet of Herostratos's psychological malady when he emphasized its fundamentally suicidal character. It remained for Mark Twain to look beneath avowed political motivation for the assassination of an empress to discover the morbid passion for infamy. Further surprises date from our own time. A decade before the World Trade Center attack, Stephen Sondheim and John Weidman's musical *Assassins* (1991) reminded us, if we were listening, that a human mind obsessed with fame had, during President Nixon's administration, conceived the idea of hijacking a jetliner for the purpose of crashing into the White House.[14]

1 The Birth of the
Herostratos Tradition

AT FIRST GLANCE, the two antagonists appear to have been mismatched—Herostratos, an arsonist of obscure origins, and the goddess Artemis, one of the most powerful deities in ancient Greek worship. The man's identity is shrouded in mystery except for the name that history attributes to him. It is a name drawn from Greek roots, and although Classicists debate its meaning, the elements of which it is formed seem to predict a nobler destiny than lay in wait for Artemis's enemy. The word *stratós* means "army" in ancient Greek, and scholars have suggested that the male appellation "Herostratos" may be translatable as "army-hero" or, alternatively, as an "army devoted to Hera," wife of Zeus.[1] The ancient Greeks customarily bestowed only one name on a child, often making a choice that was etymologically associated with a god; the firstborn son was generally named after his paternal grandfather.[2] History, unfortunately, tells us nothing about the arsonist's family and it is by no means clear whether the name by which we know him was his at birth or later came to personify him in the course of the remarkable oral and written tradition that he inspired.

It is plain, at least, that the name Herostratos was not uncommon in the Greek world. An earlier man bearing this name established a shrine to Aphrodite in his home city of Naucratis, a treaty port in Egypt, after a narrow escape from disaster at sea. Despite the tarnish brought to the name by the arsonist, we find a Herostratos among the trusted lieutenants of Brutus, who sent him on a mission to Macedonia in 44 BC to win the support of the military commanders there, following the assassination of Julius Caesar.[3]

Because of the vastness of the Greek-speaking world, Herostratos's name provides no clue to his place of birth or residence. Writers have sometimes assumed that he must have been a citizen of the predominantly Greek-populated city of Ephesus (near the modern town of Selçuk inland from the western coast of Turkey) where he perpetrated his famous crime. This supposition, however, does not give adequate weight to the far range of Hellenistic seafaring or to the large numbers of noncitizens residing in Greek city-states in the fourth century BC;[4] it is with greater insight into the ease of Aegean travel and diversity of urban populations that Alessandro Verri, in writing the first Herostratos novel, makes his antihero a native of Corinth.[5] Another void left by the historical record is Herostratos's occupation and position in society. Imaginative literature has variously presented him as a poet, an artisan, or a jack-of-all-trades, but ancients and moderns alike are prone to visualize him as a failure—lonely, unrecognized, and bitter.

The object of Herostratos's malice, Artemis (worshiped in Rome as Diana) was the daughter of Zeus and the Titaness Leto; she was the elder twin sister of Apollo, whom she miraculously helped her mother deliver on the ninth day of labor. Among the Olympians, Artemis is particularly notable for her versatility and her ambivalent roles as a sustainer and destroyer of life. A virgin deity who hunted game, particularly deer, she tried her silver bow when still young, choosing as targets two trees, "a wild beast, and a city of unjust men."[6] Despite her love of the chase, she is often represented in images as a "mistress of the animals" whose young she protects. According to one of the two Homeric Hymns in her honor, Artemis, in the company of her brother Apollo, also took pleasure in the gentler arts of music and dance:

> Yet when the archeress tracker of beasts has had pleasure enough
> From the hunt and has gladdened her mind, she unstrings her flexible bow
> And goes to her brother's great home, to Phoibos Apollo's abode
> In Delphi's rich land, to prepare for the Muses' and Graces' fair dance.
> She hangs up there with its arrows her bow that springs back from the pull,
> And wearing graceful adornments takes the lead in the dance.
> The goddesses, raising their heavenly voices, sing a hymn
> Of fair-ankled Leto, and tell how she gave her children birth,
> Who are in both counsel and deeds the best of immortals by far.[7]

Rites of passage are another of the goddess's special interests; she guides young girls to womanhood and is sometimes concerned with male rituals of transition to maturity. Despite her jealously guarded maiden state, Artemis has important maternal functions, easing the pains of childbirth as she had done for her own mother, and assuring human and animal fertility. As a goddess of the moon and its phases, she is intimately connected with women's monthly cycles. The moonlight was flattering to Artemis but from time to time she smelled the kill. Without warning she then turned fearsome as a dealer of sudden death to women in labor as well as to men who offended her, such as Actaeon, whom she turned into a stag and had torn apart by his own pack of fifty hounds after he had committed the impropriety of seeing her naked.[8]

In Ephesus, on the Ionian coast of western Asia Minor, Artemis assumed traits of the great mother goddess worshiped as Cybele in a temple at a site near modern Ankara. The cult statues in the Ephesus Museum emphasize the fecundity of the Ephesian Artemis: "Although the nodes on her chest were once thought to be breasts, it has become apparent that they represent the testes of bulls sacrificed for her."[9] This powerful divinity not only made the countryside flourish but also caused the important port and trading center of Ephesus to thrive under her patronage.

The origins of early settlements in western Asia Minor are hazy. Greek legend fancifully regarded the Amazons, redoubtable female warriors from far reaches of the ancient world, as the first inhabitants of Ephesus, and the claim of Athens to have colonized all the cities on the Ionian coast is also disputed. The Ephesians from their beginnings devoted themselves to the worship of Artemis. Successive versions of her temple (called the Artemision) were situated in a marshy plain about a mile to the northeast of the town, near the hill of Ayasoluk; as the shrine grew in magnificence it came to be ranked among the Seven Wonders of the Ancient World. Philo of Byzantium, a scholar and engineer who described the Seven Wonders in a text written in Alexandria, Egypt, in about 225 BC, ecstatically praises the Artemision: "The Temple of Artemis at Ephesus is the only house of the gods. Whoever looks will be convinced that a change of place has occurred: that the heavenly world of immortality has been placed on the earth."[10]

Selahattin Erdemgil, director of the Ephesus Museum, attributes the construction of the magnificent Archaic Artemision in the early sixth century BC to intercity rivalry. Just before 570 BC construction of a widely admired Temple of Hera was completed in Samos. The competitive Ephesians engaged the

Cretan architect Chersiphron and his son Metagenes to design a great shrine to Artemis that would outshine the Samians' achievement. The construction of the new Artemision (which, according to Pliny the Elder, "occupied all Asia Minor for 120 years") was in progress when King Midas of Lydia occupied Ephesus in about 561 BC and placated its citizens by contributing generously to the project. Midas's beneficence may also have had the political objective of establishing worship of Artemis as a state religion to replace cults supported by powerful local clans. The temple, built almost entirely of marble and in accordance with the Ionic order, was of unusually large dimensions (380 by 180 feet, according to Director Erdemgil) that dwarfed those of the Parthenon. Two rows of columns surrounded the temple on its four sides. Pliny, who visited the later Hellenistic temple built at a higher elevation on the same design, counted 127 columns in all; thirty-six of the columns were carved with reliefs. The eight-column western facade of the building afforded a fine prospect of the city and harbor. Museum director Erdemgil refers to a calculation that "the architraves supported by the columns weighed twenty-four tons," and adds: "Considering the equipment available then, it is difficult to comprehend how such heavy pieces could be lifted twenty metres and placed on the columns. The people believed that Artemis herself came and placed the architrave on the columns."[11] In fact, Pliny informs us, the architect Chersiphron achieved this marvel "by filling bags of plaited reed with sand and constructing a gently graded ramp which reached the upper surfaces of the capitals of the columns." Lying under some fifteen feet of alluvial deposit, the site of the Archaic Temple and its successor (the Hellenistic Temple) was identified in 1870 as a result of excavations conducted by architect John Turtle Wood on behalf of the British Museum.[12] In ancient times the site had been on the seaboard but the land has moved a few miles westward as a result of silt accumulation in the Caystros River.

In 356 BC the Temple of Artemis that King Croesus had sponsored was burnt to the ground. The story of the catastrophe, as pieced together from the surviving ancient sources, can be quickly retold: The temple is said to have been destroyed on the same night (most likely July 20 or 26)[13] on which Alexander the Great was born. The fire, which caused widespread shock and lamentation in Ephesus, was attributed to arson committed by Herostratos, who was promptly arrested. Placed upon the rack, he confessed that he had conceived the crime to satisfy his appetite for fame. With the purpose of foiling his objective, the Ephesians, in addition to ordering the execution of Herostratos, adopted a decree banning the mention of his name.

Although in most respects the traditional narrative of Herostratos's crime cannot be confirmed from nonliterary sources, archeological finds have uncovered physical proof that the Archaic Artemision was, indeed, destroyed by fire. Anton Bammer and Ulrike Muss, successive directors of the ongoing Austrian excavations of the site, report their evidence with jubilation: "This is one of those rare cases in which the historical report is archeologically verifiable, since many of the sculptured column drums and pedestals as well as the *sima* frieze [under the temple's eaves] show traces of a fire."[14] John and Elizabeth Romer have surmised that Herostratos may have succeeded in setting the temple ablaze by torching its "enormous timber roof."[15]

The surviving literary works from which the crime and its aftermath have been reconstructed were produced over a period of more than 250 years; the first of them appeared three centuries after Herostratos's death, and thus it hardly furnishes fresh historical evidence. With only one exception, the authors treated their subject anecdotally or by way of illustration of a religious or moral precept and therefore seized only on isolated details that suited their narrative or stylistic purposes. The earliest source to come down to us can be found in a passage on the manifold activities of the goddess Diana (Artemis) in Cicero's On the Nature of the Gods (*De Natura Deorum*), a philosophical work that he composed in 45 and 44 BC, the last years of his life. Noting the identification of the goddess with the light-bringing and wide-wandering moon, he explains that she was called Diana "because she made a sort of *day* in the night-time." The invocation of her assistance at the birth of children was due to the equivalence of "occasionally seven, or more usually nine, lunar revolutions" to the period of gestation. This consideration led Cicero to pass along a clever observation made, as he recalled, by Greek historian Timaeus (ca. 356–260 BC), about Diana/Artemis's conflicting duties on the night of her Ephesus temple's destruction: "Timaeus in his history with his usual aptness adds to his account of the burning of the temple of Diana of Ephesus on the night on which Alexander was born the remark that this need cause no surprise, since Diana was away from home, wishing to be present when Olympias [Alexander's mother] was brought to bed."[16]

In his supplementary treatise, On Divination, Cicero mentioned again the simultaneity of Herostratos's fire and Alexander's birth. Relating these twinned events to his subject of divination, he also referred to the delirium of Asian magi over the portents to be read into the Ephesian calamity: "Everybody knows that on the same night in which Olympias was delivered of Alexander the temple of Diana at Ephesus was burned, and that the magi began to cry out as the day was breaking: 'Asia's deadly curse was born last night.'"[17] The curse would be fulfilled, of course, when the newborn Alexander became Asia's conqueror.

Plutarch (ca. 46–after 120 AD), in his life of Alexander, also adopted the tradition that stated Herostratos's arson and Alexander's birth both occurred on the same date. He retold the joke about Artemis's preference of midwifery to fire fighting but cited Hegesias of Magnesia as the author of "the conceit, frigid enough to have stopped the conflagration." He sounds a more somber note, however, in recalling the despair of visiting Asian magi over the loss of the holy sanctuary: "And all the Eastern soothsayers who happened to be then at Ephesus, looking upon the ruin of this temple to be the forerunner of some other calamity, ran about the town, beating their faces, and crying that this day had brought forth something that would prove fatal and destructive to all Asia."[18]

Both Cicero and Plutarch, in the passages cited, continued to honor the decree suppressing mention of the arsonist's name; their texts, in fact, do not disclose that the fire was willfully set. Some earlier writers, however, had already ignored the ancient prohibition against mentioning the name of the arsonist. Transgressors against the Ephesian ban on memory followed the lead of Theopompus of Chios, a Greek historian (born ca. 378 BC) who was living at the time of the fire but has left posterity only fragments of his works, an account of the last years of the Peloponnesian War (*Hellenica*) and a world history beginning with the accession of Philip of Macedon (*Philippica*). The first extant work to name Herostratos as the arsonist is the *Geography* of Strabo (64/63 BC–21 AD at least), who in the course of describing the history of the Artemision, noted: "But when it [the temple] was set on fire by a certain Herostratus, the citizens erected another and better one, having collected the ornaments of the women and their individual belongings, and having sold also the pillars of the former temple. Testimony is borne to these facts by the decrees that were made at that time."[19]

A Roman historian during Emperor Tiberius's reign, Valerius Maximus, published around 31 AD his *Memorable Doings and Sayings* (*Factorum ac dictorum memorabilium libri*), a collection of illustrative examples for citation by rhetoricians. One of his entries, entitled "Of Appetite for Glory," may be the first self-standing essay to cite Herostratos's case as an example of the pursuit of negative fame through a criminal act. After beginning his discourse with references to the laudable (though self-seeking) inclination of military commanders to immortalize authors who have celebrated their victories, Valerius progressively veers toward repellent examples of quests for glory:

Alexander's "insatiable" appetite for fame, and Aristotle's small-minded insistence on literary credit. As the pitch of his sermon rises in intensity, Valerius refers to "the design of those who in their desire to be remembered forever did not scruple to gain notoriety even by crimes." He refers first to the assassination of Philip of Macedon by Pausanias, who, having asked Hermocles "how he could suddenly become famous," was advised that "if he killed an illustrious man that man's glory would redound to himself." To crown his admonitions, Valerius turns from the celebrity killing of Philip to the sacrilegious violence of Herostratos against a famous shrine. Perhaps sardonically, he credits Theopompus's "eloquent genius" as prompting the earlier historian to overlook the Ephesian decree (although Valerius purported to approve the ban as "wisely" imposed). For the only time in known ancient sources, Valerius also refers to Herostratos's confession under torture:

> Here is appetite for glory involving sacrilege. A man was found to plan the burning of the temple of Ephesian Diana so that through the destruction of this most beautiful building his name might be spread through the whole world. This madness he unveiled when put upon the rack. The Ephesians had wisely abolished the memory of the villain by decree, but Theopompus' eloquent genius included him in his history.[20]

Two other Roman authors mention Herostratos by name. One of the moralizing animal fantasies of Aelian (Claudius Aelianus), a *pontifex* assisting in public rites at Praeneste near Rome (170–235 AD), suggests that Herostratos should be classed with enemies of the gods. In his *On the Characteristics of Animals,* the author praises Black Sea mice that pay reverence to Hercules on an island named for the god: at the maturity of the grapes preserved for sacrifices, the rodents prefer to quit the island rather than touch the sacred fruit even involuntarily. Aelian contrasts the reverent mice with two atheists, Hippon and Diagoras, "and Herostratus, and all the rest in the tale of heaven's enemies, how would they have kept their hands off the grapes or other offerings—men who preferred by one means or another to rob the gods of their names and functions."[21]

A longer historical perspective of the Artemision's destruction is established in the geographical summary, *The Excellent and Pleasant Work* (*Collectanea Rerum Memorabilium*), written by Gaius Julius Solinus after 200 AD. Solinus notes the paradox that the temple was earlier spared by ravages of Xerxes's wars only to fall victim to the lone arsonist:

The beauty of Ephesus is the Temple of Diana, built by the Amazons, such a royal piece of work, that when Xerxes set fire on all the temples of Asia, this one alone he spared.

But this gentleness of Xerxes exempted not this holy church utterly from that misfortune, for one Herostratus to the intent (to purchase himself an everlasting fame by his mischievous deed) did set this noble piece of work on fire with his own hands, and when he had done it, confessed it to win himself a continual name.[22]

The geographer, after noting that the temple was burned on the day that Alexander the Great was born in the Macedonian capital of Pella, ended his account of the temple on the happy note that "the Ephesians afterward repaired it, more beautiful and stately than it was before."

The earliest surviving text to cite Herostratos's example as illuminating a later act of violence is *The Passing of Peregrinus,* a mocking reportage by the Greek satirist Lucian (ca. 120–after 180 AD). This work, in the form of a letter to a friend, Cronius, invokes the precedent of Herostratos's impious arson to elucidate the self-immolation of Peregrinus shortly after the close of the Olympic Games of 165 AD. At the previous Olympiad four years before, Peregrinus had cannily whetted his public's anticipation by preannouncing his intentions. In his narrative of the suicide, which he witnessed, Lucian depicts Peregrinus as a parricide, adulterer, pederast, and sham preacher, actuated throughout his life by a love of notoriety. After a short-lived conversion to Christianity, Peregrinus returned to his earlier profession as a Cynic philosopher. Taking his cue from Brahman suicides, Peregrinus, before Lucian's eyes, threw himself onto a pyre he had built in a pit about six feet deep, at Harpina, twenty furlongs from the sacred precincts of Olympia. Intended to be awe-inspiring, the end of the sixty-year-old Peregrinus filled Lucian with contempt. In a speech delivered by an unnamed speaker (probably Lucian himself) prior to the Cynic's fatal leap, the fire at Ephesus is recalled: "But you have heard, no doubt, that long ago a man who wished to become famous burned the temple of Ephesian Artemis, not being able to attain that end in any other way. He himself [Peregrinus] has something similar in mind, so great is the craving for fame that has penetrated him to the core."

Lucian was not swayed by Peregrinus's asserted humanitarian motive and feared the baleful influence that his act would have on those inclined to criminal conduct: "He alleges, however, that he is doing it for the sake of his fellow men, that he may teach them to despise death and endure what is fearsome. For my part, I should like to ask, not him but you, whether you would wish malefactors to become his disciples in this fortitude of his, and to despise death and burning and similar terrors."[23] In these exhortations, Lucian seems prescient of realities we face again: that desire for personal glory cannot be disguised by ideological catchwords or ennobled by suicide; and that it is dangerous to inspire the ill-intentioned to regard death and burning as trifles.

After these Classical literary sources for Herostratos's biography have been arrayed and summarized, several key questions require further reflections:

First

What was the motive or combination of motives that led Herostratos to burn the Artemision? The ancients concurred that Herostratos was moved by a craving for a fame that would be infinite in time ("everlasting fame," in Solinus's words) and/or in space ("spread through the whole world," according to Valerius Maximus). His plan to achieve such glory through crime is a distortion of what C. M. Bowra has termed the "heroic outlook" of the ancient Greeks. Bowra defines the essence of the heroic outlook as the "pursuit of honour through action."[24] The heroic ideal highly valued military valor in service of the city-state, and the deeds of the brave were celebrated as enduring beyond the tomb. Bowra argues that the Greeks' "vague and uncertain" thoughts about physical survival in the afterworld made the notion of perennial glory "a consolation for the shadowy doom which awaited them in the grave."[25] Similar comfort was drawn by great poets from the prospects of lasting fame for "work that sheds a special radiance on the subjects which it celebrates," and "in [poetry's] ability to outlive themselves they saw something akin to the unageing security of the gods."[26] For bravery or literary radiance Herostratos had substituted an act of devastation that was rendered memorable by its unprecedented and heinous character. As Valerius Maximus observed, Herostratos had expanded the range of violent crime by adding the element of sacrilege. To Valerius, however, another factor was at play that singularizes crimes against a famous person or institution—a process through which the attacker absorbs and wears as his new identity the celebrity of his target.

Although the desire for lasting fame is the mainspring that tradition attaches to Herostratos's arson, other contributing motives have also been hinted or postulated. Lucian may have been the first to suggest that Herostratos was actuated by envy and a sense of mediocrity or failure, when the author commented in passing that the arsonist had burnt the Artemision to obtain fame, "not being able to attain that end in any other way." Lucian's supposition that Herostratos lacked the talent or resolve to attain fame by constructive endeavors finds confirmation in the fact that to all the ancient historians who mention the fire, the arsonist is a nobody. Apart from his name, all the historical sources, considered together, tell us nothing of the man he was when he turned to crime; after he was arrested, horrified Ephesians probably wondered who he was and what he had done in life.

Miguel de Unamuno has asserted that envy lies at the base of the Herostratic impulse (see chapter 6). Professor Gregory L. Ulmer, in his monograph *The Legend of Herostratus: Existential Envy in Rousseau and Unamuno*, theorizes that Herostratos envied the newborn Alexander and, to support this hypothesis, recreates the scene when the arson was instantaneously conceived:

> We may imagine, then, that on that evening in 356 BC, as Herostratus passed by the familiar temple, runners from the court of Philip of Macedon were announcing the birth of the prince for whom great things were prophesied. The thought of this child, born into all the advantages of life and predestined for glory, made Herostratus reflect despairingly on his own frustrated ambitions, made him rage against his anonymity, mortality, mediocrity. So, after sharing in the many jugs of wine passed about amongst the revelers toasting the King's good fortune, Herostratus took a torch from a passing procession and went into the temple, there to light a fire which is the image of the passion of envy, as well as of fame.[27]

This scenario presents us with obvious difficulties of time and place. How could Philip's runners have traveled so quickly from Pella, the Macedonian capital, to Ephesus to announce a birth that was reportedly simultaneous with the arson? And why would Ephesians revel because a foreign prince had been born? More likely, Herostratos's envy would have been aroused by men with whom he had vied or who were better placed than he in Ephesian society.

Several other hypotheses might contribute to an understanding of the extraordinary crime. Herostratos's resentment against the prosperous city of Ephesus as a whole may have turned vengeful. In attacking the city's most beautiful and famous monument, he surely dealt a blow to the Ephesians' urban pride and their sense of security. Alternatively, the arsonist's wrath may have been directed against the temple itself rather than targeting the entire Ephesian community. The mysterious incendiary's attraction to sacrilege and his enmity to the gods were underlined by both Valerius Maximus and Aelian;

perhaps prayers that he had made to Artemis or other deities had gone un-heeded or he had other reasons to have lost faith in divine providence.

Finally, the operation of self-destructive drives cannot be ruled out. The crime of nocturnal arson, such as Herostratos had perpetrated, is not easy to solve, and none of the ancient sources suggests that Herostratos made any at-tempt to escape or to elude arrest. Indeed, the very satisfaction of his hunger for fame required that he be apprehended and proclaim his responsibility.

Second

What meaning should be attached to the supposed occurrence of the fire on the same night as the birth of Alexander the Great? A thread of the Herostratos tradition is that the arson occurred on the same date (or night, as Cicero specifies) as the birth of Alexander the Great. It is difficult to know whether either Cicero or Plutarch took this legendary detail seriously; they both men-tioned the remarkable coincidence only as an excuse for citing a Greek historian's skeptical joke that a goddess much in demand cannot be in two places at the same time. Another possibility is that the suggested concurrence of the two events is only a reflection of the inclination of Classical writers to arrange history in geometric patterns, the same cast of mind that led Plutarch himself to couple his biographies as parallel lives even if the similarities that he identified were sometimes far-fetched. Hermann Bengtson refers to the dating of Herostratos's crime as "probably only a 'fable of simultaneity,' of which there are many examples in ancient and modern times."[28]

Another conceivable foundation for the link of arson with a hero's birth was the ancients' perception of history's irony: the date of a crime under-taken by a mediocrity to achieve fame was rendered memorable instead as the birthday of a great conqueror and empire builder. This hypothesis would, however, be easier to accept if the name and deeds of Herostratos had fallen into oblivion as his judges intended, and if his successors in crime had not remained active to the present day.

For Sigmund Freud, the link between the fire and Alexander, far from serv-ing a literary function, provided a mythic confirmation of his theories of pregenital phases of the libido and their effect on the formation of character. As he stated in his lecture "Anxiety and Instinctual Life," he had previously found that a "triad of characteristics which are always to be found together: orderliness, parsimoniousness, and obstinacy . . . proceed from the dissipa-tion of . . . anal-erotism and its employment in other ways." His reflections on Herostratos led him to add a further theory:

A similar and perhaps even firmer connection is to be found between ambition and urethral erotism. We have found a remarkable reference to this correlation in the legend that a certain Herostratus, from a craving for notoriety, set fire to the famous temple of Artemis at Ephesus. It seems that the ancients were well aware of the connection involved. You already know how close a connection there is between urination and fire and the putting out of fire.[29]

Freud's earlier hypothesis, to which he refers in the quoted passage, had been summarized in his article interpreting the Prometheus myth, "The Acquisition and Control of Fire": that fire (associated with sexual passion) is primitively related to urination and that "in order to gain control of fire, men had to renounce the [infantile] homosexually-tinged desire to put it out with a stream of urine."[30] When these two speculations of Freud are cumulated, the Herostratos tradition, construed as myth, may be taken to suggest that both a predisposition to arson, as well as the strong ambition that Herostratos shared with Alexander, may be character formations arising from infantile preoccupation with urethral function.

Professor Norman N. Holland, in *The I,* an exploration of the self, has defined adult personality traits that are associated with a child's urethral preoccupation:

> Clinically, a child's fixation at the urethral phase provides the basis for an adult's "antisocial personality." The character type corresponds to the all-too-familiar stereotype of the juvenile delinquent or the psychopath or sociopath: antisocial, truant, aggressive, impulsive, often in particularly violent or sadistic ways. Antisocial personalities show a marked indifference to ordinary social or moral values, do not learn from punishment, and often offer grandiose but obviously specious rationalizations for behavior. . . . Often they are charmers and manipulators, indifferent to the consequences for either the charmer or the charmed.

Holland also finds surprising confirmation for Freud's correlation of bedwetting with arson and ambition:

> Freud linked urethral erotism specifically to fire. Fire, he said, was "discovered" when some Paleolithic man found a naturally occurring blaze, say, from lightning and overcame the impulse to urinate on it and put it out. Surprisingly, statistical studies tend to justify Freud's rather odd

idea. Setting fires (or pyromania) correlates positively with persistent bed-wetting in youth among delinquents—and among arsonists and volunteer firemen. . . . Other writers have suggested that the special shame of uncontrolled wetting provides a basis for ambition: if I achieve greatly, I do not need to be ashamed. (Any ambition, of course, rests on an ability—or perhaps an inability—to think of consequences.) Still others see urination as gratifying sadistic or self-assertive needs or, alternatively, as a passive giving oneself up and foregoing control.[31]

Cleveland psychoanalyst Scott Dowling confirms, similarly, that long-term bed-wetting patients that he has known in therapy or analysis have exhibited "a bitter, pressing, persistent kind of ambition, not usually very successful."[32]

A Jungian analyst (analytical psychologist) in Brazil, Victor-Pierre Stirnimann, has noted another linkage between the ambitious drives of Alexander the Great and Herostratos. Even though Alexander's victories left him weeping that there were no more worlds to conquer, he still aspired, as Herostratos had done, to the assurance of immortality that could be provided by association of his name with the temple of the deathless Artemis. By an irony of Greek tradition recorded by Strabo, the goddess granted recognition to her destroyer but not to the hero who offered to cause the Artemision to rise again from its ashes. Stirnimann comments on the incident:

In 333 BC, the Macedonian emperor was in Ephesus, and there he saw the Artemision still being rebuilt. It is said that he offered to finance the completion of the works, *provided that he received all the credit for it and his name were carved on the temple.* The city administrators, however, managed to avoid his ambiguous generosity with a reply full of psychological subtlety: *it is not fitting that one god should build a temple for another god.*

Despite the generosity of Alexander's rejected gift, Stirnimann sees his offer as an aggressive, self-aggrandizing action that resembles Herostratos's arson:

Herostratus burned the temple while driven by a quest for immortality, and Alexander tried to finance its reconstruction exactly for the same motive. The same need to leave behind a mark, creating or destroying: perhaps Herostratus and Alexander should be understood as two faces of a single theme, with their aggressive response to the state of things, their cult to their own personality, their potential for violence. A centrifugal face and another centripetal: the one seeks to expand the world while the other tries to get hold of its symbolical center.[33]

The ambitions for either conquest or destruction, in Stirnimann's view, compensate for a lack of perceived individuality:

> This alternative is always there, especially during adolescence, when we need to metabolize the pressure to enter the adults' game, the violence of the norms over the still untamed parts of our nature. The response can be Alexandrian and self-confident, the "get out there and conquer it"; or it can be the reflux of depredation and delinquency, the transgressor Herostratus smashing shop windows during the early hours of the morning. In both movements, however, something always ends up being sacrificed: there is neither recognition nor assimilation of that inarticulate kernel of sense which is felt to pertain to each individuality. That is the reason behind the identical thirst for notoriety—it can offer some relief for what is lacking.[34]

The kinship identified in these psychological studies between the aggressive personalities of Herostratos and Alexander has also been discerned intuitively by many authors who have re-created the Herostratos story in fiction and drama.

Third

Since Herostratos needed to proclaim his guilt to achieve his objective of everlasting fame, why was his confession obtained under torture? A puzzling feature of Valerius Maximus's account of Herostratos's case is his assertion that the arsonist's confession was obtained after he was tortured on the rack. Since ancient writers agree that the purpose of the crime was to satisfy a desire for eternal fame, an essential ingredient in Herostratos's premeditated design must have been to assure that all Ephesus would give him credit for the inferno. He must have been prepared to cry his name and even his motive to all who would listen. Still, we are told, his confession was coerced by torture. Why?

The ancient Greeks generally abstained from the use of torture to compel testimony. One exception that they made to this rule, as did the Romans as late as Cicero's day, was that slaves, even if they were willing to testify, were regularly subjected to torture before their evidence was heard. In *Torture and Truth*, Professor Page duBois argues that the testing of slaves' evidence through the "process of torture" rested on the assumption that "the slave, because of his or her servile status, will not spontaneously produce a pure statement, cannot be trusted to do so."[35] Despite the prevalence of this cruel practice and its frequent reflections in Greek literature, attacks on the reliability of torture as a truth-seeking device can be found in forensic speeches. A notable example is the argument that Antiphon around 415 BC wrote for his client, Euxitheus, who was tried, partly on the basis of a slave's testimony, for the alleged shipboard murder of a fellow traveler, Herodes:

> The slave was doubtless promised his freedom: it was certainly to the prosecution alone that he could look for release from his sufferings. Probably both of these considerations induced him to make the false charges against me which he did; he hoped to gain his freedom, and his one immediate wish was to end the torture. I need not remind you, I think, that witnesses under torture are biased in favour of those who do most of the torturing; they will say anything likely to gratify them. It is their one chance of salvation, especially when the victims of their lies happen not to be present. Had I myself proceeded to give orders that the slave should be racked for not telling the truth, that step in itself would doubtless have been enough to make him stop incriminating me falsely. As it was, the examination was conducted by men who also knew what their own interests required.[36]

It appears in the course of Antiphon's argument that a member of the crew who was a free man also underwent torture. K. J. Maidment, the translator of Antiphon, notes that since the sailor was tortured, "he cannot have been born a Greek."[37] Professor duBois suggests that not only barbarians but also Greek noncitizens could become victims of torture: "In the work of the wheel, the rack, and the whip, the torturer carries out the work of the *polis* [city-state]; citizen is made distinct from noncitizen, Greek from barbarian, slave from free."[38] It is possible, therefore, that Herostratos was tortured because he was presently or formerly a slave, or a non-Ephesian by birth.[39]

An alternative explanation may rest on the extraordinary nature of the crime, the shattering impact that it had on the prestige and confidence of Ephesus. Professor duBois cites a stormy passage of Athenian history in which politicians responded to a sacrilegious outrage by urging, to great acclaim, a suspension of a decree banning the torture of citizens. In 415 BC, during the Peloponnesian War, the sacred herms (marble or stone pillars often surmounted by a bust of the god Hermes and bearing male genitals) that stood in the streets of Athens had been mutilated; two council members, accused of participating in the desecration, fled rather than face the prospects of torture and criminal proceedings.[40]

The burning of Ephesus's beloved temple could have induced a similar willingness to suspend the legal guaranties of citizens' immunity from torture. The leaders of the city must have marveled that a man of whom nobody had heard could have planned an attack of such breathtaking sacrilege. Even if he had already announced his name and motive to all within earshot, could he be believed? There was no precedent in Greek history for destroying a great temple to win personal notoriety. The Ephesians could therefore understandably have suspected that an even more sinister explanation remained unconfessed, for example, that Herostratos might have been in the employ of foreign enemies of the city. Ephesus may have been in the grip of a panic, as reflected by Plutarch's account of the soothsayers who ran through the streets predicting other disasters to follow. It may have been to still such disquiet and to sound Herostratos's criminal plan to its very depth that he was led to the rack.

FOURTH

What was the effect of the Ephesian ban on mentioning the name of Herostratos? The outraged Ephesians believed that capital punishment was inadequate retribution for Herostratos's act of sacrilegious destruction and therefore also decreed that his name should never again be pronounced. This remedy, applied only to the most grievous offenses, came to be known in Roman law as *damnatio memoriae,* damnation of the criminal's memory, that is, consignment of his name to oblivion.[41] Once the desire of Herostratos for eternal fame was confirmed under torture, the obliteration of his memory must have seemed particularly appropriate as a means not only of shaming him but of taking away the fruits of his crime.

Some light may be shed on the legal doctrine supporting the ban on Herostratos's name by considering punishments imposed in ancient Athens to control public memory of disruptive crime. In *The World of Prometheus: The Politics of Punishing in Ancient Athens,* Professor Danielle S. Allen points out that Athens applied related penal strategies of remembering and forgetting. To preserve communal recollection of a crime, official memorials of punishment were inscribed on pillars or slabs, places of execution became landmarks, or the convict was condemned to wear a binding that disgraced him forever in the eyes of his fellow citizens. Alternatively, the city could impose a penalty of forgetting, which dishonored the convicted man by requiring that "[he] disappear from the sight of the citizenry, and . . . that the city forget about a wrongdoer." Allen associates with penalties of forgetting the imposition of sentences separating the criminal physically from the body of the city, such as exile, ritual expulsion of scapegoats, and "the precipitation of wrongdoers off cliffs and onto rocks" beyond the city's borders. These punishments of exclusion served the purpose of purifying the community after it had suffered pollution by criminal offenses; the sanctions "not only admitted to the permanence of social disruption [caused by the crime] but also simultaneously required that citizens forget this fact."[42]

Finnish scholar Katariina Mustakallio, reviewing ancient histories by Livy and Dionysius of Halicarnassus, has identified four capital cases in which postmortem shaming remedies were imposed in the early years of the Roman Republic.[43] The prosecutions that she cites all addressed challenges to public order, such as treasonous association with an enemy of Rome and power grabs that the Romans termed more elegantly "aspiring to kingship." The postmortem sanctions, in addition to the obliteration of names, included the confiscation of the criminal's property by the government or its contribution to religious shrines and the demolition of the criminal's residence, a distressing remedy that broke ties with the past as well as the future since it ended the family's ability to continue ancestral household rites.

Among the examples to which Mustakallio refers, the trial of Marcus Manlius, dating from the early fourth century BC, provides the clearest historiographical evidence for recourse to damnation of memory. Unlike Herostratos, Manlius had a heroic past, since it was he whom tradition credits for saving Rome from a surprise attack by the Gauls around 390 BC; he is said to have been alerted to the incursion by the monitory cackling of sacred geese on the Capitoline Hill. In later years, however, Manlius came into conflict with the patrician faction in Rome by urging that gold recovered from a ransom collection for the Gallic invader should have been used to pay debts owed by the city's plebeians. Like Herostratos's arson, Manlius's proposal was regarded as sacrilegious, because the patrician leader Camillus had already consecrated the gold to Jupiter and ordered it stored in the god's temple. Convicted of treason in 384 BC, Manlius was, according to the Roman historian Livy, thrown to his death from the Tarpeian Rocks. The Manlian clan also imposed its private penal sanction to blot out his memory, a proscription that Mustakallio finds to have been effective: "According to Livy, the family itself proscribed members from using the name of Marcus. As far as we know, no later members of the Manlii carried the name of Marcus."[44]

Similar instances of condemned memory in the reign of Emperor Tiberius are related by Tacitus in his *Annals*. After Libo Drusus of the Scribonius family, charged with hatching revolutionary schemes, forced one of his slaves to kill him, his property was divided among his accusers; it was also proposed "that Libo's bust should not be carried in the funeral procession of any of his descendants; . . . and that no Scribonius should assume the surname of Drusus." Cneius (or Gnaeus) Piso later committed suicide or was secretly murdered while facing charges in the Senate for encouraging sedition among the military. Consul Aurelius Cotta voted "that Piso's name ought to be erased from the public register, half of his property confiscated, half given up to his son, Cneius Piso, who was to change his first name." However, "much of the sentence was mitigated by the emperor."[45] Roman emperors (such as Nero) who were regarded as notably cruel also fell victim to posthumous damnation of memory: the official acts of these rulers were nullified and their sculptural portraits were destroyed or reworked.[46]

As the Roman Empire expanded, decrees banning the memory of criminals had the practical effect of international law enforceable wherever the emperor had the desire and military force to impose the will of central government on his subjects. However, until 334 BC, when it welcomed the entry of Alexander the Great, fourth-century Ephesus was only one of the many politically weak cities of Asia Minor under Persian domination, and thus it lacked the power to project the force of its local decrees extraterritorially, except perhaps to the extent that its wishes would have been persuasive with other Greek population centers in Ionia. Although the statement of Aulus Gellius, Roman miscellanist of the second century AD, that the ban on Herostratos's name was decreed by the "common council" of Asia Minor should be discounted,[47] there was precedent for religiously centered cooperation among the Greek city-states of Ionia. Herodotus notes that in the dawn of their history the twelve Ionian cities, including Ephesus, established the Panionion (All-Ionia League) on Mount Mycale, dedicated to the god Poseidon; this sacred meeting place was the site of the Panionia festival.[48]

Wholly apart from the possible effect of pan-Ionian sympathies, the power of the offended goddess stood behind the damnation of the arsonist's name. Since Herostratos's crime was also a sin against Artemis/Diana, whose cult drew widespread allegiance in Europe as well as Asia, religious unity could have provided a basis for an observance of the memory ban that transcended political boundaries. In fact, Professor A. M. Harmon, translator of Lucian, has suggested that the prohibition against Herostratos's memory "very likely was accompanied by a curse."[49]

Such curses were far from unknown. There is evidence that around 590 BC, a sweeping and bloodcurdling curse was formulated in response to a sacrilege against a major shrine in mainland Greece. According to the orator Aeschines, the inhabitants of Cirra on the Corinthian Gulf "behaved impiously toward the temple of Delphi and its dedicated offerings." After a punitive war against the offenders, the plain of Cirra and its harbor were given as consecrated property to Delphi's presiding god, Apollo, his sister and mother, Artemis and Leto, as well as Athena Pronaia (the name under which the patroness of Athens was worshiped in Delphi). The territory of the offenders was laid waste and the oracle ordered it not to be reworked. The victorious forces swore to abide by the oracle and fortified its terms by adding a divine curse: "If anyone, city or individual or people contravenes this, let them be cursed by Apollo, Artemis, Leto, and Athena Pronaia." The specifications of the curse warned would-be violators of dire consequences: "Their land should not produce crops nor their women bear children that resemble their parents but monsters, . . . they should be defeated in war, lawsuits and debates, and both they themselves and their households and their race should perish utterly . . . and may the gods not accept their offerings."[50] The text of the ancient curse was still on file in the Athenian public record office in 330 BC, when Aeschines had occasion to cite its fulminations in his prosecution of Ctesiphon, an ally of Demosthenes.

Even a horrific curse cannot be regarded as wielding the powerful deterrent effect of the modern Iranian *fatwa* that for many years caused an English resident, Salman Rushdie, to hide in fear of international assassins. Yet many commentators have seemed to reflect the belief that the memory ban continued to influence the literature of Greece and Rome for centuries after the temple fire. The acceptance of this dubious proposition is based on the fact that some ancient writers, among them Cicero and Plutarch, refer to the destruction of the Artemision but do not name the arsonist. In no event, however, was the suppression of the name universally observed even in the early years, for Theopompus, the first historian said to have violated the decree, was a contemporary of the criminal.

In any case, the Ephesians' attempt to impose oblivion on the arsonist was destined to fail. Even if the incendiary had remained anonymous to this day, he would have achieved a sinister fame as the man who burned a Wonder of the World. Whether the ancients chose to flout the letter of the Ephesian ban by naming the hated arsonist or defined him by association with his unprecedented crime, they kept alive the memory of an emblematic act of terror.

2 The Globalization of Herostratos

As the Classical tradition spread, Herostratos became well known throughout Europe. Many works in Greek and Latin were preserved or transcribed in manuscript by the libraries of medieval monasteries and universities, and were subsequently disseminated more widely through printed editions of the original texts and of translations. The course of this process over the centuries can be observed in the case of literary sources that identify Herostratos's arson as a crime undertaken for the sake of notoriety. Lucian's works, for example, are represented by eleven important manuscripts that date from the ninth through the twelfth centuries, and principal editions were printed as early as 1496; in 1780 an English translation was issued in London. The popularity of Valerius Maximus is attested by the fact that "more manuscripts of [his] *Memorable Deeds and Sayings* survive than any other Latin prose text save the Bible"; the preservation of his work depended upon two ninth-century manuscripts, and the first English translation appeared in 1678. It seems likely that Herostratos's name and crime were also embedded in oral tradition.[1]

As early as the twelfth century, European authors made allusions to Herostratos's crime as illustrations (*exempla*) of their philosophical themes. The writers of the Middle Ages, like many of their successors, regarded the ancient destroyer as embodying the pursuit of celebrity at any cost and emphasized the paradox that negative fame often outlasts glory achieved by merit. One of the first notable medieval scholars to integrate the Herostratos tradition into his own art of Christian persuasion was the internationally renowned John of Salisbury (ca. 1115–1180). Born near Salisbury, John studied art and philosophy under Peter Abelard, and after several years on diplomatic missions to the Holy See on behalf of Theobold, Archbishop of Canterbury, he was appointed Bishop of Chartres. Earlier, his banishment from court, resulting from the displeasure of King Henry II of England, gave him leisure to complete in 1159 his principal philosophical works, in Latin, dedicated to his friend, Thomas Becket.[2]

To one of these books, John, in a fit of antiquarian humor, gave the long-winded title, *Policraticus: Of the Frivolities of Courtiers and the Footprints of Philosophers.* The argumentation in *Policraticus* is studded with quotations from Classical authors. Although doubt has been cast on the extent of John's direct acquaintance with the ancient texts that he cites, there is no reason to question his love for Greek and Roman philosophy, which he praises lavishly in his book:

> That the genius of the philosophers of antiquity had abounded and that study was advanced by them is not merely opinion but a judgment of which everyone in common is persuaded. For through study and practice these geniuses prepared for themselves a path to matters which are by nature almost incomprehensible, and with their aid many discoveries were made known to posterity for which we rejoice and at which we marvel.

Time and again John professes loyalty not only to St. Augustine but to his favorite Roman philosopher, to whom he refers affectionately as "our Cicero."[3]

Herostratos takes a bow in a chapter of *Policraticus* devoted to two natural human passions, the love of rectitude and the love of material advantage. The first, John argues, leads to the love of liberty and of the public good, and to the observance of the golden rule. Materialism, by contrast, gives rise to the desire for domination, honor, praise, and glory. Although to John of Salisbury the appetite for glory always appears to be a fault, "more deadly is the error of those who deem it worthwhile to gain notoriety even by crime." In support of this aphorism, John quotes almost verbatim but without attribution Valerius Maximus's treatment of two familiar examples, the celebrity killing of King Philip of Macedon by Pausanius, and the arson of Herostratos. To the latter passage he appends a lesson for Christians:

> With similar, nay, greater madness they are seen to aim at glory who lay waste with the fires of self-indulgence not the temple of Diana at Ephesus, which deserved destruction because of the character of its worship, but the temple of the Holy Ghost, the entire man, that is, body and soul,

that they may by this act become known to men. For they seek fame and generally attain honor from that from which it were more fitting that they suffer disgrace and punishment.[4]

Valerius Maximus was among the Classical authors with whom Geoffrey Chaucer was familiar; Professor Edgar Shannon has noted Chaucer's acknowledgment of Valerius as one of the sources for his story of Julius Caesar that he inserted toward the end of "The Monk's Tale" in *The Canterbury Tales.*[5] It is therefore possible that the introduction of the phantom of an arsonist in Chaucer's *The House of Fame* was suggested by the poet's reading of Valerius's account either in the original text, or in John of Salisbury's rendering.[6]

In *The House of Fame,* an unfinished poem by Chaucer possibly written about 1380, the narrator named Geffrey is transported in a dream vision to a palace where the goddess of Fame determines, on a case-by-case basis, whether to convert raw materials of human experience into lasting traditions. In book 3, nine groups of petitioning ghosts appear before the goddess to request good or bad reputation or anonymity. Fame's responses to the first seven delegations are highly arbitrary. Some suppliants who have performed good works are rebuffed; others desiring that their pious deeds be forgotten or idlers seeking glory unsupported by merit are treated discriminatorily. Two groups of wrongdoers then remain to be judged. The goddess, in a rare display of equity, refuses to grant fair renown to a set of traitors who have confessed the "greatest wickedness." The last crowd to besiege Fame's throne, whom Anne Worthington Prescott defines as "terrorists of their time," has chosen as their spokesman an unnamed rogue who is a transformed dream-image of Herostratos, the "very rogue that burned the temple of Isis in the city of Athens." Asked by the goddess to explain the motive for his crime, the claimant, decked out with striped hose and an ornamental bell, replies:

> I would fain have had glory even as other folk in the town had, though they were famous for their excellence and their moral virtue. Thought I, rogues have as great fame, though it be for roguery, as goodfolk for goodness. And since I cannot have the one, I will not forgo the other. And to get mend of Fame I set the temple afire. Now let our renown be blown quickly, as ever thou hopest for joy!

The goddess Fame grants the prayer by ordering Aeolus, the god of wind, to sound the black trumpet of infamy; Aeolus "puffed and blew till the sound was at the world's end."[7]

Although accurately reflecting Herostratos's desire for fame as an impious destroyer and his sense of failure in competition with industrious townsfolk, Chaucer obviously had only a hazy memory of the details of the crime. Perhaps his lapse was due to the fact that, as Professor Sheila Delany has noted, the poet's "reading was eclectic and often superficial." It is even possible that he did not have any specific literary source in mind; instead, he may have been drawing on exemplary oral traditions of Herostratos just as Professor Delany speculates could have been the case in connection with a figurative reference in *The House of Fame* to the "overreaching worldly ambition" of Alexander the Great.[8]

Jacob Burckhardt has noted that Italians of the Renaissance displayed "a boundless ambition and thirst after greatness, regardless of all means and consequences." It was a period in which Niccolò Machiavelli, quoted by Burckhardt, criticized previous writers for failing to recognize "how many who could distinguish themselves by nothing praiseworthy, strove to do so by infamous deeds." Burckhardt observed that the use of atrocious, even demonic means, when success itself was in doubt, was characteristic of "this age of overstrained and despairing passions and forces, and remind[s] us of the burning of the temple of Diana at Ephesus in the time of Philip of Macedon."[9] The violent times and ethos of the Renaissance provided fertile ground for the nurture of Herostratos's story.

Michel de Montaigne's attack on the pursuit of fame in "On Glory" (included in the second book of his essays, published together with the first book in 1580) spares neither patriot nor Herostratic villain. Only God deserves to be glorified for He is perfect in substance, but humankind, with all its defects, would do better to recognize its shortcomings in "beauty, health, wisdom, virtue and such essentials." The quest for fame is a deeply flawed enterprise for many reasons. Glory is dependent on the whims of fortune and stills the voice of conscience, inducing the belief that virtue need be practiced only before witnesses. Moreover, glory arises from the consensus of a multitude whose opinion we would despise if we considered each of its constituent members separately. History's dependence on fortune and its selective memory are also a source of disappointment for the ambitious:

> To what do Caesar and Alexander owe the infinite greatness of their renown but to fortune? How many men has she extinguished—at the beginning of their success, of whom we have no knowledge, but who brought as much courage to bear as theirs, if the misfortune of their lot had not cut them short at the birth of their undertakings. In the midst

of so many and such extreme dangers, I do not recall having read that Caesar was ever wounded. Thousands have died in lesser perils than the smallest that he surmounted. Innumerable brave deeds must be lost without recording before one turns out profitably.

Montaigne concedes that in some circumstances the enhancement of favorable reputation might be profitable, but observes that the profit motive is not everpresent in the vainglorious soul: "the excess of this malady develops to the point that many try to make people talk about them for good or ill." It is said of Herostratos, for example, that he was "more desirous of a widespread reputation than of a good one." In any event, posthumous fame meant nothing to Montaigne. When the essayist was dead he would have even less benefit from the public's whimsical recognition; he would no longer have any hold on his reputation, nor could it touch him.[10]

In the text of his essay, Montaigne erroneously identifies Pompeius Trogus, a Latin historian of Gallic origin, as the source of his reference to Herostratos. Montaigne was fluent in Latin and read Greek authors in translation; his works commonly cite Cicero and Plutarch, two contributors to the Herostratos literature. However, as in this instance, his "quotations are frequently inaccurate . . . often they appear to have been set down from memory—and Montaigne admitted that his memory was bad!"[11]

Herostratos may have been among the Classical figures that people Shakespeare's universe. R. B. Parker has noted a possible "reminiscence" of the arsonist in act 5, scene 1 of *Coriolanus* (composed around 1608).[12] In the cited passage, Cominius reports his unsatisfactory meeting with Coriolanus in the rebel leader's camp:

> "Coriolanus"
> He would not answer to, forbade all names;
> He was a kind of nothing, titleless,
> Till he had forged himself a name o'th'fire
> Of burning Rome.

Parker's belief that these lines may echo the crime of Herostratos is plausible. Not only does Shakespeare refer to the attainment of fame through a conflagration but he emphatically sounds a theme of namelessness, the condition in which the obscure Herostratos lived his life and to which the Ephesian ban on his memory sought to return him.

Geoffrey Ribbans has observed that "in Renaissance and Baroque texts there is in fact something of an underworld of Herostratus-like figures and references."[13] A prime example can be found in a passage in the second part of Miguel de Cervantes's *Don Quixote* (1615), in which Don Quixote and Sancho Panza converse about the pursuit of fame.[14] Don Quixote is annoyed that Sancho persists in believing that he has seen the knight's lady, Dulcinea, winnowing corn. She would not have appeared in such humble guise "were it not for the envy which some evil enchanter seems to display towards [the Don's] affairs." Envy, he tells his squire, is the "root of infinite evil and canker-worm of virtue! All the vices, Sancho, bring with them some manner of delight; but that of envy brings only pain, rancour and furious rage."

Sancho swears that he has "never spoken ill of any enchanter," and hasn't "enough wealth to be envied." Of those who may write his biography he has only modest expectations:

> Yet the historians ought to take pity on me and treat me kindly in their writings, if only because I've always believed in God and in all the tenets of the Holy Roman Catholic Church, and because I'm a mortal enemy to the Jews. But let them say what they will; for naked I was born and naked I am now, I neither lose nor gain. And though I chance to be put in books and passed about the world from hand to hand, I don't care a fig—let them say what they like about me.

Don Quixote, however, has thought more about posthumous fame and its gradations. The first category of fame seekers identified by Quixote ardently desire worldly renown irrespective of the means of its attainment. There was a lady, the Don tells Sancho, who was incensed that her name was not included in "a malicious satire against all courtesans"; at her demand the poet put her into a supplement, "and she was satisfied to find herself famous, even if for nothing good."

The next example that Don Quixote offers is Herostratos, who in the Don's literary imagination has become a "shepherd." He recounts the crime and the frustrated ban on remembrance:

> Another story that fits is the one about that shepherd who set on fire and burnt the famous temple of Diana, accounted one of the seven wonders of the world, only so that his name should survive to future ages; and though it was decreed that no one should speak of him, or

make any mention of his name by word or in writing, so that he should not achieve his ambition, still it became known that his name was Erostratus.

The Don's final illustration of thirst for infamy is the tale of a Roman gentleman's powerful impulse to combine a celebrity killing with the desecration of a religious building. The gentleman, after guiding Charles V through the Rotunda, a famous ancient temple, confided to the emperor: "A thousand times, most sacred Majesty, the desire seized me to clasp your Majesty and throw myself down from [the temple's cupola] so that I might win myself eternal fame in the world." The emperor thanked him for his candor and prudently commanded him never to enter his presence again.

In Quixote's idiosyncratic thought processes, the same "desire of winning fame" that is observable in this disgraceful trio from the past also inspired worldly heroes at their bravest moments: Horatius leaping from a Roman bridge; Caesar crossing the Rubicon; and the valiant Spaniards, led by the most "courteous Cortes," scuttling his ships so that he and his forces would be "stranded and isolated in the New World." The dedicated knight places his own quest for eternal glory on a higher plane: "We, Christians, Catholics and knights errant, have more to expect from future and everlasting glory enjoyed in the ethereal and celestial regions than from the vanity of fame achieved in this present transient life; which fame, however long it lasts, must finally end with the world itself, which has its fixed term." Having listened respectfully to his master's homily, Sancho still permits himself a quibble: How can the knights errant be ranked with saints, if, as the Don admits, it is a greater thing to bring a dead man to life than to kill a giant? On they wrangle until Don Quixote has the last word: It may be that there are more friars than knights errant in Heaven, but that is because the number of religious is greater and few of those are "deserving of the name of knights."

As Ribbans has noted, Juan Ruiz de Alarcón y Mendoza, one of the leading dramatists of Spain's Golden Age, includes a reference to Herostratos's arson in the 1630 comedy, *La verdad sospechosa* (*The Suspicious Truth*). The play's protagonist Don García justifies his deceitful character by invoking Herostratos's precedent:

A person who lives without being heard of,
Who only swells the population
And does what everyone does,
How is he different from an animal?

To be famous is the big thing,
By whatever means.
Let them mention my name everywhere
And gossip about me at least,
For a man, to win fame
Burned the temple of Ephesus.[15]

Herostratos's drive to win fame through sacrilege is also cited in Portugal's national epic, *The Lusíads*, by Luís Vaz de Camões (1572). The poem draws on episodes and devices of Virgil's *Aeneid* in celebrating Vasco da Gama's voyage to India in 1497 and 1498; the Olympian gods divide in fostering or opposing da Gama's explorations. At the end of canto 2, the Sultan of Malindi in East Africa asks da Gama to recount the Portuguese exploits of the past. The hospitable ruler contrasts the report he has received of "the matchless works of the Portuguese" with the inglorious tradition of Herostratos:

"Herostratus set fire to Diana's temple
Built by subtle Ctesiphon [*sic*], solely
To be known throughout the world
And remembered by the human race.
If the desire for fame can lead
To such sacrilege and atrocity,
How much better to hold in memory
One whose deeds are worth eternal glory."[16]

An early seventeenth-century image of Herostratos torching the Artemision appears in *Emblemas Morales* (*Moral Emblems*) by a Spanish canon and lexicographer, Sebastián de Covarrubias Orozco.[17] Emblem books were a popular form of illustrated literature in the sixteenth and seventeenth century. Covarrubias defined emblems as "the lines of verse which are written underneath some painting or carving and by which we give the import of some idea or conceit, be it warlike, moral, amorous or otherwise; the lines of verse thus help to make clear the author's intention in making his emblem."[18]

The woodcut (frontispiece) illustrating Emblem 55 of Centuria II (the second group of one hundred emblems) shows Herostratos at his infamous work; stylized flames engulf the upper tiers of a round, domed temple that evokes the Renaissance rather than Greek antiquity. Above the dome a banderole bears a Latin motto that proclaims, "Fame is prepared in flames." Beneath the illustration an eight-line poem (octave) in Spanish points the moral:

IN FLAMMIS FAMA PARATVR

EMBLEMA. 55.

Llega el furor de la ambiciosa fama,
A tanto estremo, que el que la apetece,
No mira si se honra. o si se infama,
O si por ello gana, o desmerece:
El Ephesino templo el otro imflama,
Cuyo nombre, con gran razõ merece,
Que pues le pretendio tan locamente,
Le sepulte el oluido eternamente.

Vn

Herostratos torching the Temple of Artemis in Ephesus, an illustration in Sebastián de Covarrubias Orozco's *Moral Emblems* (1610).

The madness of ambitious fame
Reaches such an extreme point that he who craves it
Does not consider whether it causes him honor or infamy,
Or whether he gains by it or loses merit.

A man sets fire to the Ephesian temple,
Whose name, with good reason, deserves
That since he sought it so insanely,
Oblivion buries it forever.

On the reverse side of the page Covarrubias adds a prose commentary:

A foolish man, in order to have permanent fame, without considering whether for good or ill, decided to burn the famous and celebrated temple of Diana in Ephesus, one of the so-called wonders of the world; and that depraved intention having become known, it was ordered by law that nobody should mention his name. Nevertheless he is said to have been named Erasistratus [*sic*]. Infamous glory, sinister remembrance, like those of the heretics of our times and the past, who by such a pernicious route have thought to make their memories eternal, dying stubbornly in error. For all of them this motto is very appropriate: *Fame is prepared in flames.*

The discovery of funerary urns shallowly buried in the soil of Norfolk inspired Sir Thomas Browne to write his essay *Urn Burial* (1658). The early chapters consider the variety of ancient practices in the disposition of mortal remains by interment and cremation. This theme turns the author's mind to the ways in which funeral ceremonies reflect attitudes toward the afterlife: Muslims, so Browne tells us, "think to return to a delightful life again" and are therefore "carried forth with their heads forward and looking toward their houses."

The essay's concluding section (chapter 5) is a reflection on the vanity of the human desire to find a lasting place in the memory of posterity. Even the intriguing riddles of ancient legend and archeological dating might be easier to resolve than the identity of those whose bones were deposited in the Norfolk urns with false hopes that the dead would be remembered:

What song the sirens sang, or what name Achilles assumed when he hid himself among women, though puzzling questions, are not beyond all conjecture. What time the persons of these ossuaries entered the famous nations of the dead and slept with princes and counselors might admit a wide solution. But who were the proprietors of these bones, or what bodies these ashes made up, were a question above antiquarianism: not to be resolved by man.

For Browne, to "subsist in bones and be but pyramidally extant is a fallacy in duration," particularly in the light of his belief that the world would come to an end in the year 2000. Noting the difficulty of reading "bare inscriptions" on ancient graves, Browne ridicules the human inclination "to hope for eternity by enigmatical epithets or first letters of our names."

No comfort can be drawn from remembering that a man existed if we know nothing of his life, Browne argues, for "to be nameless in worthy deeds exceeds an infamous history." Browne reminds us that "the iniquity of oblivion blindly scattereth her poppy and deals with the memory of men without distinction to merit of perpetuity," preferring the ravager of Ephesus to the world's great builders: "Who can but pity the founder of the pyramids? Herostratus lives that burnt the Temple of Diana; he is almost lost that built it." All pretensions to earthly glory, Browne concludes, are doomed to failure for "there is nothing strictly immortal but immortality." Only God, just as He "hath no beginning may be confident of no end." The "sufficiency of Christian immortality frustrates all earthly glory" and "makes a folly of posthumous memory."[19]

The ghost of Herostratos participates in a witty conversation with a fourth-century BC orator, Demetrius of Phalerum, in *New Dialogues of the Dead* (1683–1684) written by Bernard Le Bovier de Fontenelle after Lucian's ancient Greek model.[20] Demetrius, after being appointed governor of Athens, was driven from power by a naval invasion and his hundreds of statues around the city were toppled. Herostratos tells him that he would have relished the destruction of "so many statues made for the same man." The ghost of Demetrius replies bitterly that "such a wish is worthy of the man who burnt the temple of Ephesus."

Herostratos, in his meditations over the centuries, has arrived at a measured assessment of his crime and punishment. He had no reason to complain of the effect of the law that prohibited the mention of his name. The Ephesians, Herostratos tells Demetrius, were "good people who didn't recognize that to prevent his name from being spoken was to assure his immortality." And his excessive desire for notoriety that caused him to burn the Artemision had not been catastrophic when properly viewed. The citizens of Ephesus actually were lucky that his ambition had not cost them more dearly; "another man perhaps would have ruined all the city and their entire state." His motive was not different from that of the architect who had built the temple to make his name survive. The "vanity that erected the temple by the hands of another was able to destroy it by mine." The self-glorification with which Herostratos was charged could easily be detected in the rest of the human race: "A father leaves behind as many children as possible so as to perpetuate his name. A conqueror, to perpetuate his, exterminates as many people as possible."

Demetrius is not surprised that Herostratos employs all sorts of arguments to defend the actions of destroyers, but even if destruction is a method of attaining glory, there can't be any other methods less noble. Herostratos does not agree, for in his eyes, destruction sweeps history's plates clean:

> The earth resembles great tablets on which everyone wants to write his name. When these tablets are full it is necessary to wipe out the names that are there so as to inscribe new ones. What if all the ancient monuments survived? The moderns would have nowhere to place theirs. Could you hope that [your] 360 statues could stay up for long? Didn't you see that your glory took up too much space?

It is not so easy for Demetrius, even in his afterlife, to become philosophical about the fall of his statues. Once they were erected, all over Athens, wasn't it just as well to leave them standing? Herostratos does not think so and replies with his own question: Wasn't it just as well before the statues were in place that none of them be erected at all? For in the view of the temple's nemesis: "It is the passions that make and unmake everything. If reason dominated on earth nothing would ever happen."

In a separate dialogue between another ambitious destroyer often linked to Herostratos, Alexander the Great, and Phriné (a famous Greek courtesan of his period) about their respective careers, the world conqueror comes out second best. In Ezra Pound's translation, Phriné convincingly demonstrates the advantage of her peaceful occupation: "You could learn it from all the Thebans who lived in my time. They will tell you that I offered to restore at my own expense the walls of Thebes which you had ruined, provided that they inscribe them as follows: Alexander the Great had cast down these walls, the courtesan Phriné rebuilt them."[21]

An aphoristic reference to Herostratos, found in Colley Cibber's adaptation of Shakespeare's *Richard III*, has made its way into Bartlett's *Familiar Quotations*. Cibber (1671–1757) was an actor and playwright who became poet laureate in 1730. Literary foes made him pay dearly for this official recognition; parodies of Cibber and of his stylistic excesses appear in Henry Fielding's novel *Joseph Andrews* and in Alexander Pope's satirical poem *The Dunciad*. Despite these contemporary setbacks, Cibber holds a significant place in Shakespearean stage history. His reworking of *Richard III* was the preferred acting version from its introduction in 1700 until Henry Irving's successful restoration of Shakespeare's original play at London's Lyceum Theatre in 1877.

During the reign of the Cibber version, the role of Richard was played by giants of the English stage, including David Garrick, John Philip Kemble, Edmund Kean, and William Charles Macready. It was these eminent actors that familiarized London's audiences with Herostratos's crime (but not his name) in a powerful soliloquy written by Cibber for the villainous Richard at end of act 3:

> Why now my golden dream is out—
> Ambition like an early Friend throws back
> My Curtains with an eager Hand, o'rejoy'd
> To tell me what I dreamt is true—A Crown!
> Thou bright reward of ever daring minds,
> O! How thy awful Glory wraps my Soul!
> Nor can the means that got thee dim thy lustre;
> For, not mens Love, Fear pays thee Adoration:
> And Fame not more survives from Good than Evil deeds.
> Th' aspiring youth that fir'd th' *Ephesian* Dome
> Out-lives in Fame the pious Fool that rais'd it:
> Conscience, lie still—More lives must yet be drain'd,
> Crowns got with Blood must be with Blood maintain'd.[22]

Richard's monologue, in the couplet excerpted by Bartlett, cites the historical irony (noted in the previous century by Sir Thomas Browne) that fame from good deeds may not outlast reputation for evil: that, in fact, the fame of the arsonist Herostratos ("th' aspiring youth that fir'd the Ephesian Dome") outlived the memory of the temple's architect (the unmentioned Chersiphron). It is the spell of this incongruity that explains in large measure the tenacity of the Herostratos story. Cibber, however, sees beyond this familiar aspect of tradition to emphasize the lessons of terror that Herostratos's example had taught Richard: Evil means of usurpation do not dim the luster of a crown, and having gained ascendancy, a tyrant must not rule by men's love, for "Fear pays thee Adoration."

Eighteenth-century English Classical dictionaries also enshrined the memory of Herostratos while perpetuating some of the inaccuracies that had crept into his biographical details. Dr. John Lemprière's *Classical Dictionary,* first published in 1788, identifies "Eratostratus" as the preferred form of the arsonist's name, and without support from Plutarch or Valerius Maximus, the two cited sources, proclaims him "an Ephesian." William King's *An Historical Account of the Heathen Gods and Heroes* (1710) refers to the temple destroyer as "a profligate Fellow called Erostratus, who did it that he might get himself a Name, though it were for Villainy." No historical foundation, however, can be found to support the charge of profligacy, unless abandoned character is to be inferred from the crime rather than from its hazy antecedents.[23]

From the Renaissance on, the figure of Herostratos was so deeply rooted in the European psyche that his once abhorred name was in use as a commonplace term whose meaning was readily understood. Not only did he appear in the pages of literature that we now regard as classic, but he had become a catchword to be employed casually, sometimes even humorously, by pamphleteers or journalists. The name Herostratos now acquired a figurative meaning; no longer did it automatically signify an arsonist or other violent criminal, but it might also serve as an epithet thrown in the teeth of an adversary charged with unbridled conduct or aspirations.

The Cambridge-educated satirist and poet Gabriel Harvey (ca. 1550–1631) called Herostratos to his aid in a posthumous attack on the dissipated playwright Robert Greene in *Four Letters and Certain Sonnets* (1592). The hostility between the two writers grew out of their allegiance to opposing camps in the "Marprelate Controversy," a blizzard of pamphlets raised by Puritan diatribes of the pseudonymous Martin Marprelate against the Church of England. Choosing to speak nothing but ill of the recently buried Greene (an "anti-Martinist"), Harvey, in a preface to his readers, compared Greene's libels against the Harvey family to the crime of Herostratos that had been buried in the "deepest pit of oblivion":

> Vile actes would in some respectes, rather be concealed, than recorded: as the darknesse of the Night better fitteth the nature of some unlucky birdes, than the brightnesse of the day: and *Herostratus* in a villanous bravery, affecting a most notorious, & monstrous Fame, was in the censure of the wisest Judgmentes, rather to be overwhelmed in the deepest pitt of Oblivion, than to enjoy any relique, or shadow of his owne desperate glory.

In his third letter, Harvey also attacks polemicists who wish to be as "egregiously famous, as ever was Herostratus, or Pausanius [assassin of Philip of Macedon]."[24]

In the aftermath of the Louisiana Purchase, journalistic satire revealed that Herostratos had also entered American politics. President Thomas Jefferson, anxious to learn what he had bought, sent a questionnaire to residents of the New Orleans area. In his report to Congress on the information that he received, the president gushed over the fabulous treasures of the Missouri River: "There exists, about one thousand miles up the Missouri, and not far from that river, a salt mountain! . . . This mountain is said to be 180 miles long and 45 in width, composed of solid rock salt, without any trees or even shrubs on it." President Jefferson's dreams of vast salt deposits exposed him to ridicule in the Federalist press. A Jefferson biographer relates that "one Federalist wit insisted that the salt mountain must be Lot's wife" and that another spoofed the president's credulity by an epigram in the *United States Gazette*:

Herostratus of old, to eternalize his name
Sat [*sic*] the temple of Diana all in a flame;
But Jefferson lately of Bonaparte bought,
To pickle his fame, a mountain of salt.[25]

In 1794 a more significant journalist, Judith Sargent Murray, an early American champion of women's rights, referred to Herostratos in gently lampooning her own quest for literary recognition. In what was to be her last column, signed "The Reaper," for Robert Treat Paine's Federalist newspaper, the *Orrery*, Murray took the passion for fame as her subject. "Although the love of fame," Murray began, "may perhaps be considered as the mania of the mind—yet it is certainly a very powerful incentive to action." Anticipating an argument made by twentieth-century philosopher Miguel de Unamuno,[26] Murray sensed that the desire of a human being to survive in the "bosom of posterity" is "interwoven with our existence."

Murray speculates whether the ardent wishes for posthumous fame are "strong presumptive proof of the future resuscitation of the eternity of that intelligence, which is thus early taught to raise, towards undying felicity, its aspiring ideas." If nature, or nature's God, has implanted in us the irresistible disposition to seek fame, the impulse must, like its Creator, be "wise and good." But this is not always the case:

In the bosom of him, who burnt the temple at Ephesus, this phrensy of the soul was highly wrought. But, it is conceded, that the best motives, precipitated by the impetuous tide of passion, may produce the most pernicious consequences; and, although this fine principle, operating upon the turbid bosom of Eratostratus [Herostratos], produced such a singular conflagration, it would be irrational to conclude, that an incentive, so prevalent, might not generally procure the most salutary effects.[27]

Praise, according to Murray, is the minister of fame. For her own part, she confesses the encouragement she drew from a reader's "truly elegant lines" of appreciation in the previous Monday edition of the *Orrery.* From this "divine penman" she was delighted that her brow had received a "wreath so honorary."

These were the years when Herostratos was either a figure from the distant past or a theme for present laughter. However, as the centuries continued to roll on, the successors of the fabled criminal returned with a vengeance to wreak their havoc.

3 The Destroyers

FORMER SOVIET REFUSENIK Yuri Tarnopolsky, in an essay "On Loss," has written eloquently of the terrible Herostratic urge to destroy the irreplaceable:

> Deliberate destruction by war, terrorism, sabotage, vandalism, and interference falls into this category of [entropic] loss. Humans are dangerous neighbors of unique Things.
>
> Why would anybody have a desire to destroy a life or a Thing or to deface the Great Sphinx of Giza? Herostratus burned the temple of Artemis, one of the Seven Wonders of the World, in 356 BC, to make himself famous.
>
> I believe, it is related to the temperature of the social environment. Destructive urge rises not only in times of social unrest, but even among fans after a sports competition. Uncontrolled rage of animals is, probably, of the same nature.[1]

Whatever slogan the destroyers may imprint on their banners, they may be moved to annihilate a fame or a beauty that seems to block their place in the sun.

This chapter will focus on exemplary instances of attacks on "unique Things" since the late nineteenth century. The first episode cited, an abortive 1894 explosion near the Greenwich Observatory in suburban London, remains mantled in doubt. Did the bomber, who blew himself apart while leaving the observatory walls unscathed, intend to damage the building? We will never know, but Joseph Conrad, in his masterly novel *The Secret Agent*, has taught us to entertain the possibility that, pursuant to a foreign conspiracy mimicking anarchist violence, harm was intended to the citadel of English science. The other attacks to be discussed were clearly premeditated and the resulting cultural losses were mourned worldwide: the burning of Kyoto's Temple of the Golden Pavilion (1950); the shelling of the Stari Most (Old Bridge) at Mostar, Bosnia-Herzegovina (1993); and the Taliban's preannounced demolition of the Giant Buddhas in Bamiyan, Afghanistan (March 2001).

THE GREENWICH OBSERVATORY BOMBING (1894)

> After many unhappy experiments in the direction of an ideal Republic,
> it was found that what may be described as a Despotism tempered by
> Dynamite provides, on the whole, the most satisfactory description of
> ruler—an autocrat who dares not abuse his autocratic power.
> —W. S. Gilbert, *Utopia, Limited*, act I (1893)

As the last decade of the nineteenth century advanced, Continental Europe increasingly found itself the prey of terror by dynamite. On November 7, 1893, a bomb thrown by Spanish anarchist Santiago Salvador Franch from the balcony of the Liceo Theatre in Barcelona, during a performance of Rossini's revolutionary opera *William Tell*, exploded in the stalls below, killing twenty-three people and wounding forty others. John Quail, in his history of British anarchism entitled *The Slow Burning Fuse*, attributes this act of terror to revenge for the previous massacre of rebelling peasants, and quotes the comment of a correspondent for the *London Times:* "The barbarous atrocity of this deed calls for just reprisals on the part of the governing powers not only in Spain but of the combined civilized world. The outrage which has been committed against Barcelona society may tomorrow be repeated in some other large city."[2]

At the time this prediction was made, Paris was already in the grips of a cycle of terrorist outrages that began in 1892 when Ravachol (François-Claudius Koeningstein) avenged the conviction of a fellow anarchist, Henri-Louis-Charles Decamps, by bombing the Paris apartment houses where Decamps's judge and prosecutor resided. Auguste Vaillant perpetrated a more audacious crime on December 9, 1893, when he bombed the Palais Bourbon while the Chamber of Deputies was in session. Miraculously, no lives were lost despite the use of the heavy-studded nails sprayed by the exploding device. The series of attacks in the French capital resumed on February 12, 1894.

Anarchist Émile Henry ignited an explosive in the Café Terminus near the Saint Lazare railroad station, killing one person and causing many injuries. Vanity may have undone Henry because, according to crime historian H. B. Irving, the only evidence against him was the bomb's wrapping, a newspaper reporting an anarchist meeting in which Henry and his brother had taken part.[3]

Despite the dire forecast of the *London Times,* the English capital had so far been more often the scene of inflammatory speechmaking than of violent action. However, the comfortable illusion of urban peace was about to be disturbed. In the late afternoon of February 15, 1894, only three days after Henry's deadly bomb went off in Paris, an explosion rocked Greenwich Park. A "park-keeper and some school boys rushed to the spot where the smoke rose lazily among the trees" and found the mutilated body of a young man; at the time of the explosion, the victim may have been standing about forty-six yards from the wall of the Greenwich Observatory.[4] A *Times* article quoted by Norman Sherry reported the grisly discovery on the following day:

EXPLOSION IN GREENWICH PARK

Last evening an explosion was heard by a keeper of Greenwich Park on the hill close to the Royal Observatory. Proceeding thither he found a respectably-dressed man, in a kneeling posture, terribly mutilated.

One hand was blown off and the body was open. The injured man was only able to say, "Take me home," and was unable to reply to a question as to where his home was. He was taken to the Seamen's Hospital in an ambulance, and died in less than half an hour.

A bottle, in many pieces, which had apparently contained an explosive substance, was found near the spot where the explosion took place, and it is conjectured that the deceased man fell and caused its contents to explode.[5]

The victim was identified as a twenty-six-year-old French tailor named Martial Bourdin, well known among London's anarchists as the brother-in-law of H. B. Samuels. Since May 1, 1893, Samuels had served as editor of an anarchist journal, the *Commonweal.* In an article entitled "Bombs!" (published in

Facing page: Contemporary crime-scene drawing of the site of the 1894 Greenwich Observatory explosion. *National Archives, England.* The key to the drawing reads:
a. This is where apparently explosion took place (distance from place where he was found 25 yards by path).
b. This is where the man was found and still heavily stained with blood.
X X X X X Pieces of hand found [5 locations]

Main Road-way

(a) This is where apparently Explosion took place
(Distance from place where he was found.
25 yards by feet.

(b) This is where the man was found and
still heavily stained with blood.

X x x x x Pieces of hand found

the *Commonweal* on November 25, 1893) the fire-eating Samuels had welcomed the attack on the Barcelona theater as "a great and good act—not on the part of those concerned, but because of the death of thirty rich people and the injury of eighty others."[6] David Nicoll, a bitter rival of Samuels, believed that Bourdin, in contrast to his older brother-in-law, was too gentle a soul to have harbored a violent intent. In his 1897 pamphlet *The Greenwich Mystery*, Nicoll wrote:

> In his pockets were found some papers including a ticket of membership of the Autonomie Club [a center for anarchists primarily of German or French origin], that showed that his name was Martial Bourdin, well known among the Anarchists in London. But he was not a "dangerous character." He was universally looked upon as a quiet harmless young fellow, though wonderfully honest and sincere. He was no speaker, but he could sing, and he would often mount the platform at a dance or concert and sing "The Carmagnole." He was a clever tailor, and earned three or four pound a week in the busy season. [There was a strong] opinion among those who knew him as to Bourdin's harmlessness.[7]

Hermia Oliver, though, has cast doubt on portrayals of Bourdin as an innocent or a simpleton. In her account of the Greenwich Park explosion, she cites evidence of independent visits by Bourdin to France and America, his imprisonment as a teenager in Paris for trying to arrange a meeting of radical tailors in a public thoroughfare, and his copying of "recipes for the preparation of explosives" from the British Museum.[8]

Apart from the fact that Martial Bourdin was blown up by the explosion of the "infernal machine" that he was carrying, the circumstances of his death remain an intractable puzzle. At the time of the initial investigation there was disagreement concerning the cause of what appeared to be a premature detonation of the bomb. Newspapers suggested that Bourdin had stumbled, a view strongly contested by a Home Office expert on explosives, Colonel Vivian Majendie, who asserted at the inquest that the victim was, at the time of the explosion, standing facing the observatory wall and holding the bomb in his hand.[9]

There was also a wide range of speculation regarding Bourdin's motive in bringing the bomb to Greenwich Park. The most disturbing of all hypotheses was that, as Colonel Majendie testified, Bourdin had most likely planned to carry out a terror attack against the Greenwich Observatory. Other theories were somewhat less alarming to Londoners' security. Some suggested that the young anarchist had selected an underpopulated area of the city to experiment with a newly developed explosive device, perhaps intended for use on the Continent, or that Bourdin was acting as a courier charged with delivering the bomb to foreigners.

Many contemporaries and historians have treated Bourdin's brother-in-law, H. B. Samuels, less kindly. John Quail, for example, has drawn a character portrait of Samuels that would qualify him for admission to the company of Herostratos's successors. Despite his proclaimed sympathies with the oppressed and underprivileged, Samuels often found room in the pages of the *Commonweal* to quote his own inflammatory speeches and the incensed reactions that they incited among British officialdom. In Quail's view, this journalistic attention-getting brands Samuels as a seeker of notoriety:

> H. B. Samuels' consistent reprinting of these remarks and grumblings from the authorities fills out the impression of him as a determined self-publicist—he seems more pleased that his spectacular remarks should be publicized in a hostile press than annoyed that their theoretical under-pinning and their basis in mass suffering should be ignored. As time went by his spectacular remarks became more spectacular and his notoriety consequently became greater. It is difficult to believe that he did not cultivate this notoriety and it is difficult to forgive him the fact that the consequences of it fell on others.[10]

The inquest evidence suggested that Bourdin had been alone when he took a train to Greenwich. The conductor testified that he had issued only one through ticket from Westminster to the East Greenwich terminus and that the purchaser was a young man resembling Bourdin. The passenger got off at the last stop; a timekeeper heard him ask the conductor the way to Greenwich Park. In an interview with newsmen, Samuels said that he had met Bourdin in London's West End at 2:00 in the afternoon of the tragedy and had "remained in his company for a considerable time." Samuels, who, like Bourdin, was in the tailoring trade, asked his young brother-in-law whether he had had any luck finding work. When answered in the negative, he told Bourdin that if he would accompany him to the shop at which he was employed, some work might be available because they were very busy. However, after they had "walked about 20 or 30 yards together in the direction of Mr. Samuels' workshop, . . . Bourdin suddenly exclaimed, 'No, I'm not going today. I shall go back.'"[11]

Samuels told reporters that he had never seen his brother-in-law again. He was convinced, the *Morning Leader* reported, that "Bourdin did not go to

Greenwich with any intention of blowing up the Observatory. His object was . . . either to buy the explosive or to experiment." The *Sheffield Daily Times,* in its article of February 19, 1894, quoted Samuels to a more melodramatic effect:

> Had not this unfortunate accident occurred, the consequences, I feel certain, would have been terrible. I don't mean that Bourdin intended to commit any outrage on Thursday, but I do think it was the commencement of an extensive plot. I have an idea, but I have no proof of its being correct, that the manufacture of bombs for Continental purposes has been going on here for some little time.[12]

Samuels professed that it was a complete mystery to him where Bourdin had acquired the £13 in gold that had been found in his possession by the police.

In the issue of the *Commonweal* published on March 10, 1894, Samuels praised Bourdin as the heroic tester of a new terror weapon to be employed against the class enemy:

> Such a comrade was he that, at the age of 26, he undertook the conveyance of dangerous explosive compounds to a secluded spot, where none could have been injured, in order to put to the test, a new weapon of destruction, that could have furnished the revolutionary armoury with another means of terrorizing those who consciously or unconsciously consign so many innocent lives to destruction.[13]

To David Nicoll, who had preceded Samuels as *Commonweal* editor until imprisoned for incitement to violence, the eulogy paid to Bourdin as an anarchist martyr did not make sense. In his pamphlet *The Greenwich Mystery,* he commented acerbically: "A man surely does not require £13 in gold for an experiment in Greenwich Park." To account for this suspicious circumstance, Nicoll pointed in the direction of London's police, who had been subject to criticism for lack of energy in investigating the explosion. Only on the evening of the day following the explosion did Chief Inspector Melville lead a raid on the Autonomie Club, frequented by London anarchists, and H. B. Samuels was not arrested or charged. In his memoirs, Assistant Commissioner Sir Robert Anderson offered a lame excuse for Martial Bourdin's escaping the watchful eyes of the police force:

> I never spent hours of greater anxiety than during one afternoon in February, 1894, when information reached me that a French tailor named

Bourdin had left his shop in Soho with a bomb in his pocket. To track him was impracticable. All that could be done was to send out officers in every direction to watch persons and places that he might be likely to attack. His actual objective was the very last place the Police would have thought of watching, namely Greenwich Observatory.

. . . In war the guns of an enemy would no doubt spare an astronomical Observatory, for none but savages would wish to injure an institution of that kind; but these fiends are the enemies of humanity.[14]

David Nicoll found a sinister reason for the failure of authorities to prevent or solve the bombing. Evidence of the true explanation, he argued, was to be found in the resemblance of Bourdin's weapon to a bomb found on an alleged Fenian operative when he was arrested in 1884:

The bomb found on Daly . . . was a terrible weapon in its time–a metal shell, upon which the ends or lids were screwed. This was a bomb to be thrown, and exploded on contact. Among its contents was a small piece of lead, which, upon the fall of the bomb, smashed a little bottle containing sulphuric acid; the acid exploded a substance with which it came in contact. . . . Rather strange that Daly and Bourdin's bombs should resemble one another.[15]

In Daly's case there was suspicion that the bomb had been planted on him "by an agent of the Irish Police." Nicoll contended that Bourdin was the victim of a similar police plot, to which Samuels was a party. Samuels's participation in the conspiracy seemed consistent with the otherwise puzzling fact that he was never arrested in connection with the Greenwich explosion. In support of this thesis, Nicoll cited other instances in which he claimed Samuels gave explosives to anarchists or their sympathizers with the intent that they would subsequently be raided by police. Nicoll charged that Samuels stole the materials necessary for Bourdin's bomb but must have turned them over to an explosives expert. "Who loaded the bomb?" Nicoll asked. "Bourdin and Samuels were utterly ignorant of chemistry, and would most likely have blown themselves up long before the bomb got to Greenwich Park. To load a bomb is a difficult and dangerous operation, and the work requires a man who knows something of the nature of explosives."[16] Hermia Oliver's summary of the inquest testimony regarding Bourdin's bomb indicates, however, that he had an active part in loading the device. In his pocket the police found "a glass bottle in a metal cover, containing sulphuric acid;" explosives expert

Majendie expressed "perfect confidence" that Bourdin had poured as much acid from the bottle as was necessary to prepare the bomb, whose ingredients were not disclosed.[17]

Who would have profited from an explosion devised by Samuels in league with the police? According to Nicoll's theory, the secret beneficiary was Tory leader Lord Salisbury, who had just introduced into the House of Lords his Aliens Bill, which restricted the entry of dangerous immigrants, "and every new discovery of explosives, was another argument for his Lordship." The projected legislation was in response to the outcries of Conservative newspapers, Nicoll maintained, citing a shrill editorial in the *Globe:* "Society is asking how long the British metropolis will be content to afford a safe asylum for gangs of assassins, who there plot and perfect atrocious schemes for universal murder on the Continent."[18] Nicoll concluded his pamphlet by reconstructing Bourdin's purpose in going to Greenwich Park. Samuels asked him to take the £13 and the bomb wrapped in a "brown paper parcel" to a mysterious comrade whom he was to meet in the park; he was "too weak to refuse." After he had visited the scene, it seemed unlikely to Nicoll that Bourdin had ascended the zigzag path to the observatory with the intention of blowing it up: "The Observatory, which stands on a high hill facing the park gates, was doubtless suggested to Bourdin, who did not know his way, as a landmark." But according to Nicoll, the duped Bourdin would never have reached his destination:

> I suspect the police were in ambush not far from the Observatory, and he would not have escaped them. . . . What caused the explosion, perhaps a fall, shattering the glass bottle which contained the sulphuric acid. Perhaps an accidental leakage. . . . The case of Bourdin was the case of Daly over again. Only this bit of police business had a terrible termination. Not that those who got the affair up meant to kill him, they only intended to hand him over to the living death of penal servitude.[19]

According to Louise Sarah Bevington, an English anarchist who knew H. B. Samuels well, Samuels "boastingly related" that he had delivered a "new compound" to Bourdin for the purpose of experimentation. Bourdin had chosen Epping Forest as his site but his brother-in-law ordered him to go to Greenwich Park. John Quail, a historian of British anarchists, regards Bevington as a more reliable source than the hostile David Nicoll. She had herself praised dynamite in a *Commonweal* article as a "last and very valuable resource." Still Samuels cannot have been one of her favorite comrades, for she described him in a letter to Nicoll as "about the most rubbishy character possible"; the keynotes of his character were "vanity and vindictiveness."[20]

Despite Nicoll's air of assurance, the Greenwich Mystery was still regarded as unsolved when the centenary of the explosion was marked in 1994. Philip Taylor of the Royal Observatory posted on the Internet a previously published article, "Propaganda by Deed—the Greenwich Bomb of 1894," which still bows to the unyielding puzzle: "A mystery remains—why did Bourdin pick such an unlikely target as the Observatory? The small bomb was unlikely to cause any serious damage there and it was a very different target from the crowded opera houses and cafes favoured by the terrorists in France."[21] In a 1920 author's note to his novel of anarchists in England, *The Secret Agent: A Simple Tale* (1907), Joseph Conrad recalls his first impressions of the Greenwich explosion, which inspired his plot:

> I remember, however, remarking on the criminal futility of the whole thing, doctrine, action, mentality; and on the contemptible aspect of the half-crazy pose as of a brazen cheat exploiting the poignant miseries and passionate credulities of a mankind always so tragically eager for self-destruction. That was what made for me its philosophical pretences so unpardonable. Presently, passing to particular instances, we recalled the already old story of the attempt to blow up the Greenwich Observatory; a blood-stained inanity of so fatuous a kind that it was impossible to fathom its origin by any reasonable or even unreasonable process of thought. For perverse unreason has its own logical processes. But that outrage could not be laid hold of mentally in any sort of way, so that one remained faced by the fact of a man blown to bits for nothing even most remotely resembling an idea, anarchistic or other. As to the outer wall of the Observatory it did not show as much as the faintest crack.[22]

For the purpose of inventing a historical context for Bourdin's apparently senseless self-destruction, Conrad moves the events back in time to 1886. An international conference in Milan seeking "international action for suppression of political crime [doesn't] seem to get anywhere" because England "is absurd with its sentimental regard for individual liberty." (In reality, a similar conference, held in Rome in 1898, four years after the Greenwich bombing, failed to persuade England to alter its traditional policy of granting asylum to foreign dissidents.)[23] Adolf Verloc, playing a double game similar to that attributed by David Nicoll to H. B. Samuels, is a London secret agent of a Continental power, presumably Russia. Mr. Vladimir, First Secretary of the foreign embassy employing Verloc, threatens to discharge him unless he performs a provocative act that will "administer a tonic" to the Milan Conference.[24]

The provocation that Mr. Vladimir has in mind "need not be especially sanguinary," he tells Verloc. A bombing, to influence public opinion, now must go beyond vengeance or terrorism; it must be purely destructive. Palaces and churches should be spared because "the fetish of today is neither royalty nor religion." Attempts on crowned heads or presidents are not as effective as they used to be. Instead, the simulated anarchist outrage must attack science, which the ruling middle class believes in "some mysterious way is at the source of their material prosperity." Mr. Vladimir lectures Verloc as if he were a student none too bright:

> The demonstration must be against learning—science. But not every science will do. The attack must have all the shocking senselessness of gratuitous blasphemy. Since bombs are your means of expression, it would be really telling if one could throw a bomb into pure mathematics. But that is impossible. . . . What do you think of having a go at astronomy?
>
> . . . There could be nothing better. Such an outrage combines the greatest possible regard for humanity with the most alarming display of ferocious imbecility. I defy the ingenuity of journalists to persuade their public that any given member of the proletariat can have a personal grievance against astronomy. Starvation itself could hardly be dragged in there—eh? And there are other advantages. The whole civilized world has heard of Greenwich. The very boot-blacks in the basement of Charing Cross Station know something of it. See?[25]

Mr. Vladimir's plot gives us no clue to Conrad's theory regarding the reality that underlay the Greenwich Park explosion, which his author's note had termed a "blood-stained inanity" whose origin was unfathomable. We cannot know whether the narrative of *The Secret Agent* reflects Conrad's conclusions that the Royal Observatory was the intended target and that the attack was the work of an agent provocateur like Verloc, one who was bent on simulating a new, more unsettling kind of terrorism. The author's note, written thirteen years after the first appearance of the novel, can be interpreted as avowing to his readership a belief in a design to damage the famous building, for Conrad mentions having "recalled the already old story of the attempt to blow up the Greenwich Observatory." Still, ambiguity must remain, for this always subtle author may have intended the word "story" to cast the shadow of doubt. Even more subject to debate is whether Conrad's invention of a foreign-embassy plot to incite the outrage gives the author's credence to the anarchist charges of a police conspiracy, translated in the novel into international skullduggery.

These questions of Conrad's suppositions regarding the murky events of 1894 are fascinating but, however they may be resolved, they do not detract from his accomplishment. Conrad's fictive vision of the Greenwich mystery is of great historic importance because it predicts with chilling accuracy the course that terrorist violence was to take over the coming century.

Terrorism was in the process of returning to its origins in the burning of the Temple of Artemis. The act of terror, to raise the level of public dismay, must strike, with an uncanny appearance of motivelessness, at a symbol, an abstraction, that was an expression of a community's self-confidence and of a belief in its survival. Mr. Vladimir's objective of targeting an entire society and not simply its rulers or citizens leads him to reject as old-fashioned the Continental preference for royal and political assassinations and bomb throwings in restaurants and theaters. By contrast, the attack on the science of astronomy, as practiced at the observatory, will "have all the shocking sense-lessness of gratuitous blasphemy." Mr. Vladimir has learned to perfection the lesson of ancient Ephesus.

Verloc obtains an explosive device from an anarchist bomb maker, known simply by his nickname, "the Professor," who is devoting his life to the search for the perfect detonator. The Professor, of humble origin, had believed that "the sheer weight of merit alone" entitled him to "undisputed success." Indignation over the failure of his aspirations "absolved him from the sin of turning to destruction as the agent of his ambition." Conrad explains the satisfaction that the Professor and other fanatics drew from bombs:

> He was a moral agent—that was settled in his mind. By exercising his agency with ruthless defiance he procured for himself the appearances of power and personal prestige. That was undeniable to his vengeful bitterness. It pacified its unrest; and in their own way the most ardent of revolutionaries are perhaps doing no more but seeking for peace in common with the rest of mankind—the peace of soothed vanity, of satisfied appetites, or perhaps of appeased conscience.
>
> Lost in the crowd, miserable and undersized, he meditated confidently on his power, keeping his hand in the left pocket of his trousers, grasping lightly the indiarubber ball [which would detonate a bomb if squeezed], the supreme guarantee of his sinister freedom.[26]

Moving about London with his portable weapon of destruction, the Professor is one of literature's early characterizations of a would-be suicide bomber. When the terrorist is threatened with possible arrest by an old adversary, Chief Inspector Heat, he replies that he will never be taken with impunity: "I've no doubt the papers would give you an obituary notice then. You know best what that would be worth to you. . . . But you may be exposed to the unpleasantness of being buried together with me, though I suppose your friends would make an effort to sort us out as much as possible."[27] The Professor's policy is never to refuse an explosive to anybody, as long as he has a "pinch on hand." Verloc told him nothing when he requested a bomb, except that "it was going to be a demonstration against a building." The Professor had to know at least that much so that he could prepare an appropriate missile. As it was widely suspected that H. S. Samuels had done in connection with the Greenwich bombing of 1894, Verloc entrusts the weapon to his brother-in-law, who blows himself up in his failed mission. The fictional bomber is the slow-witted Stevie; his death is avenged by his sister Winnie, who stabs her husband to death with a carving knife and leaps to her death from a channel steamer. Since the principal figures in the domestic tragedy of Conrad's agent provocateur have all met violent ends, the explosion is destined to remain a mystery. As the Assistant Commissioner of Police proclaims in a social gathering: "It's difficult to say what it is, but it may yet be a *cause célèbre*."[28]

Unlike the Professor, whom Conrad ironically dubs "incorruptible" and "the Perfect Anarchist," Verloc, in the service of his middle-aged "repose and security," kept free of allegiances. His activity as a secret agent provided an essential source of income that supplemented the meager takings of his pornography shop, for which he secured protection by serving as an unpaid police informer. Although his frame of mind was revolutionary, all his fellow men, including his anarchist comrades, were fair game for betrayal:

> The practice of his life . . . had consisted precisely in betraying the secret and unlawful proceedings of his fellow men. Anarchists or diplomats were all one to him. Mr. Verloc was temperamentally no respecter of persons. His scorn was equally distributed over the whole field of his operations. But as a member of a revolutionary proletariat—which he undoubtedly was—he nourished a rather inimical sentiment against social distinction.[29]

Conrad's divergent portraits of Verloc, the Professor, and other figures in London's anarchist community are intended to illustrate his view that a profusion of motives may inspire adherence to an ideologically based movement that seeks to achieve its ends through a combination of inflammatory words and acts. Verloc, more a family man than a firebrand, is "only overcome by his dislike of all kinds of recognized labour," a trait that Conrad believes Verloc displayed in common with "a large proportion of revolutionary reformers." To Conrad "the majority of revolutionists are the enemies of discipline and fatigue mostly," but he distinguishes two other constituent groups:

> There are natures, too, to whose sense of justice the price exacted looms up monstrously enormous, odious, oppressive, worrying, humiliating, extortionate, intolerable. Those are the fanatics. The remaining portion of social rebels is accounted for by vanity, the mother of all noble and vile illusions, the companion of poets, reformers, charlatans, prophets, and *incendiaries.* (emphasis added).[30]

Although the anarchists of *The Secret Agent* are sometimes derided as stage villains, the quoted passage reflects a bewilderment, which we share, in confronting the complexity of the terrorist personality. Conrad recognizes that fanatics, best exemplified in the novel by the Professor, may be molded as much by circumstances of their lives that strike them as "humiliating" or "intolerable" as by the ideology of the moment. He also acknowledges the essential function that vanity may play in uniting as "companions" such seemingly incompatible figures as the poet, the prophet, and the incendiary. Conrad has hardly given us a terrorist's identikit, but he has thought deeply about his theme. Either or both of the two categories on which he principally focuses may spawn perpetrators of the crimes anticipated in *The Secret Agent,* acts of violence against targets fraught with symbolic power. The fanatic and the vain may act alone or in collaboration.

THE BURNING OF KYOTO'S TEMPLE OF THE GOLDEN PAVILION (1950)

> In a month from now there'll be lots about me in the papers.
> —Mizoguchi, in Yukio Mishima's novel *The Temple of*
> *the Golden Pavilion*

Japan's ancient wooden temples have often fallen prey to fires, but only one conflagration can be attributed to the advice of an art historian. Okakura Tenshin (1862–1913), an art critic and philosopher, had proposed the preservation of a thirteen hundred-year-old wall painting regarded as a masterpiece of Japanese Buddhist art; it was located in the Horyuji Temple near Nara, advertised as comprising the "oldest wooden buildings on earth." After World War II, his suggestion was implemented, but disaster followed in the early morning of January 26, 1949:

> By 1949 the most advanced scientific methods were being used in the project, but in an ironic twist of fate an electric cushion, a warmer, brought in by one of the project's workers, caught fire and led to even more damage inside the temple.

The frescoes that Okakura had sought to preserve were totally destroyed. In the wake of this tragic damage to its religious and artistic heritage, Japan, in May 1950, adopted the Law for the Protection of Cultural Properties.[31]

Fire departments in the antiquity-rich Kyoto area were spurred to take measures to protect their beloved shrines, including the world-famous Temple of the Golden Pavilion (Kinkakuji). A local fire department chief recalls:

> Following the fire at Horyuji, we started emphasizing research and [beginning in 1950], with an 8,000,000 yen aid package from the national government, 3,000,000 yen from the prefecture and an additional 8,000,000 yen start-up funding, we were making preparations to have the groundbreaking ceremony for national treasure disaster prevention work. With the Kinkaku as a focal point we had looked at water supply, positioning of our forces, access routes and fire-fighting techniques.[32]

On the first floor of the triple-tiered Golden Pavilion, in a small reading room in the southeast corner, fire prevention technicians installed an alarm designed to ring when even slight increases in temperature were recorded. However, by June 1950 the batteries of the alarm system had failed. A work order was submitted to Fuji Disaster Prevention Company at its office in a Kyoto department store. Before the needed repair was made, it was too late.

At about 3:17 A.M. on July 2, 1950, a fire at the Golden Pavilion was seen from the observation tower of the regional fire department dispatch station. By the time ten fire trucks arrived at the temple grounds, the Golden Pavilion was already enveloped in flames, and when the fire died down at 3:50 A.M. all three floors had been reduced to ashes. The firemen asked whether anyone was inside the temple and were told that there were "no people but priceless Buddhist statues." Braving the flames, several firefighters pulled out the self-portrait carved in wood by the temple's founder, Ashikaga Yoshimitsu, but "by then the head of the statue had burned off, and its original form was left all but unrecognizable."

A team of police and public prosecutors hurried to the scene of destruction. Their investigation showed that the temple "had no heating system and no electrical lines that could have started the blaze," and "that at 6:30 P.M. on the previous evening the elderly night watchman and four other security personnel had conducted their usual closing patrol and had encountered nothing out of the ordinary." One curious detail, however, was reported to the investigators: one of the temple's acolytes was missing. The man in question was twenty-two-year-old Hayashi Yoken who, while residing at the temple and performing duties there, was also enrolled as a third-year student at Otani University, a Buddhist institution in Kyoto. Hayashi had last been seen on the previous night playing *go* with Chief Priest Egawa of Seihouji Temple and could not be accounted for since.

Intrigued by this information, the investigators discovered muddy footprints in Hayashi's sitting room, which faced the temple building, and in the hallway leading to the outer garden. A brief search of the premises turned up scraps of a futon, pillow stuffing, and a wooden sandal. The investigators determined the cause of the fire to be arson and obtained an arrest warrant for Hayashi. A nationwide manhunt began, focusing strongly on the Kyoto area. At 3:00 P.M. every police station in the city dispatched officers to search Shinto shrines, Buddhist temples, parks, and shacks. At about 6:30 P.M., due to the alertness of a local resident, the hunt was over. An informant reported to the Kinugasa police station the discovery of a man wandering about at random in the mountains of West Daimonji, not far from the Golden Pavilion. A police squad took the man into custody and transported him to a hospital in an ambulance. He was identified as the wanted Hayashi.

When Hayashi was examined by the hospital staff, it was found that his life was in no apparent danger either from the large dose of sleeping pills he had taken or the knife wounds he had inflicted near his heart and below the left clavicle. Therefore he was subjected to chief detective Noritake's questioning. Hayashi confessed to Noritake:

This morning, before daybreak, I deliberately set fire to the Kinkakuji [Golden Pavilion]. At that time, I used paper and mosquito netting to start it, and after seeing the fire catch completely, I ran away and drank sleeping medicine that I had bought one week previously. Although I had planned this from the time I made the purchase, even now I do not believe that I have done anything wrong. It is said that a national treasure has been burned, but that seems more or less meaningless.

After finishing his game of *go* at 12:30 A.M. he had placed his kindling materials on top of the offertory box, which sat before the statue of Ashikaga Yoshimitsu. Around 2:00 A.M. he lit the fire with a match. Then, carrying a kettle full of water and sleeping medicine, he raced up the slope of the West Daimonji hill; on the summit, while watching the roaring fire below, he gulped down the medicine and stabbed himself in the chest.

Murakami Jikai, chief priest of the Golden Pavilion, was at a loss to account for his acolyte's crime:

> I cannot begin to understand why Hayashi, whom I had been looking after, decided to burn the temple. Just a week ago, he had been slacking in school so much that I felt the need to reprimand him severely. Other than that, even when he took a sword from the closet in my room, I scarcely said a word. Ordinarily, he is stubborn, reckless and has a strong tendency to solitude. I tried to encourage him to be more forthright and milder-mannered, but it seemed he would never improve. I had already spoken to his parents about his behavior. It is a shame that just as I was planning to ask them to take him home, this tragedy took place.

Hayashi was the son of a Buddhist priest in Maizuru; his mother, Shimako, accompanied by her younger brother, took a train to Kyoto to answer questions about her son's personality and recent mood. She told the investigators that Yoken, who stuttered heavily, was short-tempered and bashful. Professor Nakata, an adviser of students at Otani University, was reserved in his comments on young Hayashi. There were delicate matters involved, the professor said, which he was not presently at liberty to discuss, but he would say that "he has no relations with women." The university's chief of educational affairs stated that Hayashi's demeanor had been cheerful and his grades had at first been about average but then slipped worrisomely, bringing him a reprimand. In his third year Hayashi had been cutting classes, and was called into the chief's office for "encouragement." Mr. Yamada of the Kyoto city police, who was present at the hospital interviews, took a dark view of the arsonist's state of mind but pointed to the apparent instability of his emotions. He observed, "It appeared as though he felt some antipathy toward society and the monastery where he was staying, constantly wondering whether he would be able to take his own life, or whether his feelings would improve; he has been scheming to burn down the Kinkakuji for some time."

Novelist Nancy Wilson Ross was among the first to provide a brief English-language summary of the key testimony at Hayashi's arson trial, which began on July 24, 1950:

> At his trial [the defendant] said: "I hate myself, my evil, ugly, stammering self." Yet he also said that he did not in any way regret having burned down the Kinkakuji. A report of the trial, in explanation of his conduct, stated that because of his "self-hate and self-detestation he hated anything beautiful. He could not help always feeling a strong destructive desire for hurting and destroying anything that was beautiful." The psychiatrist who was called on the case analyzed the young man as a "psychopath of the schizoid type."[33]

Donald Keene, translator and historian of Japanese literature, also cites Hayashi's statement that his crime was intended "to protest against the commercialization of Buddhism (the temple was a celebrated tourist attraction)."[34] These tantalizing overviews can now be supplemented by references to a factual account of the trial, *Kinkaku Enjō (The Burning of the Temple of the Golden Pavilion)*, published by Japanese novelist Mizukami Tsutomo in 1979. At my request, Alex Cook has translated relevant passages into English in connection with the present study.

Mizukami, apprenticed at age nine in the Zen sect of Kyoto to which the Golden Pavilion belonged, met Hayashi Yoken as a middle-school student. He recalls the youth's powerful stammer (which had afflicted him since age three) and his unsettling looks:

> He stuttered as he spoke. I was taken aback twice. His stutter was extreme. The blood vessels on his neck stood out, so strained was his breathing. . . . The forehead that peeked out from under the hat on his head was strangely narrow, and the way that the fat part of his lips and his eyes slanted upward produced a slightly oppressive feeling. . . . His tanned face that was neither boyish nor mannish fascinated my eyes.[35]

When Hayashi was interrogated after his arrest, newspapers, as Mizukami recalls, variously headlined reports of his testimony: "Is the Student Monk

Insane?"; "Burning Such a Thing Doesn't Matter"; or "Man with Bankrupt Personality Fancies Himself a Hero." The content of the articles, however, was similar:

> They all deemed Hayashi mad. It was unavoidable that he would be called insane, for who could know what he was thinking as he set fire to the Kinkaku? No one could know the truth but himself, and even after coming to his senses [after shaking off the effects of the sleeping medicine that was identified as Calmotin], he continued to make pointless, rambling statements. One would think that the reporters, adding embellishments to hearsay, could hardly be blamed.[36]

Among the statements made by Hayashi at the police station were the avowals, now inseparable from recollections of the case, that he felt envious of the Kinkaku's beauty but that his "true feelings are hard to articulate"; that he "had little sense that he had done anything wrong"; and that "existence is painful for all of us, but every day, hundreds of people come through the Kinkakuji to sightsee and he felt somewhat envious of them."[37]

The trial court appointed Miura Momoshige, a professor at Kyoto University, to interrogate Hayashi for the purpose of passing on his motivation and state of mind. Mizukami provides extensive quotations from the transcript of Professor Miura's first interview with the defendant on July 31, 1950. In his answers, often obscurely expressed, Hayashi showed resentment of his treatment by Chief Priest Murakami Jikai at the temple. The priest, he claimed, had exacerbated his feelings of worthlessness, thwarted his ambition to compete for succession to his post, and impressed on his mind a view that life was meaningless:

Q. When did you start to think that you should burn the Kinkakuji down?
A. When I first came to the Kinkakuji . . . I don't remember if I did then . . . at first I thought I should just become the next chief priest, but then that became impossible. The ugly parts of me were becoming apparent to the chief priest, and they would look at me with strange looks in their eyes, thinking "even if you can quietly do the little things, can you do the big things?"
Q. You're saying the chief priest thought that?
A. Yes, the chief priest said that true good fortune is reality, and that all one needs to do is live through reality happily. But even if the chief priest and I had taken all of the same actions, the outcome would be different, and I

knew that.... the money that came in to the Kinkaku all went to the chief priest, though, so I thought that if I burned the Kinkaku, he probably wouldn't be able to say such brazen things to me....

At first, I thought that since everyone dies, one has to do something big....

The way the chief priest treated the student monks was biased; although that might have to do with how I am, this is something I thought of later, but in time, one of the three students had to take charge of the Kinkaku, and I knew that of the three people I was the lowest. Though I could accept that, the strange looks that the chief priest gave me were maddening, so I thought I would take the three and ...

Q. Get rid of the problem?

A. Yes, I had personal problems, I had personal quarrels with some of the older people. They would take the side of some of the younger apprentices as if they were more than just friends, and the chief priest also seemed to take their side.

Q. You weren't thinking of burning the Kinkaku then; when did you start to think about that?

A. Two or three weeks ago.[38]

Q. You thought to die in the flame.

A. Yeah ... The chief priest also said that suicide is meaningless.... I also started skipping school, and when I brought saké to the teacher, he would reprimand me about my conduct. He told me that it makes no difference if we wear our clothes inside out or if we wear our clothes with the outside out for the people around us; and that we only eat meals three times in order not to die. He said that everything was meaningless and living is meaningless.

Q. You started to dislike yourself ... you thought you were inferior?

A. I had feelings like that.[39]

Professor Miura also questioned Hayashi about his feelings toward the Temple of the Golden Pavilion and about his original plan to die in the flames:

Q. There were numerous other places you could have burned. Did you pick the Kinkaku because you had special antipathy towards it?

A. No, in the end, in order to satisfy my ambitions and to satisfy myself, it made the best target....

Q. So did you have a small degree of antipathy toward the bored looking masses who would come to the Kinkakuji?

A. No, I had almost none. . . .

Q. I think you said this sometime before, but did the beauty of the Kinkaku make you angry?

A. No.

Q. You felt that since the Kinkaku is beautiful, it would be better to die there?

A. Not because it was beautiful, but because I was going to burn it anyway, it would seem more heroic if I died there. . . .

Q. Why didn't you go into the fire?

A. I saw the flames and maybe I became afraid; I can't explain why I decided not to enter the fire.[40]

The professor also took note of Hayashi's disclosure that when visiting the Ousen red light district of Kyoto, he had told a prostitute, Heya Teruko: "I might be in the newspapers soon."[41]

Professor Miura's expert opinion concluded that Hayashi suffered from "feelings of persecution" and schizophrenia. Paranoid emotion was reflected in the acolyte's statements that "because of his insidious personality," he was disliked by everyone at the Kinkakuji and "was criticized behind his back"; and that the chief priest was superficially friendly but was clearly hiding other feelings about him. Miura distinguished Hayashi from mentally stable individuals who labored under similar impressions of rejection:

> Clinically speaking, we understand the difference between people who are schizophrenic and people who are mentally stable by whether or not their mental states cause them to harm themselves or society at large. Hayashi's mental state has undeniably caused him harm, and as such he should be considered to be suffering from schizophrenia and should be handled as a schizophrenic. However, his condition cannot be considered an especially acute case.[42]

In his book on the trial Mizukami singles out Hayashi's anger against Chief Priest Murakami Jikai as the determinant cause of the crime:

> In his testimony, one sees an abundance of anger towards the chief priest, who while managing the substantial financial intake of the temple, talked about the principles of being a Zen priest, and made him fetch him saké and then reprimanded him when he brought it. Where is the young Buddhist monk who has despaired of the way of life of the Buddhist teacher to go? He was openheartedly confessing

that his idea to burn the Kinkaku came about in this way. He flatly dismissed the ideas that he wanted to keep the superlative beauty of the Kinkaku to himself, that he desired revenge, that he disliked the tourists who came in droves to see the temple, all these ideas that the newspapers were promoting. The cause for his actions was in the words the chief priest said to him when he brought him his saké; he received his idea from there. His plan to commit suicide came directly from what the chief priest had said. At this important point, although Yoken had passed his test to become a monk, he had lost the confidence to go on living as a monk at the Kinkakuji. As a result, he started to neglect his work, which in turn incurred the displeasure of his teachers. His confession brings this state of affairs to light.[43]

Mizukami's analysis has been challenged by Professor Fujii Hidetada, who charges him with "defending and rationalizing" Hayashi's act.[44]

In 1956 Yukio Mishima at age thirty-one began work on a novel based on the case, *The Temple of the Golden Pavilion*, widely regarded as his masterpiece. He not only studied the newspaper reports and trial records but visited Hayashi in prison.[45] Among the factors in the enigmatic decision to burn the Golden Pavilion, Mishima focused on the hostility aroused in the arsonist by the temple's beauty. The novelist wrote the title "Jealous of Beauty" on his two working notebooks. Mizoguchi, the hero and narrator of the novel, is a young acolyte at the Golden Pavilion who is isolated from companionship by a heavy stammer and a sense that he is ugly. As a youth he came to "entertain two opposing forms of power wishes." He saw himself as a stuttering tyrant wreaking cruel punishment on teachers and schoolmates who tormented him, and at the same time, imagined himself a great artist ruling an inner world.[46]

Beauty, however, became "the first real problem" that Mizoguchi faced in his life. His father, a country Zen priest, taught him that the Golden Temple was the most beautiful thing on earth, and Mizoguchi's growing obsession with the image of the temple interfered with his attempts to establish human relations. During World War II the Golden Temple was transformed in Mizoguchi's vision into "a symbol of the real world's evanescence" since any day, for all he knew, fire from American bombers might rain down upon the temple. The end of the war with Kyoto's ancient shrines intact restored the temple's aspect of eternity, its "expression that said: 'I have been here since olden times and I shall remain here forever.'"[47]

The period of the American occupation brings Mizoguchi lessons in brutality and corruption acted out in the radiant sphere of the temple. After he stamps on the belly of a pregnant prostitute at the orders of a drunken American soldier, he protects himself against exposure by handing the temple's Superior the two cartons of Chesterfields that he had received as a reward for his despicable behavior. From this point forward Mizoguchi's life spirals downward to the ultimate catastrophe. An evil clubfooted schoolmate, Kashiwagi, preaches to him by words and deeds that "to live and destroy were one and the same thing"; and that beauty is useless. Mizoguchi is led from "small evils"[48] (such as petty theft, gambling, skipping classes, squandering his tuition funds in a brothel, and confronting his womanizing temple Superior with a photograph of the priest's geisha) to the grandiose dream of burning down the Golden Pavilion. The act of destruction had its seeds sown during a raging Kyoto typhoon, in which Mizoguchi found himself vainly urging the wind to greater strength.

In the year before his crime, Mizoguchi spent much of his time in the library of Otani University, reading translations of novels and philosophical works. He was aware of the influence that they had on him and that it was they that inspired him to perpetrate the arson, but he still claims originality: "Yet I like to believe that the deed itself was my own original creation; in particular, I do not want this deed to be explained away as having been actuated by some established philosophy."[49] While he was confronting "the waves and the rough north wind" of the Sea of Japan, the notion to set the fire "suddenly came to life." The idea had never once occurred to his consciousness; it "began to grow in strength and size as soon as it was born."[50]

As he pondered the resolution that he had formed, he attempted to give it philosophical meaning. He found a complete and ironic "contrast between the existence of the Golden Temple and that of human beings." The "apparently destructible aspect of human beings" seemed to produce an effect of immortality, while, on the other hand, "indestructible things like the Golden Temple can be destroyed. Why had no one realized this?" Mizoguchi gloried in the expectation that, in obliterating a temple that had been designated a national treasure in 1897, he would "be committing an act of pure destruction, of irreparable ruin, an act which would truly decrease the volume of beauty that human beings had created in this world." In a humorous mood, he concluded his premeditations with the reflection that his crime would have "great educational value"—people would learn that it is "meaningless to infer indestructibility by analogy." The Golden Temple's continued existence for 550 years confers no guarantee of its future, and the nation will become uneasy as it realizes that "the self-evident axiom which our survival has predicated on the temple can collapse from one day to another."[51]

The outbreak of the Korean War on June 25, 1950, confirmed Mizoguchi's "premonition that the world was going to rack and ruin." He was impelled to hurry his plan. After setting the fire, he decided against committing suicide as he had originally intended. As he gazed on the conflagration, he puffed on a cigarette, feeling "like a man who settles down for a smoke after finishing a job of work."[52]

In January 1951 Hayashi Yoken was sentenced to seven years in prison. While in solitary confinement in a Tokyo psychiatric prison, he was diagnosed as suffering with tuberculosis and schizophrenia, and was subsequently moved to another facility near Hachioji City. When he arrived in March 1953, his social behavior appeared normal and he was able to recognize the staff personnel responsible for him. He continued to practice daily Zen rituals, and medical department head Nishida heard him chanting Buddhist names. However, around July of 1953 he began to refuse meals on occasion and sometimes he would chant the words "namu amida butsu (Hail, Amida Buddha)" even though this was a formula that did not belong to the Zen sect. In the latter part of the year Hayashi, while in his cell, became subject to sudden impulses and bursts of violence; he "would have frequent auditory hallucinations, tear his futon up, plug his ears and yield to wild fantasies." According to Dr. Hisayama, who treated him, "he would claim that his food was poisoned and refuse to eat, crying, 'I am being killed.'" As a result of turning down meals, he began to suffer from malnutrition and at one point was so weakened that his life was in danger; the hospital staff gave him glucose injections and blood transfusions, and inserted nasal tubes. At the same time, his tuberculosis worsened and a large cavity in his chest was visible by fluoroscope. By September 1955, when a reporter from the *Kyoto Shinbun* visited the prison to inquire after Hayashi's condition, Hayashi had shown signs of dementia, making it difficult for him to communicate with his attendants. When the staff gave him magazines he stared at the same page, muttering the names of three sources to which he looked for protection: Professor Yukawa Hideki, a Nobel prizewinning scientist of the period; America; and Buddha. Despite the confusion of his thoughts, Hayashi formed an emotional attachment to his nurse, Horie Masa (née Arakawa). He wrote her a touching, if largely impenetrable, note:

Instructor Arakawa, help me, I beg you, even if death in prison is my unavoidable fate, please do something. Please talk to the American Occupation Authority. Death is a place that I do not mind, but there's a sad pain I cannot bear to think of. Instructor Arakawa, my crime and my breaking the glass against the rules and throwing away my food, please forgive it all.

And, in an apparent reference to hallucinatory obsessions, he added: "Please forgive my china tango and the chicken-thing."[53]

Because of the illnesses from which he suffered, Hayashi received a sentence reduction of two years and four months and on September 29, 1955, was released from prison. He returned to a lonely world; his mother had committed suicide by throwing herself from a moving train shortly after the arson and his father had died of natural causes. Hayashi did not survive his parents long, dying in March 1956.

It would be a mistake to accept the apprentice monk's morbid obsession with beauty as a definitive explanation of the burning of the Golden Pavilion. Other elements in the circumstances of the crime and in Hayashi Yoken's personality merit more consideration than they usually receive. Even before Hayashi's clouded motives are examined, it is tempting to speculate whether his arson design was not implanted or at least accelerated by the example of the recent fire at the Horyuji Temple.

We tend to associate the copycat crime impulse with the imitation of prior crimes that have received wide publicity, but one of Japan's most famous arsons was inspired by an accidental fire of a year before. A Kabuki Glossary tells the story of love and devastation:

> Oshichi was a 16 year-old girl, daughter of a vegetable store (Yaoya in Japanese) owner, living in the district of Hongo in Edo (the current Bunkyo-ku ward in Tokyo). In 1681 Oshichi fell in love with a young priest whom she met at his temple while seeking shelter from a large fire. Hoping to see him again, she set fire in 1682 to her own home, causing a massive blaze that destroyed a huge section of Edo. She was arrested, tried and condemned to be executed for arson. She was burnt alive to pay for her crime. . . . Yaoya Oshichi became a legend and a leading character in several Kabuki plays.[54]

The interaction of accidental and criminal fires in Japan's past is also the subject of Mizoguchi's meditations in Mishima's *The Temple of the Golden Pavilion.* The student monk cites six famous temples ravaged by fire between 1249 and 1582, including the Enryaku Temple destroyed by the warlord Nobunaga. The prevalence of fires, Mizoguchi reflects, made it feasible to hide arson:

Wherever a fire might be, it could call to another fire and its voice would immediately be heard. The reason that the temple fires mentioned in the old records were never attributed to arson, but were always described as accidental fires, spreading fires, or fires caused by warfare, is that even if there had been someone like myself in the old days, all he would have had to do was to hold his breath and wait somewhere in hiding. Every temple was bound to burn down sooner or later. Fires were abundant and unrestrained. If only he waited, the fire, which was watching for its opportunity, would break out without fail, one fire would join hands with another fire and together they would accomplish what had to be accomplished. It was truly by the rarest chance that the Golden Temple had escaped being burned down.[55]

In keeping with these ancient memories, a copycat mechanism may have driven a complex of grievances and wishes that Hayashi, the stutterer, had not found other means to express.

The Temple of the Golden Pavilion, serving a double mission as religious shrine and tourist attraction, became a symbol to many, and perhaps to Hayashi, of the commercialization of Buddhism. Zen master Sawaki, for example, wrote in 1972: "For what purpose were Kinkakuji and Horyuji and all of the other old temples built? Certainly not for monks to practice Buddhism there. Just to raise coward monks there like cattle or sheep. Therefore, it is no surprise that there are monks who set fire to the Kinkakuji."[56] Public criticism of temple corruption is reflected in Mishima's novel. Mizoguchi overhears two men in a third-class carriage speculate that the annual income of the tax-exempt Golden Temple must exceed 5,000,000 yen while the operating costs could not exceed 200,000: "Well, what happened to the balance? Quite simple! The Superior let the acolytes and the apprentices feed on cold rice while he went out every night by himself and spent the money on geishas in the Gion district."[57]

Egami Taizan, a junior apprentice to Hayashi in 1950 and later administrative director of the Shoukokuji denomination to which the Golden Pavilion belongs, blames the arson on rigorous temple discipline and the unsettled war years. "I saw it," he told the *Kyoto Shinbun* in 2002, "as just the action of a youth who lived through the trying period of the war and its aftermath, and who spent his entire adolescence in a strict temple."[58]

In a critique of *The Temple of the Golden Pavilion* in her *Mishima: A Vision of the Void* (originally published in 1980), Marguerite Yourcenar regards the "hatred of Beauty," emphasized in the novel, as falling short of a full elucidation of the crime. "Typically," she comments, "the writer preserves only one of the guilty motives, in which frustrated ambition and rancor seem to have had a part."[59] Yourcenar likens the real-life arsonist and his fictional counterpart as victims of a stutter and ugliness that caused isolation from friendship and incited bullying and ridicule.

The longing of the novice monk for recognition is underscored by Mishima himself in a crucial episode of the novel that is based on the testimony of Heya Teruko at Hayashi's trial. Shortly before perpetrating the arson, the apprentice monk Mizoguchi revisits a prostitute, Mariko, intending to use up funds that his Superior has given him for his university tuition and, as a result of this transgression, to precipitate his expulsion from the Golden Temple. After their sexual encounter is over, Mizoguchi becomes exasperated with Mariko, who lectures him against frequenting brothels. He is determined that she not remember him as a callow youth whom she had scolded but as a man rendered heroic by a great crime:

> I only wished that Mariko would experience some premonition from the fateful fact of having met me. I wished that she would come just a little closer to the knowledge that she was lending a hand in the destruction of the world. After all, this should not be a matter of indifference even to this girl. I became impatient and finally blurted out something that I should not have said: "In a month—yes, in a month from now there'll be lots about me in the papers. Please remember me when that happens."[60]

In this social outcast who dreams of being noticed Yourcenar perceives what has escaped other critics—the figure of Herostratos: "In the end, he will be arrested atop the hill that looms above the temple, stuffed with a surfeit of cheap cakes that overburden his stomach accustomed to the meager postwar rations. This pitiful Erostratus, who simply wishes to live, has renounced his planned suicide, for which he had already bought a knife."[61]

Hayashi Yoken was not subjected to a formal ban on memory such as was imposed in ancient Ephesus. Yet it is possible to glimpse the outlines of a tacit understanding among many who knew him that the destroyer of one of Japan's most treasured shrines should not become a celebrity. Although his name appears in the Kyoto press and in Mizukami's book about the trial, Hayashi's contemporaries prefer to consign him to oblivion. In 2002 reporter

Nose Masayo interviewed Mizushima Keiji, a fishing guild chief who had been one of Hayashi's classmates. Mizushima spoke of the arson with evident repugnance: "It is something that I never forget, but even at class reunions no one mentions it. I think it has become a taboo subject." The monks of the Golden Pavilion have shown similar reserve. Hayashi's name does not appear either in Nose's article or in other columns gathering recollections of the fire by temple personnel. Egami Taizan, a fourteen-year-old apprentice monk at the time of the blaze, discreetly recalls the arsonist: "He was a taciturn, introverted person. . . . As an elder apprentice, he had an air of dignity. It was awful to learn of his involvement."[62]

Egami also offered the observation that his fellow novice was "reticent and genuine," but he could not say more about his temperament. He recalled the sound of the bamboo flute that the young man played on the roof of the storage warehouse and how he taught then adolescent Egami Judo techniques.[63] The inclination among the Buddhist priesthood to omit any reference to the arsonist's identity has continued. In 2003 Arima Raitei, the Golden Pavilion's head priest and chair of the board of directors of the Kyoto Buddhist Church, also left the Golden Pavilion arsonist nameless in an article about the restoration of the temple.[64]

Even Western commentators until recently have omitted mention of Hayashi's name. Nancy Wilson Ross, in her introduction to the first American edition of Mishima's novel, *The Temple of the Golden Pavilion*, in a translation by Ivan Morris, keeps the incendiary anonymous even while quoting from the trial report. Marguerite Yourcenar's critical study of Mishima's work reflects on the arsonist's character but does not pronounce the dread syllables of his name. This long silence in the West was broken in 1994 when Donald Keene wrote dismissively of Mizukami's book about Hayashi's trial:

> The novelist Minakami [or Mizukami] Tsutomo . . . published *Kinkaku Enjō* [*Burning of the Kinkaku*], a factual account of the destruction of the famous building. Minakami (who was trained as a Zen priest) had actually known Hayashi Yōken, and his book confirms that, to all appearances, he was a totally uninteresting person; but that is about all it adds to what the reader already knew from Mishima's free but respectful treatment of the facts.[65]

> The treaty was concluded in the name of the "Powers Invisible." For the
> gods of each people were unknown unto the other people.
> —Gustave Flaubert, *The Temptation of St. Anthony,* pt. 5

In 1557 Sultan Suleiman the Magnificent commissioned the Ottoman architect Mimar Hajruddin to build what became known as the Stari Most (Old
Bridge) across the Neretva River in Bosnia-Herzegovina, southwest of Sara-
jevo. The span, regarded as Hajruddin's masterpiece, divided the city of Mostar
(or "Bridge-keeper"), to which it gave its name. Over the centuries the Stari
Most became Mostar's landmark and a link between its peacefully cohabit-
ing ethnic communities, including Croats on the west bank and Muslims on
the east. The bridge also served as a free passageway between Europe and
Asia, because, as Amir Pasic has noted, "from the seventeenth century, the
Neretva river was the west border of Islam."[66] The dominant groups of Mostar
residents lived side by side with Orthodox Serbs and Sephardic Jews.

Rebecca West, in *Black Lamb and Grey Falcon* (1941), a classic account of
her journey through Yugoslavia on the eve of the Second World War, was
overwhelmed by her view of the Stari Most:

> Presently we were looking at that bridge, which is falsely said to have
> been built by the Emperor Trajan, but is of medieval Turkish work-
> manship. It is one of the most beautiful bridges in the world. A slender
> arch lies between two round towers, its parapet bent in a shallow angle
> in the centre.
>
> To look at it is good; to stand on it is as good. Over the grey-green
> river swoop hundreds of swallows, and on the banks mosques and white
> houses stand among glades of trees and bushes. . . . The river might be
> running through unvisited hills instead of a town of twenty thousand
> inhabitants.[67]

The idyllic scene that West visited remained undisturbed for the half century
that followed. Sarah Jane Meharg has described the life of the bridge in times
of peace prior to the Bosnian conflict:

> It was a narrow, ivory-coloured limestone structure, peaked in the
> middle, with steep inclines on both sides, 30 metres long and 20 metres

high. It was declared the most beautiful of bridges in the world when it was completed. It was wide enough to accommodate foot travel, and many locals would stroll along it on their evening walk. It was where people met to discuss their business, their lives, and their families. It became a place of romance, where teens received their first kiss. The Bridge of Mostar resonated with rites of passage. It was considered one of the greatest historical monuments of the Balkans.[68]

During the war in Bosnia-Herzegovina the Stari Most came under fire from both Serb and Croat forces. In May 1991 the bridge sustained its first damage when Serb artillery "blasted it in two places and leveled much of the surrounding neighborhood." The Bosnian Muslims "draped old tires over the side of the bridge and erected scaffolds over its walkway in a futile attempt to deflect shells." In the following two years, Serb and Croat shells damaged the stone towers at the ends of the bridge.[69] The final catastrophe occurred in late 1993 under a deadly fusillade from the Bosnian Croats. Suha Özkan, secretary-general of the Aga Khan Award for Architecture, mourns the tragic event:

On the morning of November 9, 1993, the first shell hit the leg of Stari Most bridge in Mostar. Shelling of this same spot continued with chilling accuracy, one shell after another, as if attackers had finally found an historical opportunity for destruction. After several hits, the pediment was smashed, and the elegant, arched backbone of the bridge collapsed into the water with a tragic splash, as if the Neretva River was shedding tears for the millions of people who had now lost a cherished piece of memory. For them, the Stari Most Bridge was as significant as the nave of Hagia Sophia, or the top of the Empire State Building, the approach to the Taj Mahal or the heights of Machu Picchu; its presence surpassed any function.

It took [the architect] and his workers nine years, from 1557 to 1566, to build the bridge which was destroyed in perhaps less than thirty minutes.[70]

After the Stari Most collapsed into the river, a spokesman for the Bosnian Croats, who planned to establish their capital in Mostar, admitted that their gunners had the ancient structure in their crosshairs. He claimed, however, that the bridge was appropriately considered of strategic importance because Muslim positions were located nearby.[71] His words were not persuasive to the Croatian journalist Slavenka Drakulic, who wrote:

We expect people to die. We count on our own lives to end. The destruction of a monument to civilization is something else. The bridge, in all its beauty and grace, was built to outlive us; it was an attempt to grasp eternity. Because it was the product of both individual creativity and collective experience, it transcended our individual destiny. A dead woman is one of us—but the bridge is all of us forever.[72]

The military justification offered for the targeting of the bridge did not impress Suha Özkan, who had witnessed with satisfaction the prewar restoration of historic Mostar. To Özkan the attack on the Old Bridge was a part of a wider attempt to "erase the physical presence of Islam" in Bosnia-Herzegovina. To convey the ferocity of this premeditated campaign to annihilate nationhood's monuments, Özkan had recourse to the precedent set by the antipathy of Herostratos to a Wonder of the Ancient World:

> The reasons behind the destruction of the cultural heritage throughout former Yugoslavia will remain as incomprehensible as Herostratos' destruction of the temple of Artemis in Ephesus, simply because it was beautiful. Stari Most's beauty had become its reason to be—after catalyzing Mostar's initial development in the sixteenth and seventeenth centuries, it served the town well in the twentieth century through its sheer presence.[73]

The name of Herostratos echoed again in March 2001 when the Taliban regime demolished two colossal statues of Buddha in central Afghanistan. These objects of veneration, like the Temple of the Golden Pavilion, attracted the fury of sacrilegious destroyers. The two Buddha figures were carved into niches incised in the sandstone cliffs of Bamiyan, a town on the Silk Road located about 125 miles northwest of Kabul. The precise dates of their construction are disputed, but it is estimated that they rose to their commanding heights of 175 and 125 feet during the period from the second century through the fourth and fifth centuries AD. They were "covered with mud and straw mixture to model the expression of the face, the hands and the folds of their robes." The larger statue, painted in red, was "thought to represent Vairocana, the 'Light Shining throughout the Universe Buddha.'" The smaller image, in blue, "probably represents Buddha Sakyamuni, although the local Hazara people believe it depicts a woman."[74]

On February 26, 2001, the supreme leader of the Taliban regime, Mullah Mohammed Omar, in an edict published by the Taliban-controlled Bakhtar

News Agency, ordered the destruction of all statues in Afghanistan, including pre-Islamic figures such as the Giant Buddhas. Mullah Omar declared:

> In view of the fatwa [religious edict] of prominent Afghan scholars and the verdict of the Afghan Supreme Court it has been decided to break down all statues/idols present in different parts of the country. This is because these idols have been gods of the infidels, who worshiped them, and these are respected even now and perhaps may be turned into gods again. The real God is only Allah, and all other false gods should be removed.[75]

The threat to a cultural heritage that had enriched not only Afghanistan but the entire world immediately raised international outcries. Spokespersons for the U.S. State Department and the European Union as well as for foreign ministries of countries throughout Europe and Asia strongly urged a reversal of the threat of cultural desecration. The United Nations General Assembly issued a condemnatory resolution backed by a similar action of the Security Council. Secretary-General Kofi Annan also cautioned: "Destroying any relic, any monument, any statue will only prolong the climate of conflict."[76] His efforts to dissuade the Taliban from implementing their decree were seconded tirelessly by UNESCO Director General Koichiro Matsuura, who expressed "feelings of consternation and powerlessness" in face of the Taliban's unshakeable resolve. The Dalai Lama also voiced his distress, telling the *Times of India:* "I am deeply concerned about the possible destruction of the Bamiyan statues of the Buddhas at a time when there is closer understanding and better harmony among different religions."[77]

From East and West came offers to save either the Buddhas or smaller statues. On March 4 the press reported from Islamabad that Taliban Foreign Minister Wakil Ahmad Mutawakil had "rejected an Iranian offer to take Afghanistan's historic Buddha statues into safe-keeping." This rebuff overshadowed the visit by UNESCO envoy Pierre Lafrance, who had recently left Islamabad for Afghanistan on a mission to save the statues.[78] On March 2 Philippe De Montebello, while despairing of rescuing "what is hewn in the rocks," suggested the formation of an international consortium to bid for statues of a reasonable size and to place them in a secular environment "where they are cultural objects, works of art and not cult images."[79] The Association of Art Museum Directors, representing 175 American art museums, stated that it would "stand by any effort" to retrieve the artworks.[80] Another proposal was made that the

Buddhas of Bamiyan should remain in place but should be screened from fundamentalist eyes by the erection of a concrete barrier.

These pleas around the globe went unheeded as the Buddhas were dying a slow death. As early as March 3, 2001, Taliban Information Minister Qudratullah Jamal told the Associated Press that soldiers had already begun firing mortars and cannons at the heads and legs of the Buddhas. The minister added in a matter-of-fact tone: "Our soldiers are working hard to demolish their remaining parts. They will come down soon."

By March 11 the demolition of the two Buddhas was announced to have been completed after attacks by tanks, artillery, mortars, dynamite, anti-aircraft weapons, and rockets. Taliban Information Minister Jamal almost asked for sympathy as the wreckers sought rest from their labors. He commented: "The destruction work is not as easy as people would think. You can't knock down the statues by dynamite or shelling as both of them have been carved in a cliff. They are firmly attached to the mountain."[81] It was reported that "the Taliban directing the onslaught later cheered and had their photos taken above the piles of rock and dust."[82]

The extinction of the Buddhas was an even more unsettling spectacle of anticultural terrorism than the destruction of the Bosnian bridge. In her article "Identicide and Cultural Cannibalism: Warfare's Appetite for Symbolic Place" (published in November 2001 but most likely written before the World Trade Center attack), Sarah Jane Meharg cites the Old Bridge at Mostar and Afghanistan's Grand Buddhas as two features of "symbolic landscapes" that "create a particularity of place, [and] also act as narratives of collective memory that underpin the cohesion and identity of groups." The attack on the historic bridge by Bosnian Croat forces exemplifies what Meharg calls *identicide,* "the act of destroying vernacular and symbolic places during war with the intention of erasing cultural identity and a sense of social belonging." Meharg distinguishes this kind of onslaught from a related atrocity that she terms *cultural cannibalism,* which describes "the intentional elimination of symbolism representing a culture, perceived as threatening or contested." The latter concept applies to the Taliban destruction of the Buddhas:

> Identicide occurs when groups contest and aim to destroy one another's places of identity, while cultural cannibalism is a diagnostic tool for the destruction of shared world culture and heritage for immediate political, religious, or ideological goals. The Taliban, for example, are aiming to destroy a contested Buddhist landscape impregnated with historical Afghan significance to reach the short-term goal of creating a pure Is-

lamic state. They are in fact, destroying shared cultural patrimony, and cannibalizing culture.

One of the strongest expressions of outrage at the Taliban action came from the neighboring country of Uzbekistan. On March 3, 2001, in the Uzbek military newspaper *Vatanparvar* (*Patriot*), a state news agency commentator, A. Karimov, expressed concern for the safety of sites associated with Uzbek history in Afghanistan. After suggesting that the Taliban decree might have been conceived as a bargaining chip to ease pressure on Osama bin Laden, Karimov looked more deeply into the mind of Mullah Omar, the Taliban leader:

> This is another move intended to liven up the political trading. The inhuman decree is aimed at taking advantage of the secular states' weakest link—their aspiration to preserve the [universal] historical and cultural heritage.
>
> Here another idea comes to mind. What have people not done in the world in order to gain fame, and to ensure that their deeds left an indelible trace in the pages of history? One of them was Herostratus. In order to ensure his immortal fame, he chose the simplest and vilest way. He burned down the great temple of Diana at Ephesus. Thinking about it, one may believe that the Taliban have chosen Herostratus's way of attracting the international community's attention to their problems.

One of Karimov's readers was Victor-Pierre Stirnimann, a Jungian psychologist. Stirnimann points out that the Buddha was not represented in human form until the tolerant Sarvastivadin ("everything-exists") school absorbed Greek influence as a result of Alexander's conquests. He notes that the Buddhas of Bamiyan were culturally important as "a product of the first contacts between two civilizations, the East and the West."

Stirnimann sees hostility to Western commercial values hiding behind the Taliban's professed religious antagonism to the giant "idols":

> Idolatry is forbidden in Islam, but there was probably more in this iconoclastic drive than first met the eye. The statues had not been worshipped for centuries, and thus represented no threat; in fact, they were little more than remains from a forgotten past. Moreover: if radicalism and religiosity were the only reasons for blowing them up, why turn their destruction into a world press event? *They were only stones,* as the mullah has allegedly said. But the mullah also said, when Western institutions

offered to buy the statues: *we prefer to be remembered as the destroyers of statues, rather than as the sellers of them.*

. . . . By preferring to destroy them, instead of taking advantage of the hegemonic rules of commerce and interchange, they wanted to make a statement. They wanted to carry out a symbolic act, and they aimed it at a public. We may have seen it as an act of cultural self-destruction. It was also an act of terrorism against the West, against something deeply symbolic to their adversaries.[83]

With approval Stirnimann cites Uzbek journalist Karimov's reference to Herostratos's criminal desire for fame as presaging the Taliban determination to leave an indelible mark in history. "Herostratus, indeed," Stirnimann broods. "Could he be a clue, a pre-figuration to lead our way to a deeper understanding of it all?" Stirnimann and many others explored this question as they addressed the events of September 11.

4 The Killers

Assassinations of prominent victims have been numerous throughout history and the circumstances of the attacks are often mysterious and particularized. It may therefore be more difficult to identify a Herostratic desire for fame as a major stimulus to such a crime than to find such motivation behind the destruction of a symbolic building. The Herostratos syndrome is most likely to be a factor in assassination when one or more of the following circumstances can be established, as in each of the cases in this chapter:

1. The assassin had no grievance against the victim.
2. The assassin expressed to another person or persons, often on slight acquaintance, a desire to see his name or action in the media or to be remembered in history.
3. The assassin writes a memoir, diary, or correspondence either before, during, or after his crime, often with the express intention that his writings will come to the attention of a wide or future audience.

In *Criminals Painted By Themselves,* Raymond Hesse cites Herostratos as an early example of the same mind-set that causes criminals to write "literary works" immortalizing their misdeeds: "Since Herostratos, who burned the famous temple of Diana to leave a famous name in history, the mentality of the criminal has not changed. Herostratos, moreover, achieved his purpose. If he had lived as a peaceable *bourgeois,* who would cite his name today?"[1]

With the guidance of Hesse's observation and of commentators who have seen Herostratos's traits in some assassins—even those who proclaimed themselves humanitarians—a new look may be taken at some of the killers who have haunted us since the late nineteenth century. The crimes to be considered will be the successful or attempted assassinations of an empress, an entertainer, and several political leaders. Two examples of a related phenomenon, multiple killings, will also be discussed.

THE ASSASSINATION OF A "ROYAL," EMPRESS ELISABETH OF AUSTRIA (1898)

In the last years of her tragic life, Empress Elisabeth of Austria appeared in an official capacity at only one function, Hungary's millennial celebration in 1896. She had long borne her imperial duties with distaste and in her final decade was afflicted with depression over the loss of her beloved son, Crown Prince Rudolf, who had died with his young mistress, Baroness Mary Vetsera, in the "love suicides" at Mayerling in 1889. The international press disseminated rumors that Elisabeth was emotionally disturbed. *Il Secolo* of Milan, for example, wrote in 1893, "The empress-queen Elisabeth suffers from incipient insanity. Every evening hallucinations trouble her. She thinks that Crown Prince Rudolf is still a child and at her side."[2] Even before Rudolf's death, Elisabeth had thrown herself into a round of foreign travel. One of her favorite destinations was Switzerland, but by the 1880s even that peaceful locale became associated in her mind with thoughts of danger because of the country's policy of granting asylum to anarchists. In one of her "Winter Songs" of that period, she wrote:

> People of Switzerland, your mountains are splendid!
> Your clocks keep good time;
> But for us great danger is posed
> By your brood of regicides.[3]

In September 1898 the empress was taking a four-week cure in Territet near Montreux. On Friday, September 9, she left the resort for a visit to Baroness Julia Rothschild in Pregny, traveling incognito in the company of a court lady, Countess Irma Sztáray. After three hours with the baroness, Elisabeth and her attendant went on to Geneva, where she had ice cream at her favorite pastry shop and bought toys for her grandchildren. At the Hotel Beau Rivage, the empress registered for an overnight stay under the name of "Countess von Hohenembs." Her secret, though, was ill kept by the hotel management, which followed its usual policy of publicly disclosing the arrival of a royal guest. At 6:00 P.M. on September 9, the Beau Rivage gave notice of Elisabeth's arrival to three Geneva newspapers, as well as *Le Figaro* and the Paris edition of the *New York Herald*. The *Journal de Genève* reported Elisabeth's visit in its morning edition of Saturday, September 10.[4]

On Saturday morning, Elisabeth, accompanied by Countess Sztáray, visited shops in Geneva, a city that she knew well, and enjoyed a brief walk, returning to her hotel around 1:15. Countess Irma hurried Elisabeth along, for their boat, the *Geneva,* was scheduled to depart for Montreux in less than half an hour. Elisabeth and Irma left the Beau Rivage at 1:30, and a short walk would bring them to the boat's landing only a few hundred meters from the hotel entrance. Elisabeth, dressed in her accustomed black, carried a fan in one hand and a parasol in the other. A man was loitering on their route, leaning on a fence that ran along the lake, and as the two women were about to pass by, he ran toward them, looked quickly under the parasol to verify his target, and stabbed Elisabeth in the chest with surgical accuracy. According to the later report of the attorney general, Elisabeth fell from the violence of the shock; she was then helped back to her feet by Irma and a bystander and, without support, continued her walk to the quay. Unaware of the nature of her injury, she replied to the worried inquiry of her lady of honor about the reason for her distress: "I don't know; my chest hurts." As soon as she came aboard, she fainted and was unconscious for several minutes. When she came to, she could barely mutter the words, "What happened to me?" when she lost consciousness again. The boat, which had just entered open waters, turned back toward the landing. The empress was carried to the hotel on an improvised stretcher, but the doctors who were called to her bedside could not save her. An autopsy revealed a triangular wound eighty-five millimeters deep, caused by an "elongated and pointed" instrument that had cracked the fourth rib, pierced the anterior wall of the left lung, torn the pericardium, and entered the left ventricle of her heart.[5]

After his attack on Elisabeth, the assailant took flight down a city street, until his way was blocked by a narrow-gauge railroad switchman, who shouted for police assistance. Two hours later, a concierge found the criminal's weapon on his escape route: it was a sharp triangular file that had been crudely set into a wooden handle. The arrested man told police that his name was Luigi Lucheni; that his crime was motivated by anarchism; and that there were many other anarchists in Lausanne and Geneva who were ready for similar action. In a manifesto published by an Italian journal, *Don Marzio,* after his capture, he concluded with a slogan that he was to repeat often: "The day is not far off when real humanitarians will cross out all their present writings; one alone will be more than sufficient and that will be: WHOEVER DOESN'T WORK DOESN'T EAT."[6]

The police learned that Lucheni was born in 1873 at a Paris hospital for publicly "assisted" children. He was the illegitimate son of Louise Luccheni, a servant from the region of Parma, Italy, and an unnamed father, perhaps Louise's master or the son of her master. A week after Luigi's birth, Louise formally abandoned her son to the Public Assistance of the City of Paris. Raised in foster homes, and a manual laborer at age nine, he worked in construction on the Parma-La Spezia railroad in 1889. Beginning in 1894, he served in an Italian cavalry regiment and two years later was posted to Ethiopia, which had become an Italian colony in 1890. In October 1896 Lucheni received a decoration, certified by the minister of war as recognizing his services in the African military campaigns; Luigi remarked afterward that the award was for a lost battle that he had missed. On his return to Naples, he served for ten months in the squadron of Captain and Prince Ramiero de Vera d'Aragona, who regarded him as his best soldier: "[Lucheni] is always disciplined and diligent in all the requirements of service. He rides well, is excellent as a mobile infantryman, and because of his intelligence and obedience, he is specially employed for patrols with the best results."[7]

After leaving the army, Lucheni found that these words of praise were not matched by official gratitude. Although his three and a half years of service entitled him to a government position, his repeated applications for a job as a prison guard went unanswered. The best employment he could find after leaving the army in December 1897 was in the household of his former commander, Captain Vera d'Aragona, who unfortunately proved less easy to please as a domestic employer.

Parting with the captain on March 31, 1898, Lucheni set out on a course of European wanderings that strangely converted him in less than six months from an honored army veteran into a self-professed anarchist and the assassin of an apolitical empress. Setting out for Genoa by steamer, he passed through Turin and crossed the Alps on foot into Switzerland. On May 20 Lucheni took lodgings in a pension located in an Italian quarter of Lausanne. Recent disorders in Milan had inspired the weekly publication of the *Agitatore*, addressed to Italians in Switzerland. Lucheni became an avid reader of radical periodicals, attended anarchist meetings in Lausanne and Neuchâtel, and on August 18, hawked anarchist street songs. To a former regimental comrade, he wrote: "The anarchist idea is making surprising progress here. Please also do your duty with our comrades who are not yet up to date."

There are reasons to doubt the firmness of Lucheni's ideological commitment. After leaving Prince d'Aragona's household, he made several unsuccessful efforts to return to his domestic employ. Maria Matray and Answald Krüger, in their study of the assassination, remark skeptically: "The anarchist Lucheni persistently tried to become the servant Lucheni once more." Two days before the crime, the prince's lady was still on his mind. He sent his ex-employer's wife a picture postcard from Geneva showing the very scene where the murder would be committed. To Matray and Krüger, this postcard furnishes persuasive evidence that Lucheni was, in Schiller's words, a criminal out of "lost honor."[8]

Before the assassination, Lucheni told his roommate Giacomo Sartoris that he would like to kill a person of importance who was well known, so that the newspapers would talk of the event. While receiving workers' compensation for an injury to his right index finger, Lucheni acquired his murderous iron file, which a carpenter friend, Martinelli, fitted into a wooden handle at his request. Lucheni chose the file, he later explained, because he could not afford a dagger.

The murder of a page-one personage became Lucheni's obsession, but he wavered regarding the choice of his victim. During his preliminary interrogation, he claimed that he had come to Geneva to kill Bourbon Prince Henri d'Orléans only to find that the prince was no longer in the city. It was solely as a spontaneous modification of planning, he told his questioners, that he had fallen back on the idea of assassinating Elisabeth, whose visit to Geneva had been announced in the press.[9] However, since news of the empress's arrival was first published on the morning of the murder, police suspected that Lucheni had been alerted by word of mouth or by surveillance of Elisabeth's movements.

A trial in Geneva (which had abolished capital punishment) required only one day. The defendant's cause, hopeless in advance, was not aided by his grandstanding behavior in court. Entering the courtroom with the swaggering walk of a sailor, and with a permanent smile on his lips, Lucheni seemed detached from the proceedings, "as if someone else was on trial." "Yes, it's me!" he called to assembled journalists, and blew a star's kisses to the audience. After the indictment was read, Lucheni was questioned about his motive. In apparent contradiction of his pretrial effort to portray himself as an altruistic killer, he now claimed that he had been impelled by "misery," by his mother's rejection on the day of his birth, and by being put to work when he was still a child. Asked what he expected to accomplish by his crime, he replied melodramatically, "To avenge my life!"[10]

In his closing argument, Attorney General Georges Navazza urged a different interpretation. Despite his belief that the assassination was not the work of Lucheni acting alone, Navazza argued that, since the conspiracy was impossible to prove, the jury must focus solely on the defendant's motive. Navazza saw in Lucheni a boundless vanity that was moved to crime when his mind was seized by a hazily conceived notion of anarchism. At the end of his speech, Navazza was skeptical about the possibility of the defendant's rehabilitation: "Nothing in this man reveals the awakening of his conscience: there is nothing, nothing on his face, but this perpetual grin of an individual satisfied with the accomplishment of his work!" The attorney general argued for the consignment of the killer to "eternal oblivion." In his defense argument, Lucheni's court-appointed counsel, Pierre Moriaud, conceded that pride and vanity had played a larger role in the crime than misery, but contended that the real culprits were the theoreticians of anarchy. As if on cue, Lucheni, after being sentenced to life imprisonment, shouted as he was led away, "Long live anarchy; down with the aristocrats."[11]

Scientific experts could not agree on the assassin's mental condition. Before the trial began, the celebrated theorist of inherited criminality, Cesare Lombroso, reported that Lucheni presented "a great number of physical characteristics common to epileptics and pure criminals."[12] Dr. Auguste Forel, a psychiatrist who testified at the trial, took issue with Lombroso's conclusions. Forel believed that resentment, poverty perhaps, and certainly vanity, had prepared the way for Lucheni's impressionability and feeble intellect to succumb to the blandishments of anarchism; violent impulses had also been at work. Another witness, criminal jurist Alfred Gautier, concurred in finding Lombroso's analysis of the defendant ill-founded and also inveighed against excessive reliance on psychiatry in criminal justice: "If every contradiction of character is evidence of an illness, it is not only Lucheni but all of us who are sick."[13]

The news of Empress Elisabeth's assassination came to Mark Twain at an Austrian summer resort near Vienna. Powerfully moved by the sadness and the novelty of the event, he quickly penned his reactions in an article, "The Memorable Assassination," which was published posthumously in the collection *What Is Man?*[14] The first unusual feature of the case to seize upon Twain's imagination was that the victim was not a powerful ruler but an empress; he maintained that "the murder of an empress is the largest of all large events" and that "one must go back about two thousand years to find an instance to put with this case." Moreover, the expansion of the world's boundaries and the acceleration of communications had wrought an immense change in the impact of a great crime:

> The world is enormous now, and prodigiously populated—that is one change; and another is the lightning swiftness of the flight of tidings, good and bad. "The Empress is murdered!" When those amazing words struck upon my ear in this Austrian village last Saturday, three hours after the disaster, I knew that it was already old news in London, Paris, Berlin, New York, San Francisco, Japan, China, Melbourne, Cape Town, Bombay, Madras, Calcutta, and that the entire globe, with a single voice, was cursing the perpetrator of it. . . . this is the first time in history that the entire surface of the globe has been swept in a single instant with the thrill of so gigantic an event.

An irony of the calamity was that "the miracle-worker who has furnished to the world this spectacle" was

> at the bottom of the human ladder, as the accepted estimates of degree and value go: a soiled and patched young loafer, without gifts, without talents, without education, without morals, without character, without any born charm or any acquired one that wins or beguiles or attracts; without a single grace of mind or heart or hand that any tramp or prostitute could envy him; an unfaithful private in the ranks, an incompetent stone-cutter, an inefficient lackey; in a word, a mangy, offensive, empty, unwashed, vulgar, gross, mephitic, timid, sneaking, human polecat.

Lucheni illustrated to Mark Twain the lesson that "no man has a wholly undiseased mind," and that "one of the commonest forms of madness is the desire to be noticed, the pleasure derived from being noticed." Twain predicted that the obscure assassin of the blameless and charitable empress would swiftly outstrip all other pursuers of fame or notoriety; that "if there is a king who can remember, now, that he once saw that creature in a time past, he has let that fact out, in a more or less studiedly casual and indifferent way, some dozens of times during the past week."

The humanitarian motive that some found behind Lucheni's crime struck Mark Twain as a sentimental invention. He was persuaded that the world had witnessed a startling modern example of the Herostratic "hunger for notoriety":

Some think that this murder is a frenzied revolt against the criminal militarism which is impoverishing Europe and driving the starving poor mad. That has many crimes to answer for, but not this one, I think. One may not attribute to this man a generous indignation against the wrongs done the poor; one may not dignify him with a generous impulse of any kind. When he saw his photograph and said, "I shall be celebrated," he laid bare the impulse that prompted him. It was a mere hunger for notoriety. There is another confessed case of the kind which is as old as history—the burning of the temple of Ephesus.

Mark Twain's intuitive vision of Lucheni as a fame seeker is confirmed by Brigitte Hamann, Empress Elisabeth's twentieth-century biographer. Hamann describes Lucheni's mood as he faced trial: "He was in high spirits and full of pride over his act, which he was unwilling to share with anyone else: he emphasized that he was a lone assassin and could claim the 'glory' of the crime for himself alone. He saw the murder as the high point of his life and wished to suffer the death penalty."[15] According to Hamann, Lucheni had been "seized" by the ideas of international anarchism, with which he became acquainted in Switzerland; but he knew nothing of Elisabeth except what he read in the newspapers. To him, Hamann maintains, "she was a crowned head, whose murder would make headlines and would make the name Lucheni famous."

Only recently Santo Cappon has revealed a previously unknown dimension of Lucheni's commitment to the perpetuation of his fame. In 1998, Cappon published the long-lost childhood memoir written by Lucheni in his prison cell under the title *Story of a Child Abandoned at the End of the Nineteenth Century, Written by Himself.*[16] In his accompanying narrative, Cappon argues that the mysterious disappearance of Lucheni's manuscript in March 1909 was the cause of violent behavior on the part of the prisoner, who had been calm a long time; on October 19, 1910, Lucheni was found hanging by a strap fixed to a window hinge in a punishment cell.

In his memoir, which he had intended to continue into the years of his youth, Lucheni retained his strong purpose that the world not forget him. However, after years of reflection in solitude, ideology was not on his mind; he was "very anxious" that future readers should absorb one lesson—that in his formative period he had been denied love. He asked his readers to consider that his childhood

> was deprived of the most ordinary pleasures and joys that all children enjoy; that . . . it enjoyed no friendship, no fellowship, no society of

friends of his own age. That it was also deprived of education, of advice, of consolation and of sympathy; all indispensable things, it seems to me, to prepare worthily a child destined to pass his mature years with others having the same duties to fulfill.[17]

These words of introspection and of self-pity came much too late to spare the life of the empress. In the same volume that includes Lucheni's memoirs, Cappon includes another reflection of the killer's psyche, a photograph of a "jovial Lucheni flanked by two gendarmes" conducting him to a preventive prison prior to his trial. On Lucheni's face, memorable forever, is the self-satisfied grin that appalled Attorney General Navazza.

Mark David Chapman, Murderer of John Lennon (1980)

In his rapidly cycling moods, the celebrity killer Mark David Chapman, born in 1955, experienced feelings of worthlessness and grandiosity. To Jack Jones, who interviewed him for more than two hundred hours at Attica prison, he said in explanation of his murder of John Lennon: "I was an acute nobody. I had to usurp someone else's importance, someone else's success. I was 'Mr. Nobody' until I killed the biggest Somebody on earth."[18] Before the murder, however, he liked to tell his wife, Gloria, that "ever since he was a kid he knew he was meant for greatness, that he was destined to be someone big."[19] He was encouraged in this belief by his mother, who often fled to her young son's bedroom to escape marital violence.

On a morning after his sleep was disturbed by sounds of a quarrel in his parents' bedroom, Mark was visited by an apparition of the "Little People," who seemed to inhabit the walls of his bedroom and acclaimed him as their king. He could not remember when they had first come to him but they were to return at emotional junctures of his life. The Little People witnessed a childhood and a coming-of-age that passed through many phases typical of the 1960s generation. After suffering indignities at the hands of schoolyard bullies, Mark began to experiment with psychedelic drugs as to which the Beatles' *Magical Mystery Tour* album had first piqued his curiosity. In 1970 he ran away from his suburban Atlanta home in the hope of finding a sense of belonging among the drug "freaks" of Miami. His job as a carnival security guard and his hippie acquaintanceship proved equally disappointing and within months the prodigal returned to his dependent mother and unaffectionate father.

By 1971 Mark Chapman had remade himself once more, giving up drugs for born-again Christianity. Michael McFarland, a new friend who invited him to play guitar in a Christian rock band, recommended that he read *The Catcher in the Rye*. When Mark finished the novel, he was swept by a new conversion—to the personality of the book's hero, Holden Caulfield, and his campaign against phoniness. A childhood friend observed that Chapman had undergone a "true personality split," resolving to be "the best Christian in the world" and expressing what Jack Jones calls "an intense loathing for the musical heroes of his childhood: John Lennon and the Beatles." Lennon was replaced by Todd Rundgren as Mark's favorite rocker.

For several years Mark Chapman's discovery of religious faith led him to fruitful service on behalf of the Young Men's Christian Association. As a camp counselor, and subsequently assistant program director, he was popular with his young charges, who called him by his preferred nickname, Captain Nemo, borrowed from the protagonist of Jules Verne's *Twenty Thousand Leagues under the Sea*. Nemo, the Latin word for nothing, was an apt emblem of Mark's struggle with low self-esteem, and the children's admiration gave him the feeling that "Those were the greatest days of [his] life. [He] was Nemo and everyone in camp loved [him]."[20]

Early in 1975 Chapman was selected by the YMCA's international camp counselor program for summer work in Beirut, but Lebanon's civil war terminated his stay there in less than a month. Instead, Mark was offered employment at a YMCA-operated resettlement camp at Fort Chaffee, Arkansas, where he helped Vietnamese "boat people" refugees. The highpoint of the recognition that he received for his service was a handshake from President Gerald Ford.

It was at this point that Mark Chapman's life began an irreversible slide. Joining his fiancée, Jessica Blankenship, at Covenant College, a fundamentalist Presbyterian school in Tennessee, he fell into a depression and could not keep up with his classwork. After his return to Georgia, he sought the comfort of familiar work at the YMCA camp only to come into personal conflicts that challenged his memories of prestigious service in the past. He later told Jack Jones, "My YMCA identity fell apart, when I was stripped of that is when the clouds really started getting dark and I started slipping into an abyss that ended in murder, of someone I didn't even know."[21] As a stopgap, Mark took a job as a security guard but, according to his fiancée's mother, "his personality began to change. He became quickly angry—just a trigger!"[22] In January 1977, despairing of his prospects, Chapman fled to Hawaii where (Jack Jones reports) he planned to take his life after a "last fling in paradise."[23] After Mark later confessed his intentions to Jessica Blankenship in a telephone call from Honolulu and asked for assurance of her continuing love, she urged him to return home. He complied, but when the couple's Georgia reunion failed to restore their engagement, he returned to Honolulu, committed to his suicidal purpose. For him, however, death proved no easier than life, for the hose that he attached to the exhaust pipe of his automobile simply melted away.

Mark responded quickly to treatment at Castle Memorial Hospital for depression and in 1978 was on the move once again, this time on a tour around the world. On June 2, 1979, he married his travel agent, a Japanese American woman named Gloria Abe. Despite his new responsibilities, he remained unable to find stable employment. After jobs at Castle Memorial Hospital came to an end, he drifted into all-night security jobs that left him more time on his hands than was good for him.

During his long hours at the Honolulu Public Library, his preoccupations with both John Lennon and the fictional Holden Caulfield deepened. On a library shelf he came upon Anthony Fawcett's *John Lennon: One Day at a Time;* the book persuaded him that Lennon, contrary to what he had said and sung, "was a successful man who had the world on a chain." He recalled to author Jack Jones his sense of outrage that Lennon had "told us to imagine no possessions, and there he was, with millions of dollars and yachts and farms and country estates, laughing at people like me who had believed the lies and bought the records and built a big part of our lives around his music."[24] During the same period Mark reread *The Catcher in the Rye* for the first time since he was a teenager, and found that Holden Caulfield, who dreamt of becoming a savior of children, gave him "a pseudo-identity." The blurring of Mark's personality with the two alter egos on whom he had become fixated left telltale signs that went unnoticed. Determined that he would win recognition as the Holden Caulfield of his generation, he inscribed a copy of *The Catcher in the Rye* that he gave to his wife, "To Gloria from Holden Caulfield," and his own copy, "From Holden Caulfield to Holden Caulfield."

Despite his disenchantment over John Lennon's affluent and showy lifestyle, he remained enmeshed in the superstar's personality. On October 23, 1980, when he checked out for the last time as a maintenance man in a downtown Honolulu apartment building, he signed the register as "John Lennon" and had also pasted Lennon's name over his uniform tag. He translated his mixed feelings of attraction and repulsion into a plan to murder the Beatle hero.

With a brand-new .38 caliber revolver stowed in his checked baggage, Chapman flew home from Honolulu to New York City on October 29, bent on his deadly mission. To a girl he picked up while touring the city, he bragged:

"Something is going to happen soon. You're going to hear about me."[25] His anticipated celebrity, however, was blocked by the city's strict control over the sale of ammunition; he found that he could not acquire .38 caliber bullets without being licensed and bonded. In all innocence, an old Georgia friend, now a sheriff's deputy, solved his problem. Mark flew to Atlanta on the pretext of a sentimental journey and persuaded the deputy to supply him five cartridges with "real stopping power" in case he should be attacked on New York City's "frightening" streets; the bullets were hollow-pointed, designed to explode on impact.

Although all the components of murder were now in his hands, Mark stepped back from the brink of action. On November 12 he arrived in Honolulu, one day after having phoned Gloria from New York to confess that her love had saved him from carrying out his plan to kill Lennon. In the course of a month, however, his homicidal resolve strengthened again. He returned to New York City on Saturday, December 6. Two days passed in fruitless watching at the entrance of the celebrity-favored Dakota apartment building, 72nd Street and Central Park West, where Lennon resided, but on Monday morning, December 8, Mark Chapman awoke early to try again. Before he left his hotel he set out a display of mementos intended to catch the eyes of the police when they would search his room after the murder. Jack Jones describes the arrangement that he devised:

> Before leaving the hotel, Chapman had neatly arranged and left behind a curious assortment of personal items on top of the hotel dresser. In an orderly semicircle, he had laid out his passport, an eight-track tape of the music of Todd Rundgren, and his little Bible, open to The Gospel According to John (Lennon). He also left a letter from a former YMCA supervisor at Fort Chaffee, Arkansas, where, five years earlier, he had worked with refugees from the Vietnam War. Beside the letter were two photographs of himself surrounded by laughing Vietnamese children. At the center of the arrangement of personal effects, he had placed the small Wizard of Oz poster of Dorothy and the Cowardly Lion.[26]

He took his station among the Lennon fans who watched outside the Dakota for sightings of their idol. His actions near the doorway reflected the odd mélange of his feelings toward the world-famous musician and activist. At first Mark's love for Lennon seemed to take the upper hand. In the early afternoon he caught sight of Lennon's five-year-old son, Sean, escorted by his nanny. Jack Jones re-creates the scene:

As he was introduced to John Lennon's son, Chapman stepped forward and uncurled the sweaty fingers of his right hand from around the chunk of steel. Sliding his hand carefully from the deep pocket of his coat, he knelt on one knee before Sean Lennon. He wrapped his fingers around the child's tiny hand.

"I came all the way across the ocean from Hawaii and I'm honored to meet you," he said. The child stared at him blankly and sneezed.

Chapman smiled.

"You'd better take care of that runny nose," he said. "You wouldn't want to get sick and miss Christmas."[27]

In the evening Mark's long wait was rewarded: he saw John Lennon and Yoko Ono leaving the Dakota entrance. As he stood thunderstruck, Paul Goresh, a freelance photographer, reminded Mark of his announced intention to obtain the superstar's autograph on the latest Lennon-Ono album, *Double Fantasy*, which he had purchased the day before. Without speaking a word, Mark held out the album; Lennon laughed in acknowledgment of his fan's attachment and signed, "John Lennon. December, 1980." Thrilled to have acquired the collector's item, Mark offered Goresh $50 for a picture of his magic encounter with Lennon.

But Mark did not wait for a report from the photographer's studio. A little before 11:00 o'clock that night Lennon and Yoko Ono returned to the Dakota from a recording studio. When Lennon emerged from the limousine, Chapman, assuming a combat stance, rapidly fired four bullets into his target's back; the fifth shot went astray. Arrested as Lennon lay dying, Chapman told police officers: "I am the Catcher in the Rye." They bagged as evidence a copy of the Salinger novel that Mark had bought that morning; as he had previously done on his Hawaii copy, he had written an inscription "To Holden Caulfield from Holden Caulfield," but added below: "This is my statement."

After forgoing his original plan to use his trial to publicize *The Catcher in the Rye*, Chapman pled guilty to second-degree murder and was sentenced to serve a term from twenty years to life in Attica prison. Before the disposition of his case, he was examined by a series of forensic psychiatrists. Dr. Naomi Goldstein, appointed by the court to pass on Chapman's competency to stand trial, reported that the defendant "had an insatiable need for attention and recognition ... [and] grandiose visions of himself." He had avowed to her his mixed feelings about Lennon; he did not hate him but thought he was a phony, just as he was portrayed in Anthony Fawcett's book. He added revealingly, "I admire him in a way. I wished someone would write a book about me."[28]

Dr. Daniel Schwartz, on the basis of his examination of the defendant, had been prepared to opine at trial that Chapman was schizophrenic and also suffered from a "narcissistic personality disorder" causing him to crave attention and fame. Dr. Schwartz believed that the defendant was in the grips of a confusion with his victim's identity; he noted that Chapman, like Lennon, had married a woman of Japanese origin who was a few years older; had entered the rock star's name on a name tag and work log; and had given up his employment after learning that Lennon had become a househusband. Another defense expert, Dr. Richard Bloom, agreed that Chapman was schizophrenic and the victim of delusions of grandeur. According to Dr. Bloom's findings, as summarized by Jack Jones, Mark Chapman "was unable ever to unify the various elements of his personality into a cohesive and recognizable self."[29]

At the sentencing hearing, District Attorney Allen Sullivan did not introduce any psychiatric testimony. In his speech, he described Mark Chapman as a remorseless killer who "remains only interested in himself, his own well-being, what affects him, what's important to him at the particular moment." The defendant's "primary motive," Sullivan argued, was "personal aggrandizement, to draw attention to himself, to massage his own ego."[30]

Mark's only contribution to the proceedings was to read aloud a passage from *The Catcher in the Rye*.

Some American Political Assassins

In *American Assassins: The Darker Side of Politics* (1982), and a sequel relating to John Hinckley's attempt on the life of President Reagan,[31] Professor James W. Clarke argues that there has been excessive reliance on pathology theory to explain political assassinations. On the basis of his study of sixteen successful and would-be assassins, Clarke proposes a more refined approach that would divide assassins into four types. Two groups are outside the scope of this book: Type I assassins, who "view their acts as a probable sacrifice of self for a political ideal" and do not recant "or seek clemency or personal publicity," and Type IV assassins, who "are characterized by severe emotional or cognitive distortion that is expressed in hallucinations and delusions of persecution and/or grandeur."[32]

Clarke's two remaining classifications overlap to a significant extent with what is in the present study defined as the "Herostratos syndrome." The related groupings in Clarke's classification are:

Type II assassins, who experience "overwhelming and aggressive egocentric needs for acceptance, recognition and status." According to Clarke, these assassins (among whom he numbers Lee Harvey Oswald and Samuel Byck) are neurotics who suffer "a deprivation of love and affection" and are inclined to "project personal motives on public objects." There are always "significant others" in their lives and their "exercise of power in a public manner generates the attention that had been denied in the past."

Type III assassins, consisting of psychopaths or sociopaths (among whom Clarke includes Arthur Bremer and John Hinckley), who "believe that the condition of their lives is so intolerably meaningless and without purpose that destruction of society and themselves is desirable for its own sake."[33]

The distinctions that Clarke attempts to make between these categories are not easy to apply to biographical facts. One could argue, for example, that John Hinckley's vain pursuit of Jodie Foster resulted in a Type II rejection of love. Moreover, it is far from clear that Type III enemies of society do not seek public attention as fervently as the Type II assassins who kill to compensate for personal failures. Indeed, Clarke's conclusions emphasize the significance of media exposure to cases of both Type II and III assassins: "The one characteristic that post-1963 Type II and III subjects shared was a need to do something spectacular that would guarantee the public exposure each desired."[34] In Professor Clarke's scheme, Lee Harvey Oswald falls into Type II since "Oswald's motive in the assassination was personal and compensatory rather than political." Among the disappointments redressed by the crime were his "disillusionment with an unwelcoming Russian bureaucracy after his defection to the Soviet Union;" loss of a job that he blamed on the FBI, and his resentment of the agency's surveillance; and his wife's sexual taunts and refusal to live with him.[35]

In *Case Closed,* Gerald Posner suggests, on the basis of comments of Oswald recollected by two fellow marines, that he may also have been influenced by a desire for fame. According to Mack Osborne, Oswald once made "some statement to the effect that one day he would do something which would make him famous." To Kerry Thornley, Oswald was more expansive on this theme: "He wanted to be on the winning side so that 10,000 years from now people would look in the history books and say, 'Well, this man was ahead of his time. . . . ' He wanted to be looked back upon with honor by future generations. He was concerned with his image in history."[36] These quotations encouraged Rudolf Augstein to give the title "Herostratus in Dallas"[37] to his 1993 review of *Case Closed* in *Der Spiegel,* the German news magazine that Augstein founded. The review concludes, "Oswald was in fact concerned about his place in history. Herostratus of Ephesus may have thought similarly in 356 BC, although we know nothing more of his motives or fate. He and Oswald were no doubt kindred spirits."

Like Oswald, three failed assassins of American politicians, Arthur Bremer, Samuel Byck, and John Hinckley Jr., have a place among the followers of Herostratos. Of widely differing social backgrounds, they are united by personal frustrations and a passion to be remembered.

Arthur Herman Bremer

On May 15, 1972, a twenty-one-year-old stalker of politicians, Arthur Herman Bremer, shot Alabama Governor George Wallace, a Democratic presidential candidate, as he shook hands at the conclusion of a rally at a shopping center in Laurel, Maryland. Of the five .38 caliber bullets fired, one struck his spine and left him paralyzed below the waist. Professor James W. Clarke describes the appearance of the gunman, who would inspire the character of Travis Bickle, played by Robert DeNiro in director Martin Scorsese's terrifying film *Taxi Driver:*

> Shortly before the Governor's speech, a blond crew-cut, and pleasant-looking young man parked his 1967 Rambler Rebel in the shopping center lot and joined the gathering crowd. Arthur Bremer was becoming a familiar face at the recent Wallace rallies. Dressed in red, white, and blue combinations of jacket, shirt, and tie, adorned with huge Wallace campaign buttons, and always smiling beneath silvery sunglasses, Bremer appeared to be one of the Governor's most loyal and enthusiastic supporters—a male Wallace groupie of sorts. Applauding, whistling, and shouting enthusiastically, even in indifferent crowds, Bremer was hard to miss.[38]

Cornelia Wallace, then the governor's wife, recalls the sudden attack:

> And then all of a sudden, I heard, da, da, da-da-da. And then time just stood still. I thought they'd shoot him again. And so I jumped on top of him, trying to cover up his head and his heart and his vital organs, his lungs. And, uh, there just wasn't anybody around him. Well, the Alabama bodyguard had been shot and blown out and knocked down. The Secret Service agent that was—these two were supposed to protect his body—got shot in the jaw and was vomiting and vomiting blood. So I just kept saying, uh, he, he was dazed and he didn't speak, and I kept saying, "George, I'm going to take you home. I'm going to take you home. And we're going home now." And, uh, finally, all of a sudden somebody was pulling me away from him. I kept begging him, I said, "Let—don't take me away from my husband now. Please don't take me away from my husband now."[39]

Southern historian Dan T. Carter observes that the assailant was not the kind that Wallace would have expected:

Wallace, by the mid-1960s was certainly aware that he was a figure in danger. That is we'd had the assassination of Kenn-, the two Kennedy brothers and Martin Luther King, and he often talked about the danger that he had. But I think he always anticipated the kind of uh, political ideologue, somebody who opposed him, uh, uh, finding him at some moment and shooting him. George Wallace, the most intensely, ideological, political candidate of the 1960s, uh, ends up being shot by somebody who just wants to get his picture on the front page of "The New York Times."[40]

Arthur Bremer grew up in Milwaukee, the fourth of five children raised by parents described by a social worker as "an amiable, bland, white unsophisticated couple . . . from a low socioeconomic background." Mrs. Bremer "was given to erratic hostile outbursts at both her husband and her children" and compensated for her lack of warmth with interest in little blond Arthur's cleanliness. Arthur's father, according to Professor Clarke, "insulated himself from [his wife's] attacks with alcohol.[41]

Following graduation from high school, Arthur took various low-paying jobs as busboy and janitor. In October 1971 he struck his father in an argument and moved out of the family home. While on his own, the young man, still a virgin, made clumsy and unsatisfying experiments in relations with women. A date with a fifteen-year-old girl at a rock concert before Christmas 1971 was spoiled by erratic behavior resulting in his being reported to a policeman, and his date's mother soon afterward told him, to his dismay, that her daughter would not see him again. As he looked back on his brief friendship with the girl as the happiest time of his life, Bremer's thoughts turned to killing himself or others under circumstances that would catch the public eye. Professor Clarke relates that Bremer planned to "tie [a] rope to the railing of a busy midtown bridge [in Milwaukee], then shoot himself while perched on the rail so that he would drop to hang as a grisly spectacle for passing commuters." Alternatively, he envisioned hijacking an armored car, which he proposed to park in a busy intersection where he could "kill as many people as possible with rifle fire through the vehicle's slit windows."[42]

In the search they made of Bremer's automobile after his attack on Wallace, police found the pages of his handwritten, misspelled diary that covered the previous period of less than six weeks; he had buried the first part of the diary in Wisconsin.[43] As the pages discovered in the car begin, on April 4, 1972, Bremer is bent on the assassination of President Nixon. Harding Lemay, who contributed an introduction to the manuscript of the diary when it was published the following year, was struck by the fact that "he expresses no animosity toward President Nixon, who is merely the vehicle through which Arthur Bremer will achieve stardom."[44]

Bremer writes, "This will be one of the most closely read pages since the Scrolls in those caves."[45] He holds to his overweening expectations of fame despite life's disappointments, such as the failure in his encounter with a New York City masseuse in April 1972: "I'm as important as the start of World War I I just need the little opening & a second of time. Nothing has happened for so long, 3 months, the 1st person I held a conversation with in 3 months was a near naked girl rubbing my erect penis & she wouldn't let me put it thru her."[46] At the foot of this page, Bremer prints in capitals, FAILURES, one of his preoccupations together with his sense of inadequacy. He is obsessed by failure with women and by the frustration of his plans against Nixon's life. His self-loathing is reinforced by sensitivity about his short stature ("Some of the weeds between the curbs & the sidewalks are taller than me 5'6").[47] He also recognizes the excessiveness of his worry that his clothes may not be pleasing. Comparing himself unfavorably with Senator Robert F. Kennedy's murderer, Sirhan Sirhan, in whom he took great interest, Bremer sneers at his own focus on how he should dress for the moment of assassination:

And I was concerned, overly concerned with my appear[e]nce & composure after the bang bangs. . . .

I will give very little if ANY thought to these things on any future attempts.

After all does the world remember if Sirhan's tie was on straight?[48]

Disappointed by his inability to come within shooting range of Nixon in Ottawa, Bremer, on May 4, 1972, recorded his decision to change targets; he had decided that "Wallace will have the honor of—what would you call it?"[49] His principal reservation about his new choice was not based on his views of Wallace's politics but on a nagging anxiety that a Southern governor's killing would not merit international attention:

It seems I would of done better for myself to kill the old G-man Hoover. In death, he lays with Presidents. Who the hell ever got buried in 'Bama for being great. He certainly won't be buried with the snobs in Washington.

SHIT! I won't even rate a T.V. enteroption [interruption] in Russia or Europe when the news breaks—they never heard of Wallace. If something big in Nam flares up I'll end up at the bottom of the 1st page in America. The editors will say—"Wallace dead? Who cares."[50]

Scarcely more than a week before the assassination, George Wallace does not dominate Bremer's thoughts about what he would achieve by the killing. An upsurge in the would-be murderer's grandiosity suggests that, if he decides not to kill himself, the sale of his diary could harvest vast profits from a gullible public:

Hey world! Come here. I wanna talk to ya!

If I don't kill—if I don't kill myself I want you to pay thru the nose, ears & belly button for the beginning of this manuscript. The 1st pages are hidden & will preserve a long time. If you don't pay me for them, I got no reason to turn 'em over—understand punk!?

One of my reasons for this action is money and you the American (is there another culture in the free world?) public will pay me. The silent majority will be my benifactor in the biggest hijack ever![51]

In Bremer's mind, the "hijack" of the public's dollars has supplanted his earlier fantasy of seizing an armored car.

On Sunday, May 7, 1972, Bremer's diary entry indicates that he was still wavering as to the choice of his victim. "Yesterday," he writes, "I even considered McGovern as a target." In fact, the identity of his target was a matter of relative indifference to him, as was the possibility that he would not survive his moment of glory: "If I go to prison as an assissin (solitary forever & guards in my cell, etc.) or get killed or suicided what difference to me? Ask me why I did it & I'd say 'I don't know,' or 'Nothing else to do,' or 'Why not?' or 'I have to kill somebody.'"[52]

After a trial at which eight psychiatrists and two clinical psychologists divided along adversarial lines on the issue of Bremer's insanity, the jury found him guilty of attempted murder; the trial judge's sentence of sixty-three years' imprisonment was reduced on appeal to fifty-three years. Arthur Marshall had argued for the prosecution that Bremer was seeking glory and regretted that Wallace had not died. Professor Clarke cites only one "faintly remorseful" remark by the defendant when the trial judge asked him, in the sentencing hearing, whether he had anything to say: "Well, Mr. Marshall mentioned that he would like society to be protected from someone like me. Looking back on my life I would have liked it if society had protected me from myself."[53]

In the public courtroom, Bremer could not bring himself to express his frustrations and motives with the same intensity that sometimes lends an odd eloquence to his illiterate diary.

Samuel Joseph Byck

In 1974 Samuel Joseph Byck, a forty-four-year-old unemployed Philadelphia salesman and recently divorced father of four children, identified the Nixon administration as the source of all his woes. He sought satisfaction from his political enemies through a plan of violent revenge that he called "Operation Pandora's Box." His ingenious scheme was simplicity itself. He would hijack a commercial airliner and, brandishing a homemade incendiary device, would order the crew to crash into the White House. Until the attack on the World Trade Center invited us all belatedly to "connect the dots," Byck has been one of the least well-known of America's would-be presidential assassins. The attempted hijacking was not well timed to hold the public's attention for long. Reports of Byck's failed takeover of a Delta plane at the Baltimore-Washington International Airport, even though it resulted in three deaths including his own, competed with news of Watergate, including anticipated criminal charges against H. R. Haldeman and John D. Ehrlichman, developments in the Patty Hearst kidnapping, and the release of ransomed *Atlanta Constitution* editor Reg Murphy.

Samuel Byck's life had been beset with disappointment and unhappiness. Dissatisfied with his low income as a tire salesman, he applied to the Small Business Association in the spring of 1969 for a loan of twenty thousand dollars to finance his own tire business, but was turned down. He quarreled with his more successful brothers and became increasingly depressed. In November 1969, shortly before the rejection of his SBA loan application, he was admitted to a psychiatric hospital and for two years after his release around Christmas received care for a "manic-depressive illness." Professor Clarke has described how Byck came to blame his problems on the Nixon administration: "The more he read and thought, the more he became convinced that his economic difficulties, which were directly responsible for his rapidly deteriorating marriage, were the result of a corrupt, constitution-subverting political regime in Washington. He became a strong McGovern supporter and an outspoken critic of the Nixon administration."[54] He was questioned by the

Secret Service in late 1972 for allegedly threatening the assassination of President Nixon but, according to a Secret Service spokesman, the U.S. attorney's office in Philadelphia declined to prosecute when Byck was committed to Philadelphia General Hospital in January 1973 for mental observation.[55]

Byck, however, continued to brood on his political grievances, including the still-rankling rejection of his SBA application. On Christmas Eve, 1973, Byck, costumed as Santa Claus, picketed the White House, carrying a placard declaring, "Santa sez, 'All I Want for Christmas is My Constitutional Right to Peaceably Petition My Government for a Redress of Grievances.'" Although another of Santa's placards called for Nixon's impeachment, Byck turned, as the New Year arrived, to his design for a violent end to the administration he hated.

A weakness in the security arrangements at the Baltimore Airport provided Byck with an opportunity for armed intrusion. Pier C in the eastern wing of the airport, unlike the principal pier, had not been sealed off by a security screen and was open to the general public. On Friday morning, February 22, 1974, shortly before Delta's scheduled 7:15 A.M. flight to Atlanta, Byck, dressed in a black raincoat that was at odds with his sunglasses and carrying a gasoline bomb in a suitcase, entered Pier C without attracting notice and concealed himself behind a wall near a metal detector at the departure gate. As passengers were boarding, he suddenly emerged from his hiding place and fired several shots from a .22 caliber pistol into the back of the head of a security guard, who died instantly. Dashing along the ramp toward the plane, he "waved his gun at four boarding passengers and yelled, 'Get out. Get out.'" One of the passengers whom he had spared later remarked: "He looked like any other passenger except for that gun. It was all I really noticed."[56]

Once aboard the jetliner, Byck ordered the crew to "fly the plane out of here." When the pilot told him that the plane's wheels were blocked and its doors unsealed, Byck fired three shots into the cockpit wall and warned that "the next shot will be in your head." Exasperation now overwhelmed what little rationality remained to him: "Byck then shot both pilots and grabbed an unidentified woman passenger pulling her into the cockpit and telling her 'Help this man fly the plane.'" The copilot was killed and the pilot critically wounded.

Retribution came from the weapon of the airport guard whom Byck had shot. A policeman fired the dead guard's powerful magnum through the six-inch porthole of the plane's door, hitting Byck twice in the chest. The wounded hijacker then shot himself in the right temple, bringing the violence to an end. A Maryland police superintendent commented that the loss of life would have been greater had Byck's bomb been detonated aloft: "It was not a professional job but if he had opened it [the suitcase] in the air there would have been an explosion and burning and in all probability it would have destroyed the aircraft."[57]

Byck purported to see himself "as a political terrorist, like those in Northern Ireland and the Middle East."[58] Yet there is no doubt that he was powerfully motivated by a desire for publicity surpassing that accorded to earlier assassinations (whose chronology he had photocopied) and to a recent aerial invasion of the White House grounds. According to a report in the *Washington Post*, Byck called the *Philadelphia Inquirer* on the Monday before the attack; his purpose was "to discuss the paper's account of an Army private who stole a helicopter and landed on the White House lawn [on Sunday, February 17]. Byck ended the conversation with the paper's reporter by saying, "*I may have something for you later on. I'm not ready to break it now*"" (emphasis added).[59] The expectation of posthumous glory did not fully satisfy Byck, because he longed to observe at close hand the amazement that his daring would incite. On the night prior to the hijacking attempt, Renée Goldstein, who lived in the apartment below Byck in Philadelphia, saw him outside her door, holding an armful of books. When she asked what he was studying, he answered: "I am going to make a bomb." Her reaction must have been disappointing: she did not believe him.

On the same date on which he attempted to pique Mrs. Goldstein's curiosity, Byck undertook a far more ambitious campaign of self-advertisement. He described "Operation Pandora's Box" for posterity on an hour-long tape, mailing copies to many celebrities, including Leonard Bernstein and columnist Jack Anderson. At the same time Byck posted a letter to U.S. Magistrate Jean Dwyer in Washington, enclosing a Delta Airlines flight schedule with a circle drawn around the Atlanta departure he had targeted. On February 27, under the headline "Posthumous Fame Sought by Hijacker," the *Washington Post* quoted the beginning of the tape that Anderson had received:

> My name is Sam Byck, and I am hoping that some day—I'm hoping by now that you will have read about me in the newspapers and if I'm not successful you probably don't know who I am and it won't make much difference.
>
> I call myself a grain of sand on the beach called the U.S. of A.

In a separate article in the same issue of the *Post*, Anderson included verbatim Byck's taped description of his plan, still somewhat vague in details and resembling only slightly his rampage at the airport:

I will try to get the plane aloft and fly it towards the target area, which will be Washington, D.C., the capital of the most powerful, wealthiest nation of the world. By guise [sic], threats or trickery, I hope to force the pilot to buzz the White House—I mean, sort of dive towards the White House. When the plane is in this position, I will shoot the pilot and then in the last few minutes try to steer the plane into the target, which is the White House.

Byck continued to tape-record his intentions until the final hour of his life, when he sat in his car at the Baltimore-Washington Airport. "If I had sort of an after wish," he wistfully confided to the recorder, "I would like to be alive, after I'm dead, I would like to be alive ya know, for about a week afterward to see what, eh, what people say and think, not that it makes any difference, I, eh, what they say or think about me, I mean they'll have their own opinions, but I want to see who sheds an honest sincere tear, who's really gonna miss me." One of his last concerns was to leave behind an indisputable claim of criminal originality:

I wonder if they'll figure that I'm a product of these two plots that are going on. One in California with Patricia Hearst and the other in Atlanta with the editor. I wonder if they'll think that all this crap triggered me off. If they do, they're a bunch of damn fools because I've been planning this thing for well over a year. Planning it, thinking about it, trying not to think about it and I realized that at once I had conceived it, once I had conceived the Pandora Box, the Mission Pandora Box that it would be the downfall of me. And so it shall be. It's the end.[60]

Samuel Byck's terrestrial return was not what he had had in mind. In 1991, played by the actor Lee Wilkof, he appeared as a character in the musical production of *Assassins,* with music and lyrics by Stephen Sondheim and book by John Weidman, presented by Playwrights Horizons in New York City. In scene 9 Byck, wearing his Santa Claus suit, records a tape for Leonard Bernstein:

You know the world's a vicious, stinking pit of emptiness and pain. But not for long. I'm gonna change things, Lenny. I'm gonna drop a 747 on the White House and incinerate Dick Nixon. It's gonna make the news. You're gonna hear about it and I know what you're gonna ask yourself: What kind of world is this where a decent, stand-up guy like Sam Byck has to crash a plane into the President to make a point? You're gonna wonder if you want to go on living in a world like that. Well, lemme tell you, Len. You do. And you know why? So you can keep on writing love songs!

His attitude toward Bernstein turns hostile when he reflects on how little the musician and the other celebrities on his mailing list have done for him. But Operation Pandora's Box and the eternal fame it assures will be his revenge against them all:

> You knew where I was. You *all* did. And you know what you did? You left me there! . . . You had your chance and now it's too damn late! . . . I'm outta here! I'm history, Lenny! Understand? I'm *history!*[61]

John W. Hinckley Jr.

In February 1980 twenty-five-year-old John W. Hinckley Jr. stood outside the Dakota apartment building in New York City, mourning for John Lennon, whose murder, he later told a psychiatrist, had stunned him. Hinckley's outpouring of grief on the ex-Beatle's death was but the latest expression of a deep-seated preoccupation with homicide and celebrity. Professor James W. Clarke informs us about Hinckley's passion for books on these themes:

> Hinckley's tastes in reading ran toward the lives of violent people. Not ordinary husband-kills-wife stuff, but books and articles about people whose crimes had, in some sense, achieved celebrity status for them— mass and serial murderers, skyjackers—and it would be hard to name a book he hadn't read about assassins.[62]

Sometimes Hinckley turned to biographies of political figures, like Ronald Reagan and Edward Kennedy, but he devoured everything written about John Lennon: "John Lennon was his hero. He had read every book and had clipped every article he could find about the slain Beatles star, all of whose albums he had collected since childhood."[63]

John Hinckley was born in Ardmore, Oklahoma, in 1955, the youngest of three children. His father, Jack, after service as a naval officer, threw himself into a hard-driving business career, first in the employ of Carter Oil Company and eventually as an entrepreneur in the petroleum industry. Jack's mother, Jo Ann (nicknamed Jodie) reminds Professor Clarke of the devoted housewives who populate sitcoms of the 1950s. Following Jack's road to success, the Hinckleys moved fourteen times in the first five years of their marriage; in 1958 the family resettled in Dallas. Jack, according to Professor Clarke, treated his withdrawn youngest child with disdain, harping on the superior accomplishments of the older children and resenting John's dependence on his mother's protection. In 1973, when John graduated from high school, Jack decided that his son should leave home to major in business at Texas Tech in Lubbock. Professor Clarke describes John Hinckley's psychological state in the years that followed:

> It was during the seven lonely years of what he considered to be his exile that John Hinckley's social withdrawal became so complete that he gradually withdrew psychologically into a world of his own making, losing his capacity to think clearly or rationally in the midst of his fantasies.[64]

While at college, Hinckley continued to seek the attention of his parents, who had moved to a Denver suburb. In April 1976 he wrote that he had left college for Hollywood and was trying to sell some of his songs there. In July he cheered them with two news items, both invented: that he had made a contact at United Artists and that he was dating a young actress named Lynn Collins. After his parents' subsidies ran out, he was back home in Colorado. In response to his father's demands that he seek employment, he became a busboy at a nightclub. After several months, he returned briefly to Texas Tech where his father, recognizing belatedly that John had not inherited the genes of commerce, had recommended a new major in liberal arts. Although John remained in Lubbock until the winter of 1979–80, his class attendance was sporadic. In early 1980 he returned home "for medical examinations arranged by his parents in response to his complaints of sleeplessness, headaches, and physical weakness."[65] When no physical ailments were identified, he saw a psychologist employed by his father's company.

What John failed to tell his parents was that while visiting Hollywood in 1976 he came under the thrall of *Taxi Driver*, which he saw about fifteen times. In the ensuing years Hinckley became obsessively interested in Jodie Foster, a young actress (bearing his mother's nickname) who played Iris, a prostitute, in the film. After he learned in 1980 that Foster would begin undergraduate study at Yale in the fall, he "left letters and poems in her mailbox and had two awkward conversations with her which he recorded."[66] In a New Year's monologue that he tape-recorded in 1981, Hinckley indicates that his thoughts about Lennon and Foster had become intertwined:

John Lennon is dead. The world is over. Forget it. . . . It's just gonna be insanity, if I even make it through the first few days. . . . I still regret having to go on with 1981 . . . I don't know why people wanna live.

John Lennon is dead. . . . I still think—I still think about Jodie all the time. That's all I think about really. That, and John Lennon's death. They were sorta binded together. . . . [67]

After his disappointment at Foster's lack of interest in his approaches, Hinckley redirected his celebrity hunt to the political arena. In the style of *Taxi Driver*'s protagonist, Travis Bickle, who plans to assassinate a presidential candidate, he tracked President Carter in Columbus and Dayton during September and October 1980. There was no ideological motive in his pursuit of Carter, for only the voice of the American electorate ultimately determined his choice of victim. In March 30, 1981, Hinckley wounded President Reagan and three others in a burst of exploding "devastator" bullets outside the Hilton Hotel in Washington, D.C.

Before leaving his hotel room for the Hilton, Hinckley wrote a letter, which was never mailed, to Jodie Foster:

Dear Jodie:

There is definitely a possibility that I will be killed in my attempt to get Reagan. It is for this very reason that I am writing you this letter now.

As you well know by now I love you very much. Over the past seven months I've left you dozens of poems, letters and love messages in the faint hope that you could develop an interest in me. Although we talked on the phone a couple of times I never had the nerve to simply approach you and introduce myself. Besides my shyness, I honestly did not wish to bother you with my constant presence. I know the many messages left at your door and in your mailbox were a nuisance, but I felt that it was the most painless way for me to express my love for you.

I feel very good about the fact that you at least know my name and how I feel about you. And by hanging around your dormitory, I've come to realize that I'm the topic of more than a little conversation, however full of ridicule it may be. At least you know that I'll always love you. Jodie, I would abandon the idea of getting Reagan in a second if I could only win your heart and live out the rest of my life with you, whether it be in total obscurity or whatever.

I will admit to you that the reason I'm going ahead with this attempt now is because I cannot wait any longer to impress you. I've got to do

something now to make you understand, in no uncertain terms, that I'm doing all of this for your sake! By sacrificing my freedom and possibly my life, I hope to change your mind about me. This letter is being written only an hour before I leave for the Hilton Hotel. Jodie, I'm asking you to please look into your heart and at least give the chance, with this historical deed, to gain your love and respect.
I love you forever,
John W. Hinckley[68]

The defense's theory (resulting in an acquittal for insanity) was that Hinckley, in a psychotic state at the time of the shooting, had shot the president with the intent of making an impression on the indifferent Jodie Foster. One of the prosecution's expert witnesses, Dr. Park Elliott Dietz, while conceding Hinckley's desire to win Foster's attention, opined on direct examination that the assassination attempt also reflected a desire for fame resulting from the defendant's narcissistic personality disorder that fell short of psychosis:

A. He had felt rejected by Jodie Foster as early as September [1980], after his first efforts to contact her, and, as he later described, he was angry about what she had done, that is, that she had not responded to his calls as he hoped. To win her attention, to be able to impress upon her, here is John Hinckley who loves her, to make her remember him, was a goal for which he was willing to sacrifice a great deal. But it was not entirely a sacrifice, as I will show, because in addition to winning her attention, he wished to have fame and notoriety.

Q. Is that a separate goal?

A. Well, they are linked in this way, but it is a goal that I will show separate evidence for.

Q. All right. Do you have anything more to say about the goal insofar as it relates to a serious mental disorder?

A. Only to say that my first impression without the facts was that that could well reflect a serious mental disorder.

Q. Where do you stand today?

A. That it does not.

Q. Why?

A. Because I have had the opportunity to obtain the facts, to speak with him, and to determine that indeed that was a goal that developed out of his experiences in life and which he feels he has accomplished. . . .

Q. You mentioned the goal of—I believe it is—fame?

A. He displayed a considerable concern with the media, as I will show . . . [a]nd he indicated his interest in assassination through not only the things I have referred to already, but comparisons he made between himself and other assassins.

Q. Does the fact he had the goal or purpose or whatever of fame show that he had a serious mental disorder?

A. No, the goal of becoming famous is not limited to those who are mentally disordered. In Mr. Hinckley's case, it does relate to [the] narcissistic personality disorder that I have diagnosed.

Q. Briefly, why is that?

A. That is because with narcissistic personality disorders, the view of one's self as special and more important than others may translate itself into a concern with becoming both the center of attention and famous to the extent of wanting to be in the media, wanting to be in history books.[69]

The prosecution, through Dr. Dietz's direct testimony, had presented a strong basis for concluding that Hinckley was a narcissist who precisely fit the Herostratic matrix: he was a loner unable or unwilling to pursue a successful career through his own efforts and focused instead on instantaneous acquisition of fame through an attack on a celebrity and his consequent identification with his media-worthy victim. On cross-examination, however, the defense counsel sought a concession from Dr. Dietz that the dividing line between narcissism and delusion may not always be easy to draw:

Q. And is it fair to characterize this idea of fame [as] an idea of grandiosity?

A. Well, it is a grandiose concern and a grandiose preoccupation if one continues it to the point of fantasizing unlimited success, unlimited fame, and so on. It is not a grandiose delusion, which is another matter altogether.

Q. If it were a grandiose delusion, it then, of course, would it not, become a personality feature associated with the disease of schizophrenia?

A. Yes. Well, yes. Grandiose delusions are often found in schizophrenia as in other disorders, and that is when a person believes that they already are successful or famous or has a delusion—of being Napoleon or Jesus Christ— examples of grandiose delusions.

Q. Well, there are other grandiose delusions short of thinking you are Napoleon, are there?

A. Yes there are.[70]

In light of the jury's verdict that Hinckley was not responsible for the shooting of President Reagan and his aides, we are left with the sobering lesson that a Herostratos among us may escape criminal punishment.

Shared Herostratic Features of Chapman, Bremer, Byck, and Hinckley

The cases of Chapman, Bremer, Byck, and Hinckley evidence to varying degrees the three special features proposed at the beginning of this chapter to help distinguish Herostratic assassinations from others in which self-glorification is not a significant factor:

1. Neither Bremer nor Hinckley had any animosity against the political leader he attacked. Bremer, like Empress Elisabeth's assassin Lucheni, changed his targeted victim with ease, based on convenience of access; Hinckley initially stalked President Carter and would likely have continued to pursue him had he won reelection. Byck conceived grievances against the entire Nixon administration, but his political hostility, as Professor Clarke has noted, appears to have been a projection of family and business setbacks.

2. As the arsonist Hayashi Yoken had done, both Chapman and Byck confided to acquaintances their intentions to win headlines. Chapman passed along his hint to a girl he hardly knew, and Byck, champion of impromptu confession, teased both a reporter and a neighbor with allusions to his hijacking scheme. The criminals' observation of reaction to these face-to-face disclosures supplemented the less palpable rewards of posthumous fame.

3. Bremer's diary and Byck's audiotapes recorded for a public audience the development of their murder plans. To Bremer, the possibility of the diary's becoming a best seller almost reconciled him to the prospect of surviving the attack on Wallace. Byck's grand design of distributing his taped revelations to celebrities not only assured wide publication in the press but also associated him irresistibly with the fame of his addressees. Hinckley's last letter to actress Jodie Foster, though never sent, probably was intended to serve similar twin purposes.

As the discussion of the Unabomber and the Columbine High School killers will show, the passion for self-documentation is also found in cases of serial or mass murder.

The modern successors of Herostratos have understood that an unexceptional crime will not hold the attention of a public sated with violence or win them the place in history to which they aspire in their most grandiose dreams. Attacks on prominent victims have provided a reliable shortcut to the headlines, but sheer horror is an alternative route. Recent years have introduced the phenomenon of multiple murders influenced by a desire for lasting fame. The mass killer elbows other crime news off the front page by the scale of one day's carnage. The serial murderer holds a community or even a nation in terror over a period of time; members of the public wonder whether they fit the unknown slayer's pattern of victim selection, or whether it is the apparently random nature of the attacks that threatens their everyday lives.

The Herostratic wish for fame can be detected in both the Columbine High School massacre and the serial crimes of the Unabomber.

Ted Kaczynski (The Unabomber)

Alston Chase, in *Harvard and the Unabomber: The Education of an American Terrorist* (2003), has observed that "ever since he was a boy," Ted Kaczynski, dubbed the Unabomber by the FBI because of his early attacks on universities and airlines, "had identified closely" with novelist Joseph Conrad, and "reportedly used 'J. Konrad' as an alias on occasion when taking trips to deposit or mail his bombs." Kaczynski's favorite among Conrad's novels was *The Secret Agent*. Overlooking the book's scathing portrayal of London's anarchists as misguided or self-seeking, Kaczynski focused on the character of the Professor, who secretly gratifies his sense of power and assuages career disappointments by making bombs and working to develop the perfect detonator.[71]

During the seventeen-year period from 1978 to 1995, Kaczynski, a brilliant mathematician who gave up his teaching career at the University of California to live alone in the woods of Montana, mailed or delivered sixteen bombs, killing three and injuring many others as the deadliness of his explosive weapons increased. He acquired the reputation of an antiscience ideologue through his selection of victims associated with university programs in technology, mathematics, and business; air travel; behavior-modification psychology; and genetic engineering. After his attacks were already in progress, he also evinced an interest in environmental issues. The Unabomber's onslaught against technology is the subject of his manifesto "Industrial Society and its Future," published under his coercion in 1995. Although it would be imprudent to underestimate the role that philosophical convictions appear to have played in

Kaczynski's crimes, a remarkably similar series of bombings that began in the late nineteenth century cautions that professions of social dogma may mask the contribution of personal motives. Between 1894 and 1909 a vengeful Swedish chemist and inventor, Martin Ekenberg, sent a variety of cleverly disguised package bombs (including a Parker pen cylinder and a perfume flask) to four men; he believed that three of the addressees had frustrated his business projects, and the other was an attorney-agent with whom he had become embroiled. Two of his targets were seriously hurt, and in another case Ekenberg's bomb exploded in a post office, injuring three employees. The bomber attempted to give the last two outrages a political coloration in the wake of a large-scale Swedish strike in 1909. He wrote to newspapers under the name "Justus Felix" (the "just and lucky man," a name drawn from the hero of a children's story), attributing the attacks to a socialist assassination bureau. After a professional colleague recognized Ekenberg's handwriting in a letter from the self-proclaimed socialist enforcer, the bomber was tracked down and arrested in London, where he hanged himself while awaiting extradition.[72]

In *Harvard and the Unabomber*, Chase argues that the Unabomber Manifesto "embodied the conventional wisdom of the entire country" in Kaczynski's formative years and that its message was found "in virtually every school and college textbook, every book on ecology or natural philosophy, every environmental best-seller for more than a generation. It was nothing less than the contemporary American creed."[73] The introduction of the manifesto sounds the keynote that "the Industrial Revolution and its consequences have been a disaster for the human race" and that they "have subjected human beings to indignities, have led to widespread psychological suffering . . . and have inflicted severe damage on the natural world." According to Kaczynski, "the most important of the abnormal conditions to which modern society subjects people" is "lack of opportunity to experience the power process."[74] The power process, for which Kaczynski believes human beings probably have a biological need, consists of a goal, effort, and attainment of the goal, often involving the exercise of autonomy. Science and organization-dependent technology, the manifesto argues, have demanded mass conformity with the industrial "system." Technical advances derive from the pursuit of research intended not to benefit humanity but mainly to serve as the scientist's "surrogate activity," fulfilling his personal drive for power. Kaczynski pursues this argument with vehemence:

> Also, science and technology constitute a mass power movement, and many scientists gratify their need for power through identification with this mass movement. . . .

Thus science marches on blindly, without regard to the real welfare of the human race or to any other standard, obedient only to the psychological needs of the scientists and of the government officials and corporation executives who provide the funds for research.[75]

The power motive, Kaczynski urges, is also dominant among "leftists," among whom he places not only socialists and communists of the old left, but those professing "the spectrum of related creeds that includes the feminist, gay rights, political correctness, etc., movements."[76] In words that may damn his own conduct as well, he writes of his leftist enemies: "Leftists may claim that their activism is motivated by compassion or by moral principle. . . . But compassion and moral principle cannot be the main motives for leftist activism. Hostility is too prominent a component of leftist behavior; so is the drive for power."[77]

Another target of Kaczynski's attack is modern technology that is "developing ways of modifying human behavior" to better serve the needs of society. Among the techniques against which he inveighs are the use of antidepressant drugs, surveillance, alteration of learning preferences in the direction of the sciences, and genetic engineering.[78] Chase believes that Kaczynski's hostility to behavior-modification techniques, and his molding as a terrorist, were due to the devastating effect of his participation as a Harvard College student in a deceptive and confrontational experiment devised by psychology professor Henry A. Murray to assess "personality development among gifted college men."[79] It is Chase's theory that Kaczynski's ineradicable memory of the Murray experiment gave rise to recurrent nightmares during his graduate years at the University of Michigan, in which he would assault or kill psychologists who were trying to control his mind, or their allies.[80] As he told the court-appointed psychologist Sally Johnson, he began to have "fantasies of revenge against a society that he increasingly perceived as evil and obsessed with enforcing conformism through psychological controls."[81]

Kaczynski's retaliatory feelings were also aroused by many people who he believed had injured him or disturbed his peace of mind. Among the principal targets of his mounting rage was his family. His parents' pressures for academic accomplishment and a more active social life translated in his mind to psychological abuse for which he demanded an apology in his lonely adult years. His brother David he regarded as a traitor for abandoning the rebellious political views they had shared and for marrying a "bourgeois" woman. Unwelcome noise near his Montana hideaway jarred his nerves, according to Chase: "The sounds of chain saws, snowmobiles, jet planes, prospectors, and helicopters drove him to new heights of rage. So he, too, took up monkey-wrenching—stringing wire across trails in hopes of garroting backcountry bikers, shooting at helicopters, and destroying logging and construction equipment." Kaczynski also recalls that he smashed up the interior of a vacation house belonging to "motorcycle and snowmobile fiends."[82]

Like his predecessor Martin Ekenberg, Kaczynski ultimately found that his desire for personal revenge could only be assuaged by serial killing. In the journals that he kept from 1969 on, Kaczynski emphasizes that this personal motive overwhelmed ideological conviction as a driving force. Before he bought the land for his cabin in Lincoln, Montana, he entered a summary of his motivation that began and ended with an emphasis on revenge:

> My motive for doing what I am going to do is simply personal revenge. I do not expect to accomplish anything by it. Of course, if my crime (and my reasons for committing it) gets any public attention, it may help to stimulate public interest in the technology question and thereby improve the changes [*sic*] for stopping technology before it is too late; but on the other hand most people will probably be repelled by my crime, and the opponents of freedom may use it as a weapon to support their arguments for control over human behavior. I have no way of knowing whether my action will do more good than harm. I certainly don't claim to be an altruist or to be acting for the "good" (whatever that is) of the human race. I act merely from a desire for revenge. Of course, I would like to get revenge on the whole scientific and bureaucratic establishment, not to mention communists and others who threaten freedom, but, that being impossible, I have to content myself with just a little revenge.[83]

Furthermore, in 1977, the year before his first bombing, Kaczynski stressed that it was revenge, not "philosophical or moral justification," that underlay his ambition to kill victims in many walks of life:

> I emphasize that my motivation is personal revenge. I don't pretend to any kind of philosophical or moralistic justification. The concept of morality is simply one of the psychological tools by which society controls people's behavior. My ambition is to kill a scientist, big businessman, government official, or the like. I would also like to kill a Communist.[84]

As is true of many assassins of the Herostratic type, Kaczynski desired not only to receive credit and publicity for his crimes but also to create a lasting autobiographical record of his actions and thought processes. Although his famous *nom de guerre*, the Unabomber, was invented by the FBI, he had himself included in many of his devices the initials FC (which, as he later explained, stood for "Freedom Club") so that he would acquire the identity of a serial bomber. The notebooks appeared at first glance intended to defeat elucidation. Chase notes that Kaczynski kept in his Montana cabin "lab notebooks, written partly in Spanish, in which he carefully documented the design, construction, and deployment of 245 explosive devices."[85] His personal journal, thousands of pages long, was "written partly in code, partly in Spanish." If, however, it was Kaczynski's objective to stymie investigation by forswearing English, his substitution of America's second language, Spanish, did not seem the best guarantee of privacy. Even the employment of code was mysteriously ineffective. Although Chase asserts in a legend to a reproduced page of Kaczynski's "secret journal" that "the code would have been virtually 'unbreakable,'" the Unabomber conveniently left the key in his cabin, where the FBI was able to find it without difficulty. Moreover, in an entry in a coded journal page deciphered by the FBI, Kaczynski even confesses an expectation that he will have readers: "This may surprize [*sic*] reader considering some things reported in these notes."[86]

The notoriety that the Unabomber craved was his due, he believed, because he was a "special" person. In an undated entry in his journal, he wrote, "I tended to feel that I was a particularly important person and superior to most of the rest of the human race. It just came to me as naturally as breathing to feel that I was someone special."[87] After the 1993 bomb attacks on Dr. Charles J. Epstein, a famous geneticist, and Yale computer science professor David Gelernter, Kaczynski's campaign for publicity accelerated into a flurry of a dozen letters. The last of these mailings were made on June 24, 1995, when he circulated his manifesto to the *New York Times,* the *Washington Post,* and *Penthouse,* promising that if it was published he would "permanently desist from terrorism." His sixteenth bomb, mailed on April 24, 1995, had resulted in the death of Gilbert Murray, president of California Forestry Association in Sacramento. That bomb was mailed on April 20, the day after Timothy McVeigh's attack on the Alfred P. Murrah Building in Oklahoma City. Although Kaczynski's bomb had been manufactured before the Oklahoma City attack, it is possible that the Unabomber's manifesto blackmail and its aftermath had been influenced by the wish to regain ascendancy among American terrorists. On the same day as he circulated his manifesto, he mailed a fresh threat to the *San Francisco Chronicle* that would not, by its terms, be quelled by any publication of his philosophy: "WARNING: The terrorist group FC, called Unabomber by the FBI, is planning to blow up an airline out of Los Angeles International Airport sometime during the next six days."

Four days later, satisfied with the additional publicity that the latest menace had brought him, Kaczynski wrote again, explaining that the airline bomb warning had been "one last prank" intended "to remind [the public] who we are." Yet Kaczynski's hunger for revenge was not appeased by the issuance of the manifesto. When he was arrested on April 3, 1996, authorities found under his bed a completed bomb, identical to the last exploded device that had killed Gilbert Murray.[88]

To avoid the prospect that his trial counsel would attempt to prove his insanity, and in exchange for the federal government's agreement not to seek the death penalty, Kaczynski pleaded guilty to thirteen bombings that killed three victims and seriously injured two others. He also acknowledged responsibility for all sixteen of the Unabomber attacks. On May 4, 1998, he was sentenced to life imprisonment without parole. On August 11, 2003, it became apparent that fame was still on his mind. The Associated Press reported that he had "asked the government to return his personal papers, and other materials, including a bomb seized by the FBI" and "his voluminous autobiography." He requested that these and other items confiscated when he was arrested in Montana should be shipped to a University of Michigan archive already containing more than fifteen thousand of his papers. Conceding that the legal issue, which was before a federal judge, was complex, Kaczynski said that the release should be authorized for the sake of posterity.

The Columbine High School Massacre (1999)

When Eric Harris drove into the parking lot of Columbine High School in the Denver suburb of Littleton on the morning of April 20, 1999, his senior-year classmate Brooks Brown "started cussing him out" for missing a test. Harris had patched up his friendship with Brown after having long been extremely hostile to him. Their falling-out had a small beginning—Brooks had overslept and failed to drive Eric to school on time. But Eric's petty grievance escalated to the point that he posted a death threat against Brooks on his Web site amid wild rantings about blowing up and shooting everything he could. When Brooks's parents reported the contents of Eric's Web site to the police, they took no action and failed to inform the Browns that Eric and his friend Dylan Klebold had recently appeared in court to answer for breaking into a van to steal electrical equipment.[89] Brooks was also unaware that Eric had told a probation officer in connection with the eleven-month "juvenile diversion" program in which he and Dylan participated following their smash-and-grab offense that he had "experienced homicidal and suicidal thoughts."[90]

Eric's old animosity was not on Brooks's mind when he approached him in the school parking lot on April 20, but he was startled by his friend's response to his words. Eric "looked straight at [him]" and said: "Brooks, I like you now. Get out of here. Go home."[91] Without knowing the reason for Eric's warning but fearing that his erratic friend was planning a prank as their graduation approached, Brooks obeyed. As he lingered on a street nearby, the meaning of Eric's words became all too plain. Explosions in the parking lot announced the beginning of the Columbine massacre. Harris, eighteen, and his friend Dylan Klebold, who was seventeen, invaded the school armed with a semiautomatic rifle, two sawed-off shotguns, a semiautomatic handgun, an assortment of knives, and seventy-six homemade bombs; their explosives were carried in duffle bags, backpacks, and ammunition pouches strapped to their bodies. The two youths shot twelve students and a teacher to death, wounded twenty-one others, and finally turned their weapons on themselves. A timeline constructed by the Jefferson County Sheriff's Department disclosed that the two gunmen fired their first shots at about 11:19 A.M. and killed the last victim at 11:35 A.M.[92] By shortly after noon, the killers had committed suicide. Within this brief period, Harris and Klebold fired a total of 188 rounds. The sheriff's report also estimated that if two twenty-pound propane bombs, placed in the school cafeteria on the morning of the attack and rigged with a timer set to detonate the explosives at 11:17 A.M., had worked as intended, most of the 488 people in the room would have been killed or severely wounded.[93] As events unfolded, the principal scene of slaughter was the library, where gunfire claimed ten lives before Harris and Klebold shot themselves.

Brooks Brown, long suspected of complicity because of his timely flight from the schoolyard, speculates about sources of the killers' rage in *No Easy Answers: The Truth Behind Death at Columbine* (2002), which he coauthored with Rob Merritt. Brown rejects the commonly espoused theory that the boys' passion for video games ignited their fury:

> Video games may have given them a place to direct their rage—but something else caused their rage in the first place. Something caused them to cross the line of fantasy and embrace imaginary worlds like *Doom* and *Duke Nukem* as an alternate reality.
>
> When Eric and Dylan got into the world of video games, they loved it, because it was a world with definite rules. Those rules were preset,

and they could not be broken. For a young man in a world like ours, it was a godsend. In the real world, the rules change constantly—and you could be in trouble at a moment's notice. But video games are different.[94]

Dismissing the public's charges against violent video games, Brooks Brown looked elsewhere to account for the disorientation and anger of the killers, and particularly of Eric Harris, whom he regarded as dominating his confederate.

The son of an air force officer, Eric "had been moved around all his life, and had known the difficulties of trying to fit in at one strange school after another."[95] Moreover, he "had a slight chest deformity" and "when Eric would take his shirt off in P.E. class, the bullies were ready and waiting to mock him." Brown believes that the marines' rejection of Eric's enlistment application in the spring of 1999 was due to his taking an antidepressant and also "perhaps because Eric hadn't disclosed his medical history regarding his chest deformity."[96] At Columbine Eric and his friends were the targets of persistent bullying from the school athletes, who derided them as "queers" and "computer nerds." The outcasts' feeling of victimization was reinforced by their impression that the "jocks" formed an elite group favored by the school administration and automatically exonerated in any physical confrontations with the "nerds" or the hapless freshmen:

> One guy, a wrestler who everyone knew to avoid, liked to make kids get down on the ground and push pennies along the floor with their noses. This would happen during school hours, as kids were passing from one class to another. Teachers would see it and look the other way. "Boys will be boys," they'd say, and laugh.
>
> The problem was that the bullies were popular with the administration. Meanwhile, we were the "trouble kids," because we didn't seem to fit in with the grand order of things. Kids who played football were doing what you're supposed to do in high school. Kids like us, who dressed a little differently and were into different things, made teachers nervous. They weren't interested in reaching out to us. They wanted to keep us at arm's length, and if they had the chance to take us down, they would.
>
> The bullies liked to propel paper clips at us with a rubber band. If a teacher saw you get hit, he or she did nothing. But as soon as you threw it back, or did something to defend yourself, you were done. The teacher would grab you and you would be in the office. We were the "undesirables," and the teachers were just waiting for an excuse to nail us. The bullies knew it.[97]

Making a virtue of their estrangement, Harris's clique adopted black trench coats as their distinctive antiestablishment garb and became known, under circumstances that police investigators could not reconstruct, as the "Trench Coat Mafia." Harris wore these outer garments to their killing field.

However, investigators of the massacre did not all accept Brown's theory that the killers were motivated by a desire to take revenge against athletes. The reporting team for *Time* asked rhetorically: "Why, if their motive was rage at the athletes who taunted them, didn't they take their guns and bombs to the locker room?" And they immediately answered their own query: "Because retaliation against specific people was not the point. Because this may have been about celebrity as much as cruelty." FBI agent Mark Holstlaw, whose Associates Team was responsible for identifying all the killers' friends and associates, agreed that desire for fame was the key to the attack: "They wanted to be famous. And they are. They're infamous."[98]

The quest of Harris and Klebold for perennial infamy is evident in their scheduling of the massacre. Their criminal forerunner Herostratos did not prearrange his crime to fall on a significant date; only after his death did the early molders of his tradition emphasize his permanent place in history by inventing a simultaneity between his arson and the birth of Alexander the Great. But Harris and Klebold left nothing to chance or to their chroniclers. Instead, they wrapped their record-setting school slaughter in the vestments of Nazi atrocity by choosing to strike on the birthday of Adolf Hitler.

The same preoccupation with celebrity that timed their attack also moved them to leave detectives and the public a record of their ambitions to be remembered as peerless butchers. They spent their last nights in their basements filming three hours of video footage that was summarized by *Time* in its issue of December 20, 1999. The reporters, Nancy Gibbs and Timothy Roche, were struck by the competitive drive of Harris to outdo the school killers of the past:

> Above all, they want to be seen as originals. "Do not think we're trying to copy anyone," Harris warns, recalling the school shootings in Oregon [by Kip Kinkel in 1998] and Kentucky [by Michael Carneal in 1997]. They had the idea long ago, "before the first one ever happened."
>
> And their plan is better, "not like those f——s in Kentucky with camouflage and .22s. Those kids were only trying to be accepted by others."[99]

Harris and Klebold listed many groups that they hated, embracing much of the world that they had known in their brief lives—African Americans, Hispanics, Jews, gays, "f——ing whites," and, the reporters add, "the enemies who abused them and the friends who didn't do enough to defend them." Klebold hoped to kill 250 of them. When the massacre was over, the immortality would begin. The reporters recall the duo's gloating:

> Even when it is over, they promise, it will not be over. In memory and nightmares, they hope to live forever. "We're going to kick-start a revolution," Harris says—a revolution of the dispossessed. They talk about being ghosts who will haunt the survivors—"create flashbacks from what we do," Harris promises, "and drive them insane."[100]

As he concludes his taping session, Harris takes pain to fix it precisely in time for archival purposes. It is 1:28 A.M., March 15. Klebold "says people will note the date and time when watching it." He also ruminates about future Hollywood battles over the film rights, according to the *Time* report: "'Directors will be fighting over this story,' Klebold said—and the boys chewed over which could be trusted with the script: Steven Spielberg or Quentin Tarantino." FBI agent Holstlaw finds the videotapes consistent with the two boys' hunt after fame and their suicidal impulses: "You have two individuals who wanted to immortalize themselves. They wanted to be martyrs and to document everything they were doing."[101]

David J. Krajicek, journalist and former Columbia University journalism professor, has detected traits of Herostratos in the Columbine killers, as well as in the Unabomber and his rival, Timothy McVeigh. In his article "Nobody Loves a Crime Reporter," Krajicek cautions the press against catering to these bloodstained publicity seekers:

> The modern media conundrum of crime celebrity is familiar to us even if the name Herostratus is not. Recent cases suggest journalists should pay heed to a crime culture in which fame and infamy have grown increasingly synonymous. Timothy McVeigh, the Oklahoma City bomber, seemed to be angling for legend status. The two boys who murdered classmates and a teacher in suburban Denver in 1999 before killing themselves left videotapes anticipating their own media immortality. The Unabomber was so keenly aware of his image that he made it known he wanted to be called Ted (not Theodore) Kaczynski.
>
> When someone commits a criminal act purely to attract celebrity, are journalists facilitators? On the other hand, how can we ignore the acts of

some publicity-seekers? A mass killing is news. Bonnie Bucqueroux, co-ordinator of the Victims and the Media at Michigan State University, says the reading and viewing public has come to expect details about perpetrators.

"The truth is that evil is a compelling thing to look at," she says. "The question is, how much do we pander to our curiosity, and to what extent do we want to show our children that this is a viable way to garner attention, because we know from our kids that those who can't get attention through positive behavior will turn to negative behavior to get attention?"[102]

The valid concerns about media glorification of Herostratic killers was magnified exponentially when journalists were compelled to face the horrors of September 11, 2001.

5 Herostratos at the
World Trade Center

THE NAME OF HEROSTRATOS rose spontaneously to the minds and pens of professional and amateur writers who recorded their early impressions of the attacks on the World Trade Center. This chapter will concentrate on two principal works in which a Herostratos pattern was observed: *Dostoyevsky in Manhattan,* a book by French philosopher and human rights activist André Glucksmann; and "The Terror and the Temple," an essay by Victor-Pierre Stirnimann, a Jungian analyst (analytical psychologist) in Brazil.[1] To demonstrate the pervasiveness of references to the Herostratos prototype, Internet sources such as online journalism and electronic mailing lists will also be cited.

The final stage of Herostratos's globalization has been his invasion of cyberspace. When the Twin Towers and the Pentagon were struck, news readers and viewers around the world placed articles and messages on the Internet to draw parallels between the shocking American catastrophe and the arson in ancient Ephesus. Remarkably, the postulation of the Herostratos analogy in online writing and chatter was generally unaffected either by the degree of the writer's sympathies with the United States or by the fact that al-Qaeda's concerted attacks on Manhattan and Washington, unlike the burning of Diana's temple, were apparently motivated by ideology.

"Welcome to the Third Millennium!" This was the mournful refrain of a prose poem that Italian literary critic Peter Patti published in his telecom journal, *Binario 1 (Track 1),* two days after the destruction of the World Trade Center. Patti worried about how we would explain to our children that the toppling towers with which they had become familiar from so many films, mostly

The September 11, 2001, attack on the World Trade Center. © Reuters/CORBIS

American, had become an urban reality. It was difficult, Patti wrote, to "understand the mentality of a kamikaze terrorist who goes to his death with the certainty of being glorified afterward (but where? in his village of stones and misery?)." The answer to this riddle lay in the distant past, for the suicidal destroyer "sets fire to the temple, as Herostratos had already done millennia before him. 'What a madman!' we say, shaking our heads. But knowing that people are mad, and that the world is a madhouse doesn't help us live more securely."[2]

A little over two hours after the Manhattan attack, an open letter was posted on a religious bulletin board, "Have Theology Will Argue." While cautioning against "blind retaliation in anger," the writer warned "the cowards who think they have gained something by displaying the blackness of their hearts" that "we will not forget you." The letter drew a response that insisted on greater precision of thought even at a moment of emotional turmoil: "Not quite a coward, per se, but a Herostratus."[3]

One of the post–September 11 remembrances of Herostratos was imbued with chauvinism. In October the *San Antonio Business Journal* published a guest comment by Carlos Freymann, "It is best not to kick a sleeping giant." In Freymann's highly spiced words, "ignorant warriors" whose "brain does not function the same in all members of our genus" had "destroyed thousands of lives and one of the true wonders of modern times." He cited the ancient precedent: "These structures, icons of this nation's might and its progressive form of capitalism, were to last for centuries, if not forever. But blinded by primeval hatred against America, and led by a modern Herostratus, the damnable suicidal beings used human occupied missiles to crush the spectacular high structures."[4]

On September 20, 2001, a more thoughtful use of history was made in *GloboNews.com* of São Paulo, Brazil. "From antiquity to the modern era," its comment began, "great monuments and icons of historical significance have been victims of attacks like those that leveled the twin towers of the World Trade Center in New York, and part of the site of the Pentagon in Washington." The author referred to the "myth" that "the young Herostratos had ruined the Artemision moved by the impulse to conquer fame and eternal recognition." Citing Professor James Higginbotham of Bowdoin University, the editorialist continued, "There are interesting parallels between tragic events of antiquity and the attacks perpetrated against the United States in the past week. The struggle against a dominant culture and the desire to break the barrier between dominator and dominated are motives impelling attacks of hatred, intolerance and violence."[5]

On September 20, 2001, *Largeur.com* initiated a discussion on increased violence in Switzerland. A contributor signing herself "Hildegarde" related the phenomenon to what she termed the "Herostratos syndrome." She asked whether suicidal followers of the ancient destroyer would become more common and answered her own question in the affirmative:

I fear that they will be more numerous in future times in preferring a criminal and spectacular death to an obscure and lonely destiny.

To all of them we must say that they are mistaken. We won't remember anything about them. Herostratos is the proof that this imbecilic temptation to drag along innocent people to death in order to attract attention to themselves is anything but a heroic act; it is simply a crime, a murder, whatever its scale.[6]

The "psychological consequences" of the World Trade Center terror were the subject of an editorial posted on the Web site of St. Petersburg, Russia's Rosbalt News Agency in November 2001. The author, Natalia Starichkova, Rosbalt's issuing editor, treated with equal skepticism reactions based on fear, anger, or a kind of cowardice that expresses itself in "political civility" toward religious extremism. Starichkova also quoted a recent discussion in *Izvestiya* of the Herostratic element in terrorism: "If we agree that terror is basically a psychological case, the Herostratus phenomenon is likely to be a description of the terrorist's psychology. Highlighting of terrorism in mass media is a trigger for the Herostratus phenomenon. Every showing of a shop's explosion, mass murder and falling skyscrapers gives birth to more and more terrorists." Unpersuaded by *Izvestiya*'s argument, Starichkova regarded the proposal to control media coverage as another outbreak of emotionalism in response to September 11. "Well, what a pretty choice! We should either hide our fears (i.e., from a psychological point of view, bury the problem), or transform this fear into persistent anger and fiery revenge (and who will be our victims, may I ask?), or prohibit mass media from speaking about terrorism."[7]

While Russian editors differed concerning the wisdom of news restraints, a German journalist inveighed against the heroization of terrorists. Torsten Kleinz's recollection of the ancient ban on Herostratos's name was wakened in December 2001 when *Time* nominated Osama bin Laden as Person of the Year. Kleinz's angry article "How Many Osamas must there be?" appeared online in the German-language magazine *Telepolis*. Kleinz referred to the failure of the Ephesians' attempt to suppress the arsonist's name: "The plan did not succeed. Still today we know the name of the attacker, Herostratos."[8] The same problem was presented in the United States; but "must a gruesome crime turn someone into a media star?" Kleinz recognized that the *Time* selection was not intended as a distinction but to identify what Henry Luce had defined as "the person or persons who most affected the news or our lives, for good or for ill this year." Kleinz noted that in 1999 Adolf Hitler and Yitzhak Rabin were running neck and neck for Person of the Twentieth Century until Elvis Presley overtook both. When the votes were counted for Person of the Year in 2001, Rudy Giuliani vanquished Osama. It was a happy result, Kleinz commented, for bin Laden intended his death, like his life, to be a major media event. The journalist referred to interviews of Osama's ex-wife, Sabiha, with the *National Enquirer* and

Russia's TV 6: "Bin Laden planned a melodramatic end. If he were cornered, bin Laden would command his eldest son to kill him before rolling cameras. When pictures of the dying terrorist leader were shown around the world, a second wave of terror would begin."

According to Jean Daniel's editorial in the online issue of *Le Nouvel Observateur* for the week of September 26, 2001, bin Laden, like Herostratos, sought immortality:

> In Greek antiquity it was said that Herostratos had burned the Temple of Artemis . . . only to assure his immortality. That is undoubtedly what bin Laden also sought in attacking the towers of the World Trade Center. But we should manage to have the Islamic strategist spoken of as people spoke of Herostratos: with shame and contempt. It's not that way yet in a part of the world, but we can't rule that out for the future.[9]

Yet the hope that Herostratic criminals will suffer oblivion has failed mankind in the past; magazine cover portraits and television spectaculars were not essential to assure eternal memory. As Pascal Ory noted in an online article in *France Culture* in April 2002: "Everyone has forgotten the names of the magistrates, the priests, the journalists of Ephesus in ancient times, but the name of the incendiary has remained engraved in the collective memory. . . . The Herostratuses, for humankind, are, like all monsters, unforgettable."[10]

The first two anniversaries of the Twin Towers attack have occasioned further reflections on the relevance of Herostratos's crime. In an allusion to the role of Artemis as a moon goddess, *Nexos,* a student publication of EAFOT University in Medellín, Colombia, published on the Internet "Herostratos, the Airplane of the Moon, One Year after Its Collision." While regretting that the retaliation in Afghanistan claimed even more lives than the Manhattan terrorism, the author noted that the attack on the Twin Towers was a "vile act" beyond Herostratos's imaginings: "We can only say that the [human] plane that struck the temple mentioned in the Bible, consecrated to the goddess Artemis, was not so fatal as to serve to designate a whole complex of actions, since crimes like that in New York cannot be described in such minimal terms as those which, without intending to do so, Herostratos has established."[11]

On September 11, 2003, Jean Daniel returned to the theme of the World Trade Center's destruction. In an online edition of *Le Nouvel Observateur,* he suggested that the attack, though unprecedented in scale and location, was prefigured by the crimes of ancient destroyers. Drawing on an article that he had published in early 2002, Daniel wrote:

We did not know that the United States could be attacked in its "standing City" (Céline), this Western symbol of progress, with the arrogant and futuristic sumptuousness of aggression and the hallucinating and dreamlike aspect of drama. We did not know how intense the trauma in the depth of America's soul could become. But we knew the rest. We knew that the real power, the only power belonged from now on to the heirs of Herostratos, who burned the Temple of Artemis at Ephesus to be able to leave a name in history; to those of Nero, who was enchanted to see Rome in flames; and to those of Caligula, of whom one of his contemporaries said that the extravagance of his madness led him to think that to enter into competition with the gods, it was necessary to massacre those nearest and dearest. These three antiheroes advocated the enjoyment of evil, the ecstasy of nothingness; they wanted to transform destruction into destiny.[12]

In 1999 academic participants in an online mailing list maintained by Ohio State University's Classics Department had exchanged views on "random disaster" and Herostratos under a caption more ominous than they knew, "Toppling Towers and Burning Temples." Professor David Lupher of the University of Puget Sound regarded Herostratos as "an interesting precursor of what we tend to think of as a distinctly modern 'type,'" and a participant from Nagasaki, Alvar Minaya, likened the Ephesian crime to the burning of Kyoto's Temple of the Golden Pavilion.[13] In the autumn of 2001, the Classicists resumed their e-mail discussion in the light of the attack on the Twin Towers and the Pentagon; Professor Lupher, once again participating in the discussion, reviewed the ancient sources. The professor's vision of the pertinence of Herostratos seemed to alter as he wrote. His initial comment was that Herostratos should be considered as essentially a "self-publicist" rather than a terrorist: "He regarded his arson as his claim to fame. And he had no further 'message' to broadcast." Yet, on further thought, Lupher noted that much the same observation could be made about the modern terrorists. Those "who gave us 9/11 and the ongoing anthrax . . . scare do not seem eager to stake a public claim to their acts. Not even Osama bin Laden actually quite did so in his recent video. Nor, for that matter, do they yet seem to be offering a list of grievances, though some of their apologists seem eager to 'interpret' their acts." Professor Lupher's final reflection was that the World Trade Center attack was "something closer to 'existential terror,' or 'pure terror, unsullied by mere demands or complaints.'"[14]

While others debated Herostratos's origins and his message to the twenty-first century, an introspective Web logger stood aside from the public fray.

On September 20, 2001, Joe McCleskey, an expert on instructional videos, participated in a multidisciplinary forum on dealing with the World Trade Center tragedy in the classroom. On June 12 of the following year, he posted to his Web log a modern parable of a Herostratos who is condemned by destiny to commit his crime even if denied the fame for which he quests. On the road to Ephesus, he meets a blind old man who has intuitive foreknowledge of his intention to destroy the Artemision:

> The old man smiles. "I know many things, Herostratus. Including why you wish to burn it down."
>
> "All right then, tell me."
>
> The old man turns his cataract eyes toward the moon. "You grew up hearing stories of great men—Miltiades, Alcibiades, Leonidas. You wish men to know your name as well."
>
> Herostratus gazes at the man, speechless.
>
> "I'll tell you something else. In a very short time, your deed will be forgotten by most, while the deeds of the truly great will live on. People will quiz each other for amusement; they will ask who destroyed the Temple of Artemis, and none will recall your name."
>
> Beginning to look angry, Herostratus stammers, "Then what can I do to gain fame?"
>
> The old man laughs. "What you must do is burn down the temple. It is your fate. Now run along."
>
> After standing and looking bewildered for a moment, he continues walking down the road, torch in hand.[15]

Two weeks after the destruction of the World Trade Center, André Glucksmann and film director Romain Goupil summarized their reactions in an article in *Le Monde,* "The nihilist equation." In the following year Glucksmann developed the article's theses in his book *Dostoyevsky in Manhattan.* The title of the work reflects Glucksmann's perception that the atrocities of September 11 were acts of nihilism that can be better understood in the light of Dostoyevsky's portrayals of nineteenth-century Russian terrorists in his novel *Demons* (also translated as *The Devils* and *The Possessed*).[16]

The identification of a precedent in literature does not cause Glucksmann to deny the "newness" of the September 11 attacks. He cautions against the belief that, with the passage of time, the wound will heal as if nothing had happened. An "unforeseeable" event has taken place, and can happen again, Glucksmann warns, citing Clausewitz's dictum, "Once the boundary markers of the possible, which only existed in our unconscious, have been toppled, it is difficult to set them up again."[17]

In Glucksmann's assessment, a principal result of September 11 was to disabuse modern states of their flattering assumption that they had "a monopoly of violence." Yet recent history, from the Guernica bombing in 1937 through the destruction of the Buddhas of Afghanistan and the Mostar bridge, as well as the leveling of the Chechen capital of Grozny, had already made it plain that civilian populations and cities were targets of "urbicide," a terror that does not speak its name. Glucksmann finds that fear is enhanced by the attackers' silence:

> The act [of violence] speaks for itself. When terror is silent, it reaches maximal intensity. The violence that engulfed the World Trade Center does not ask for anything, that is, it demands everything. The absence, for weeks, of motivation, of any claim of responsibility, of any issued ultimatum, redoubles stupefaction and fear. The extremely disturbing impact of wordless violence. Its annihilating power is affirmed as nonnegotiable. In the universe of the concentration camp the victims asked, "Why?" The executioner answered: "Here there are no whys."[18]

The unresponsiveness of killers to their victims illustrates the chilling fact that the enemies of civilization's norms find the range of their choices to be limitless. Glucksmann also cites a question put to a thirteen-year-old Liberian gang leader: "Aren't you afraid that you will shoot down your brothers, sisters, father and mother with your *kalashnikov?*" The young boy answered, "Why not?"[19]

Glucksmann's image of the September 11 attackers combines Dostoyevsky's nihilists with the ancient terror of Herostratos:

> The anticity strategy is the cherished option of totalitarian violence. Dostoyevsky and his *Demons* might judiciously have subtitled the images delivered continuously on CNN: "We shall proclaim destruction . . . why, why is the idea so fascinating? We shall light fires! We shall spread legends . . . there will be a great upheaval such as the world has never seen . . ." The last seconds before the crash. Imagine the ecstasy of the piratical pilot plunging into the regal towers. I was nothing, just a featherless biped among others. From now on I am everything, I am dying and the world dies with me. In Mohamed Atta, the suicidal organizer of the hellish fire and mild-mannered son according to his papa, a Cairo lawyer, recognize Herostratos, the obscure Greek who in 356 BC burned

the Temple of Diana, one of the Seven Wonders of the World, prepared for anything, even death, to surpass Alexander in immortality.[20]

The linkage of nihilists with Herostratos is supported by their will to achieve immortality in crime and their joy in destruction. Glucksmann cites a hero of the Marquis de Sade who asserts: "I would like to find a crime whose perpetual effect is active even when I shall act no more." This wish has now been fulfilled, Glucksmann thinks, for "the insane joy in destruction for destruction's sake ravaged the twentieth century and has spilled over into the next."

Glucksmann gives back to France the dubious honor of having invented nihilism, crediting Anacharsis Cloots with the "first glorious appearance of the word" in 1793, when the president of the Jacobin Club announced that the French Republic was neither deist nor atheist but nihilist; Cloots's bold credo brought him to the guillotine. As a footnote to this historical reference, Glucksmann provides a modern definition of nihilists: "The nihilist is a man of practice rather than the inventor of a theory. He cares less about elaborating theses than about demolishing them. The nihilist abandons heaven to the clouds and takes possession of the earth as his theater of operations."[21] The nihilist grounds his sense of being in his ability to murder; updating Descartes, he maintains, according to Glucksmann: "I kill, therefore I am." On September 11 nihilists exhibited "a perfectly deliberate and totally arbitrary will to crush every soul living within a given perimeter."[22] Their massive crime was infused by the nihilists' conception of God as "the spirit of the Deluge" whose power of destruction they rivaled in extinguishing their own lives as well as those of their thousands of victims.[23]

A fundamental theorem of *Dostoyevsky in Manhattan* is that nihilist outrages are not impelled by allegiance to any particular ideology but by self-realization in the destructive act. "A specter haunts the planet," Glucksmann intones in mockery of the Communist Manifesto, and "that is nihilism. It uses ancient religions, abuses ancient ideologies and communal fervor, but it does not respect them." He urges that "Islamic nihilism is above all a nihilism and a contemporary way of living one's life and damaging that of others."[24]

Glucksmann devotes his final chapter to a praise of literature and of the insight that it provides into the dark forces perpetually at work in our lives. There is a common tendency to consider "cruelty, individual as well as collective, [to be] episodic." One sees cruelty as "a misfortune, a detour in the road of progress, an accident, a bad moment to pass through and transcend." But some great novels have reversed this perspective: "They have dissipated euphoria. Progress, development, and life-stories reemerge with necks cut, their obligatory happy ending decapitated." Glucksmann admires the freedom of these masterworks from illusion, believing as he does that the "subject of literature, par excellence, is violence seen from within, *hubris* exhibited in the assertive and swaggering logic of its display."[25]

One of the traits of Russian literature most highly prized by Glucksmann is its avoidance of facile explanations for criminal acts. Glucksmann observes that in a preparatory note for *The Idiot,* Dostoyevsky "amuses himself with the words spoken by the defender of a high-school student charged with the murder of an entire family: 'It is natural that poverty put in the mind of my client the idea of killing six people. That idea, who in his circumstances would not have had it?'" Certainly, Glucksmann adds, "the criminal was born poor, but all the poor are not born killers."[26] This is a wise reminder to those who seek universal socioeconomic causes for terrorist conduct. In the vision of Dostoyevsky, the omnipresence of terrorism cannot be so easily accounted for. Glucksmann quotes the notebooks for *Demons:* "Where did the nihilists come from? From nowhere. They have always been with us, within us, at our sides."[27]

Jungian psychologist Victor-Pierre Stirnimann's article, "The Terror and the Temple," has previously been cited in connection with issues considered in chapters 1 and 3. The article by Stirnimann appears in a 2002 collection, *Jungian Reflections on September 11: A Global Nightmare,* edited by Luigi Zoja and Donald Williams. Reviewer John Fraim has related the publication to the commitment of post-Jungians "to an approach that did not focus exclusively on psychic reality but also took into account the realities of the outer world."[28] True, however, to the Jungian tenet that "images from the unconscious, or a collective dream . . . [are] a potent source for information,"[29] Stirnimann highlights symbols latent in modern terrorism and in its ancient origins. At the outset, he observes that many have called the new kind of terrorism "symbolic," and wonders whether Herostratos "could . . . be a clue, a pre-figuration to lead our way to a deeper understanding of it all."[30]

Herostratos, so Stirnimann assumes, knew himself "as totally devoid of any trait of excellence," and it was for that reason that he "tried to immortalize his name through the only way he could find—destroying something immortal, in order to participate in the immortality of what he had destroyed." He defeated the Ephesian attempt to expunge his name from history and made himself immortal "through the unconceivable nature of his crime."[31] Stirnimann theorizes that Herostratos asked himself how "you make yourself meaningful, significant in your individual existence, when you do not possess anything of recognizable value to your own time and culture." The ancient terrorist then formulated the most radical of answers: "You can over-come your mediocrity, if only you sacrifice yourself together with a valuable offering to the Gods of your era. To destroy, but as a means to possess." The arsonist, Stirnimann further supposes, went even beyond this fundamental scheme by destroying, and thereby possessing "what was arguably the most sacred and valued place in the world he knew." By this "unthinkable trans-gression" and the certain punishment that it entailed, "his terrorism put him by force in the center of his own cosmos."[32]

Stirnimann expresses Herostratos's anguish in harsh mathematical terms: the temple destroyer protested "against the predicament that an unequal des-tiny (his insignificance as an individual) imposes upon the equality of desire (his longing for recognition)." Lashing out in anger against this unbalanced formula, Herostratos, to Stirnimann's mind, "offers an evocation or model allowing us to better figure the power of a suicide, when it is associated to a symbolic destruction of collective magnitude."[33] According to Stirnimann's analysis, the burning of the Artemision foreshadowed the destruction of Afghanistan's Buddhas and the September 11 attack because Herostratos, as well as those responsible for these two modern disasters, relied "on a funda-mental principle of terrorism, its intimate relationship with publicity." Most modern acts of devastation were meant to be seen, and Herostratos "was sure to be discovered."[34]

In concluding his analogy between past and present acts of terror, Stirni-mann laid heavy stress on "the iconoclastic component . . . , the particularly religious status of what was to be destroyed." September 11, he writes, has brought an attack "mainly against our tolerant consumerism of all images" and at the same time "the great strike against one of our temples, the World Trade Center and the architectural wonder of its high columns touching the sky." We watched the disaster "in 'real time,' the equivalent to what must have been, in 356 BC, the fire at the Artemision."[35]

To extend the scope of the proposed comparison, Stirnimann turned his attention to the victim of Herostratos's rage, the goddess Artemis. He noted many of her associations with transition—her rule "over the boundary be-tween the civilized and the savage, the space between the city and the forest," and, in human life, her special care for female puberty. What better place, he reasoned, could be chosen for a temple in honor of such a goddess than Ephesus, "at the transitional zone between the Greek world and its otherness, between the West and the East?"[36] These musings led Stirnimann to a con-sideration of Alexander the Great's career as the embodiment of "the first large globalization movement." According to Stirnimann, Alexander took a unifying Western vision of the world as a foundation for an empire, and it was from that same vision that Herostratos felt himself excluded.[37]

The parallel between the temple and the towers holds, Stirnimann argues, despite the fact that "Herostratus sought recognition, while the current terrorist seems not to mind his remaining anonymous." The apparent inconsistency of motivation dissolves, he feels, when we recognize that "the suicidal martyr becomes a hero before his people; the paranoid sending white powder through the post perpetuates himself by spreading his personal beliefs—all these violent acts have a symbolic component, and all of them are in the pursuit of some sort of abstract immortality." Stirnimann points out that "Herostratus was also anonymous when he set fire to the temple," and "his anonymity was a pre-condition for the motive and means of his crime."[38]

Stirnimann believes that "September 11 would not be feasible in a world where the Alexandrian impulse had not got close to its extreme. Technological knowledge has shortened/civilized all distances to the same extent that it has exposed our own precariousness." He counsels, however, that the World Trade Center's fall should not blind us to the activity of Herostratos's followers in other arenas of violence:

> We should not concentrate too much on the attacks. Herostratus is not to be restricted to Islamic fundamentalists; he could easily be seen as a typically American phenomenon, like the teenager who initiates a shooting at his own school. We can find his traces in Oklahoma City, or in the middle-aged citizen who massacred politicians at the House of Representatives in Zug, Switzerland, or in any young and uneducated individual from a Third World country who sees in a gun his only gateway to achievement. All willing to touch History, all dying for immortality.[39]

The works discussed above exemplify the wide range of commentaries on Herostratos's thematic relationship with the September 11 attacks. Our understanding of his relevance to other experiences of the modern era can be advanced by examining the literature that has interpreted his crime from many viewpoints since the early nineteenth century. This varied literature of Herostratos will be the subject of the next chapter.

6 The Literature of Herostratos
Since the Early Nineteenth Century

> By what strange chances do we live in History? Erostratus by a torch . . .
> —Thomas Carlyle, *Sartor Resartus,* bk. 1, chap. 7

THE LITERATURE OF the early nineteenth century began the still ongoing process of converting Herostratos from a symbol of destructiveness into a richly imagined personage. In many genres and disciplines—fiction, poetry, drama, criticism, philosophy, and journalism—writers have invented what the tantalizing brevity of ancient sources has omitted: the genesis and context of his attack on the Artemision. Speculations are offered concerning the citizenship and occupation of Herostratos and the extent to which he was known by the Ephesian community; his religious experience and love life; and his cheated hopes, a theme frequently encountered in Herostratos narrative. The emphasis placed by some authors on personal obscurity and disappointment in the life of the fictive Herostratos tends to romanticize or palliate an arson that would otherwise be viewed as a repellent act of sacrilege. Still, the dominant voices among the poets, and the virtually unanimous judgments of the most recent essayists, condemn the crime of Herostratos without qualification and cite it as a warning to succeeding generations, which have suffered time and again from similar acts of infamy.

FICTION

The first book-length work of fiction based on the life and crime of Herostratos is *La Vita di Erostrato* (*The Life of Herostratos*) by Alessandro Verri, an important figure in the eighteenth-century Milanese Enlightenment.[1] He collaborated with his brother Pietro on a scientific-literary journal, *Il Caffè* (1764–1766), which has been likened, on a smaller scale, to Denis Diderot's *Encyclopedia*.[2] Alessandro also translated *Hamlet* and *Othello* and authored plays and novels exploring themes from Roman and Greek antiquity. Verri's *Erostrato*, published in 1815, the year before his death, remains one of the most passionate interpretations of Ephesus's notorious pyromaniac.

Bearing the plain impress of the Napoleonic Wars, Verri's tale is cast in the form of a fictitious "translation" from an ancient Greek text of Dinarco, a citizen of Epidaurus. Dinarco's tale is bracketed by comparisons of Herostratos's crime with the larger-scale devastation wrought by the great men of history. The novel's introductory section notes the coincidence, "arranged by the Fates," that Alexander was born on the same night that Herostratos's arson took place. Dinarco continues:

> This man [Alexander], in order to become great, threw Asia into confusion, filled the underworld with enraged souls, left battlefields covered with skeletons that were the leavings of carrion crows. The other man [Herostratos] obtained fame through lesser injuries. In both there was the same passion: in one, unsatiated by blood and the weeping of multitudes, and in the other pacified by the firing of a temple. And yet if the craving for celebrity is madness, it is appropriate, based on its effects, to consider greater the madness of Alexander, an incomparable example of how much an audacious usurper can make fools of us.[3]

Verri gives Dinarco, his spokesman, more to say on this theme as the last words of the novel:

> Finally, to render that night [of the fire] more memorable, there occurred the birth of Alexander nicknamed the Great because of the terror of his deeds. The following morning the mages predicted that the "ruin of the world" had been born. The Macedonian's insatiable desire for glory was certainly no less than that of Herostratos, but it was nourished by vast fires and by grave misfortunes of immense nations.[4]

Against this background of historical cataclysm, Verri spins a tale that is almost pure invention; his narrator tells the pitiful story of Herostratos, a Corinthian endowed with many natural gifts but doomed to fall agonizingly short of success in all his endeavors. While he was carried in the womb of his mother Ippodamia, she dreamt continually of giving birth to torches that would burn palaces or temples. Her husband Cleante consulted oracles only to receive the disturbing advice that his child would make his parents' lives wretched. Assuming that these obscure responses hinted at parricide, Cleante ordered a trusted servant to take his infant out to sea and to abandon him on any shore to which the wind might blow his craft.

After he is adopted by Agarista, a wealthy young woman of Lemnos, life's prospects smile deceptively upon Herostratos. Across the threshold of his young manhood, however, an unbroken chain of dashed hopes awaited him. At the Olympic Games, his patriotic declamation is praised for "strong, grandiose and profound thoughts" but found wanting in vocal projection and choice of words; his lyre playing causes a sensation that faded after defects in his technical mastery became apparent; and his promising start in a two-horse chariot race came to naught when a rival jammed him as he turned a post. His next disappointment was in love, for on his honeymoon cruise with Glicistoma, they were shipwrecked in a violent storm that took the life of his bride.

Once he recovered from his grief, Herostratos turns his ambitions toward military glory. The young widower's plan to seek immortality in battle is foreshadowed when he tells his philosophy teacher Panfilo that marble memorials more effectively spur heroism than material rewards, such as gold, jewels, and "virgin beauty," which encourage a desire to prolong life's pleasures rather than inspiring willingness to die for one's country.[5] Despite Panfilo's cautionary response, Herostratos gives up his tutelage to join Theban forces in a campaign against Spartan aggressors. Once again, his lot is bitter disillusionment; though "his fierce valor was recognized, he was not able to command other soldiers."

A decisive episode in Herostratos's life plays itself out in chapter 10 of the novel. "Wearied by the injuries of fortune and his various efforts to overcome them," he seeks consolation in the company of priests dedicated to the contemplative life at a sylvan temple in the Isthmus of Corinth. Although his heartfelt eloquence on a variety of subjects wins Herostratos a warm reception from the priests, one of them soon harbors troubling doubts about the newcomer. Why is it, he asks, that a young man ardent for glory and often moved to "sublime transports of sentiment" in discussions of heroic subjects falls silent when the conversation turns to a theme even worthier of his opinions, the divine order of the universe? In reply, Herostratos frankly expresses the depths of his religious despair:

> At the moment the aspect of the sky, the sea, the fertile coasts truly fills our spirits with delightful calm and infuses our minds with a sense of a benign and well-ordered governance. But if a baleful eclipse darkens

the sun, if storms confuse heaven and sea, it seems then that a tyranni-cal genius has usurped the rule of the world. The shepherd incinerated by a thunderbolt, a ship splintered on the rocks, the laments of the farmer over a ruined harvest make it difficult for the intellect to com-prehend the justice of Jove.[6]

Despite his loss of faith in divine justice, Herostratos makes still another at-tempt to win fame, this time as an agitator urging Greeks to rise against op-pression; he reminds his audiences that all men were born with the same natural rights and asserts that "the time had come when heaven, moved to pity of our misfortunes, invites our return to the sacred principles of the origin of civil society."[7] His speeches, however, result only in public disorders and condemnation to exile. Failure upon failure had strengthened his hun-ger for glory, but now his thoughts take a negative direction: "Angered by a destiny that had frustrated his every wish, he decided to conquer, almost to insult, his destiny."[8] A former politician now converted to terrorism, he takes sail for his appointment with destiny in Ephesus.

In a final chapter, Verri's narrator Dinarco takes pains to refute the com-mon tradition that Herostratos confessed his crime for glory only after tor-ture; to the contrary, it was necessary for him to brag about the arson in order to obtain the fame that he sought. After this explanatory prelude, Dinarco quotes verbatim Herostratos's defense speech, as "transmitted to us in the memoirs of that period." Herostratos devotes the body of his oration to minimizing his crime in comparison with the ravages of Xerxes and other great destroyers. He concludes by rejecting speculation about his possible insanity:

> Immortal glory is the goal of all my thoughts. This is the ambrosia on which my mind feeds. These fragile limbs of mine are the vessel of a great and immortal soul. My body is indeed the victim of your rigor-ous sentence. My soul will return to its source, and wandering amid the music of the spheres, will hear the eternal sound of fame.[9]

By ending on this note of sympathy for Herostratos's religious hope of im-mortality in the universe, Verri prefers his novel's protagonist to the world's destroyer, Napoleon.

In the preface to his *Vies imaginaires* (*Imaginary Lives*) (1896), novelist Marcel Schwob (1867–1905), contrasting himself with historians, acknowl-edges his debt to John Aubrey's *Brief Lives* and to the character studies in

Hokusai's prints. Aubrey "never felt the need to establish a connection between individual details and general ideas." Most of the time his readers need not know whether the subject of a literary portrait was "a mathematician, a statesman, a poet or a clockmaker, but each of them has his unique trait, which differentiates him forever from other men." The Japanese artist Hokusai aspired to a similar goal, hoping that when he was one hundred years old, every line he drew to create a subject's face and figure would be alive, that is, individual.[10]

Each of the lives that Schwob concisely relates is "imaginary" in the sense that the account contains fictional elements, but at the same time every character exemplifies a distinct and often villainous or exotic category of human experience that is identified in a subtitle. The second study in the volume is devoted to "Herostratos, incendiary." Schwob's Herostratos was an Ephesian born to a violent and proud mother and a father of whom nothing was known. The boy later boasted that he was the son of fire, which the famous Ephesian philosopher Heraclitus (at the height of his career around 500 BC) had taught was the primary substance of a universe constantly in flux. Those who attended at the birth of the infant predicted that he would be subservient to the goddess Artemis. He was easily angered and remained a virgin; his face was corroded by dark lines and his complexion was swarthy, signs perhaps intended by Schwob to forecast the smoke and soot of the conflagration for which he would become famous. From childhood on, he lingered under a high cliff near the Artemision, watching the sacrificial processions. Because of his dubious parentage, he was disqualified from joining the priesthood of Artemis. He was forbidden many times by the priestly assembly to enter the temple, where he had hoped to look beneath the precious veil that shrouded the goddess's image. He was resentful of his exclusion and vowed to violate Artemis's secret.

As another key to Herostratos's crime, Schwob imagines that the young man was obsessed with his name, which "seemed to him to be comparable to no other one, just as his own person appeared to him superior to all humanity." For a while he attached himself to the philosophers who taught the doctrines of Heraclitus, but found that they were unaware of the secret part of his philosophy, "since it was enclosed within the little pyramidal cell of Artemis's treasure." Herostratos could only guess at the meaning of the precious documents, but Artemis, to whom he was devoted, took no pity on him and did not interfere with a decision of her priests to exile the ardent young man to the suburbs. From a hill overlooking the temple, he passed his nights watching "the sacred lamps of the Artemision."

When placed under torture after the fire, Herostratos confessed that the pain to which he was subjected caused him suddenly to understand why Heraclitus had taught that the soul in its best state was the "driest and most enflamed." Herostratos pursued this assertion doggedly:

> He asserted that his soul, in this sense, was the most perfect, and that he had wanted to proclaim this fact. He did not assign any other cause for his action, except the passion for glory and the joy of hearing his name mentioned. He said that only his reign would have been absolute, since his father was unknown and Herostratos would have been crowned by Herostratos; that he was the child of his own work, and his work was the essence of the world; that thus he would have been, all in one, king, philosopher and god, unique among mankind.[11]

In Schwob's account, Herostratos's destiny to burn the temple was probably revealed to him all at once. He seized one of the sacred lamps and entered the goddess's shrine, tore the veil that hid the cult image and "avidly kissed the divine stone." Catching sight of the temple treasury, he unsealed its door; ignoring the goddess's jewels, he withdrew only the ultimate object of his quest:

> But he only took out the papyrus scroll on which Heraclitus had inscribed his verses. By the light of the sacred lamp, he read them and understood everything.
>   He immediately cried out: "Fire, fire!"

In its terse conclusion, Schwob's study records the failure of the ban on Herostratos's memory and the arson's concurrence with Alexander's birth: "The twelve cities of Ionia, under pain of death, prohibited handing down the name of Herostratos to future ages. But whispers of his name have made it come down to us."[12] The night on which Herostratos burned the temple of Ephesos, Alexander, the king of Macedonia, came into the world. Like Verri before him, Schwob emphasizes that the ambition of Herostratos links him to a world conqueror.

Jean-Paul Sartre has blended Herostratos's pathological ambition with a favorite theme of existentialist fiction: the impulse to experience a sense of freedom by committing a gratuitous criminal act (*acte gratuit*). Paul Hilbert, the first-person narrator of Sartre's short story "Erostratus," has a horror of human contact.[13] Hilbert likes to reduce pedestrians to ants by viewing them in the "downward perspective" of superiority afforded by his seventh-floor balcony. When he had to "go down into the street," he was afraid of big men who would bump into him to see how he would react. He felt more powerful, however, from the day he bought a revolver.

One night Hilbert "got the idea of shooting people." He had never had sexual intercourse with a woman; when a prostitute balked at parading before him naked, he threatened her with his gun and for four successive nights dreamed of shooting "six little red holes grouped in a circle about [her navel]." As his obsession with shooting gathers force, he fantasizes about firing into crowds attending concerts at a Paris theater, and takes target practice.

A discussion of Charles Lindbergh among Hilbert's office mates sets him in quest of a "black" hero epitomizing his own secret murderous instincts. He tells his colleagues:

"I like the black heroes."

"Negroes?" Masse asked.

"No, black as in Black Magic. Lindbergh is a white hero. He doesn't interest me."

"Go see if it's easy to cross the Atlantic," Bouxin said sourly.

I told them my conception of the black hero.

"An anarchist," Lemercier said.

"No," I said quietly, "the anarchists like their own kind of men."

"Then it must be a crazy man."

But Masse, who had some education, intervened just then.

"I know your character," he said to me. "His name is Erostratus. He wanted to become famous and he couldn't find anything better to do than to burn down the temple of Ephesus, one of the seven wonders of the world."

"And what was the name of the man who built the temple?"

"I don't remember," he confessed, "I don't believe anybody knows his name."

"Really? But you remember the name of Erostratus? You see, he didn't figure things out too badly."

The conversation ended on these words, but I was quite calm. They would remember it when the time came. For myself, who, until then, had never heard of Erostratus, his story was encouraging. He had been dead for more than two thousand years and his act was still shining like a black diamond. I began to think that my destiny would be short and tragic.[14]

Coveting, like Herostratos, the widest possible recognition for his crime, Hilbert spends his leisure time drafting a letter to 102 writers who "have humanism in [their] blood." He introduces himself to them as a "monstrosity" who cannot love his fellow men and resents his inability to detach himself from their words and thoughts. He asserts that he is going out to kill only half a dozen of them simply because his revolver has six cartridges. When the decisive moment arrives, however, he proves to be a miserable failure. He shoots a big red-necked man three times in the belly but fears he may have only wounded him. After firing two more shots at random into a crowd on the street, he locks himself in the lavatory of a café. He puts the barrel of the gun in his mouth but is unable to pull the trigger. Hilbert, a failed modern Herostratos, finds that his personal weakness undermines his impulse to express himself in violent action.

A French criminal defense lawyer briefly considered pleading that the popularity of Sartre's "Erostratus" among young readers might have contributed to the decision of a gang at a Paris secondary school to murder a seventeen-year-old schoolmate, Alain Guyader, in 1948. André Billy, a journalist and biographer who was asked by Guyader's father, Raoul, to write an account of the case, dismisses the possibility that the crime was influenced by literature:

> In the course of the crime investigation, [Raoul Guyader] informed me one day that Panconi's lawyer intended to plead a "gratuitous criminal act," under the influence of Gide, Sartre and Camus. Could Panconi have become a murderer because of having read [Gide's] *Lafcadio's Adventures* [*Les Caves du Vatican*], [Sartre's] *Erostratus* and [Camus's] *The Stranger* [*L'Étranger*]? We debated the matter, considered the question from every direction, concluded that, and for many obvious reasons, the crime ... had no connection with the theory of the "gratuitous act." Undoubtedly, Maître Goutrat [Panconi's lawyer] ended up taking the same view because he adopted a different defense theory.[15]

Alain Nadaud, in his novel, *La Mémoire d'Érostrate* (*The Remembrance of Herostratos*) (1992), imagines Herostratos as a failed poet who makes the fatal decision to convert himself into an abstraction, a name that will remain forever in human memory.[16] The novel relates the double voyage of its narrator, Sextus Publius Galba, a fictional Roman poet of modest attainments, to discover traces of Herostratos in history and in Galba's own soul. The reigning emperor Gallienus, whose court Galba frequents, would rather compose vague poems or debate metaphysics with Plotinus than defend the empire's crumbling frontiers. With the avowed purpose of compensating for the under-appreciation of Galba's work, he sends him to Ephesus on a "rapid and safe galley" to research what he hopes will be the poet's masterpiece, *The Remembrance of Herostratos*. Haunted, though, by his possible resemblance to the proud, mediocre poet turned arsonist, Galba, as he embarks at the port of Ostia in the summer of 263 AD, is aware that he will be gazing inward as well as reviewing the work of his literary predecessors:

> This is what I am going to try to establish—the relationship of all those who . . . have cited his name somewhere or who, from one generation to another, sometimes without being aware, have alluded to him; in addition, if I were permitted to retrace the path that this name has traveled within me, perhaps I could at the same time explore myself and measure the extent of the ravages he has caused me.[17]

Galba's tale is cast into a fragmentary and elusive form. The adventures of the traveling poet and his reflections on Herostratos are recorded in alternating subchapters respectively headed "description" and "meditation," and illuminated (in an amusing mélange of fact and fiction) by "compilations" of references to Herostratos in ancient literature, and annotations (*scholia*) on details of the action and settings. The result of this prismatic storytelling is, no doubt intentionally, to leave the reader often as much at sea as the voyagers on the imperial galley. What, for example, are we to make of the relationship of the narrative voice of Galba in the novel with the poem of the same name that he planned to compose? In the first *scholium,* the reader is told only that we are not in a position to say "if what we read today, under the alternating headings of *descriptio* and of *meditatio,* actually constitutes, without appearing to be so, the poem itself, or simply its commentary, or even the notes that he may have accumulated with a view to the later composition of the work."[18]

Another factor complicating the identification of narrative points of view is that everyone who has a role in telling the story, Galba as well as the invented commentators, appears to be addicted to conspiratorial thinking: they hold the common belief that the Ephesians and the goddess Artemis herself have persecuted and continue to hunt down all violators of the ban against mentioning Herostratos's name. This obsession continues into the novel's epilogue, when the vengeful goddess, mistaken by Galba for his beloved slave Orphréia, shoots him dead with her arrow either for viewing her nudity or seeking to enhance the fame of her temple's destroyer.

As the novel ends, Galba's travels have been all in vain. At his death, the poet's mission remains incomplete; his galley had been captured by marauding Goths as he entered the harbor of Ephesus, and he was never to learn what memorials of Herostratos might have remained in the city. Still, in one of his last "meditations" on the ambitious poem he had conceived, he was able to hypothesize a threefold objective on the part of Herostratos in burning the Artemision:

1. To express his resentment against Artemis, the Conductress of the Muses, who had abandoned him by denying him outstanding literary gifts;
2. To punish the self-satisfaction of the Ephesians by toppling a monument that was the very foundation of their inordinate vanity; and
3. To eclipse by an insane act the fame of his city's favorite son, the philosopher Heraclitus, who had deposited the manuscript of his celebrated work at the foot of Artemis's altar.

The triumph over Heraclitus was particularly sweet, because the arson not only demonstrated that the immortality of sacrilege could surpass literary fame but also reduced to ashes the philosopher's manuscript, "of which nowadays nobody remembers the title or preserves more than fragments." Another irony consoled Herostratos, Galba theorized. Heraclitus had argued that fire was the creative element of the universe and had written that everybody would be judged and devoured by fire.[19]

Jerzy Limon, novelist and professor of English drama at the University of Gdansk (Danzig), has spun an ironic tale of short-lived Herostratic fame in Poland after World War II. In Limon's short story "The Herostratos of Bierut Street," the people of a spa town near Gdansk long for a thaw in Communist rule.[20] The advent of a new era will, they hope, be confirmed by a change in the name of the town's thoroughfare, Bierut Street, which memorializes Communist Poland's first head of state, Boleslaw Bierut.

In a period of false dawn, the townspeople acclaim unlikely heroes, none stranger than a one-legged, heavy-drinking, henpecked shoemaker who is suspected of having collaborated with the Nazis during the war because he rides an admired bicycle of German manufacture. The shoemaker first marks himself as a possible opponent of the Red regime by scoffing at May Day celebrations. When a VIP reviewing stand burns down mysteriously, the intoxicated shoemaker is found asleep on a park bench spared by the blaze, and he is sentenced to five years' imprisonment for arson. The convicted man is exuberant over the unexpected turn in his fortune: "And then began a time of which he had always dreamt. Within a few days he was famous." He was a topic of conversation throughout the country and Radio Free Europe called him a hero, a champion of free thought, and "a further victim of the Communist slave drivers from Beria's clique."[21]

On his release from prison, the shoemaker was hailed by the townspeople and even his abusive wife beamed with pride. Memories, however, were short and the town hero took to drink again: "The other residents of our street very soon forgot about the experiences of our heroic shoemaker, and today there is almost nobody who remembers him, although at the time it appeared as if he would, so to speak, attain the status of the Herostratos of Bierut Street."[22]

Unlike Limon, who found an incarnation of Herostratos in his own neighborhood, the modern Italian novelist Umberto Eco invoked the arsonist as a symbol of American crime. In a late chapter of *Foucault's Pendulum* (published in English in 1989), Eco introduces Herostratos in the guise of a copycat criminal. Although the passage in question takes a comic turn, this variation on the Herostratic theme is founded in grim reality. A copycat killer may hope for a shortcut to lasting fame through the public's association of his crime with an earlier sensation. In Eco's linkage of crimes present and past, fact mimics art: "This is what always happens. A young Herostratus broods because he doesn't know how to be famous. Then he sees a movie in which a frail young man shoots a country music star and becomes the center of attention. Herostratus has found the formula; he goes out and shoots John Lennon."[23] In spite of his apparently ironic tone, Eco has been completely faithful to reality. The film to which he makes reference is Robert Altman's *Nashville* (1980), which was once blamed for influencing Mark Chapman's murder of Lennon. The director recalled the incident on the twentieth anniversary of the former Beatle's death:

Nashville was sort of a harbinger of [the murder]. When John Lennon got assassinated, I got a call from a reporter at the *Washington Post,* and he asked, "Do you feel responsible for this?" I said, "How do you mean?" He said, "Well because in your film "Nashville" you did an assassination of a celebrity." I told him, "That's what the film is all about—do you feel responsible for not heeding my warning?"[24]

Eco, however, is not concerned with the merits of the charge against Altman, for he has his own trick to play. The Herostratos syndrome in crime reminds Eco's narrator of a similar phenomenon among vanity press authors aspiring to fame: "It's the same with the SFAS [self-financing authors]. How can I become a published poet whose name appears in an encyclopedia? . . . It's simple, you pay."[25]

The Catalan novelist Terenci Moix (1942–2003) has written a devastating group portrait of featherbrained Spanish successors of Herostratos at the millennium's end. In *Chulas y famosas, o bien, La venganza de Eróstrato* (*The Flashy and the Famous: The Revenge of Herostratos*),[26] the "private" diary of jet-setting Miranda Boronat, a self-styled "millionairess" and "woman of the world," impudently records how she and her eighty best friends pursue celebrities, admired and despised, in the spheres of aristocracy, politics, fashion, and entertainment and forever hope to achieve fame by snaring the attention of the tabloid press. Miranda's self-advertisement comes at a price; she finds that Terenci Moix, to whom she has shown her grotesque diary to relieve his case of writer's block, has copied her words verbatim in the present novel. The subtitle given by Moix (to whom Miranda refers only as "the Author") puzzles her at first when she is shocked to encounter the work in a bookstore in Seville where she has come to attend the wedding of a nobleman and a model:

My hands began to tremble. I remembered the history of the young Herostratos, the rogue who destroyed the votive church of the goddess Diana. In fact, the book bore the subtitle, *The revenge of Herostratos*. What was the point of that? Had the Author converted my experiences into a Greek novel?[27]

On further reflection, however, Miranda places herself on guard against more sinister intentions on the Author's part. Could it be that her irresponsible adventures signal the return of Herostratos's destructive spirit? She muses anew in the light of a particularly disturbing news headline: "Take care, Mirandilla, for the ferocious Herostratos is on the loose once again. He is coming to destroy. He is coming to sow chaos. Remember the temple of Diana. Remember the catastrophe."[28]

Herostratos can also be found at his violent work in plots of detective fiction. Professor Horst Bosetzky, a German master of detective fiction who signs his work with the abbreviation "–ky," has written a short story entitled "You Can Then Forget Herostratos" (1994). The opening scene is set in a high school philosophy class. The overbearing teacher, Konrad Klenzke, lectures about Kant's insistence that life must have a goal. To illustrate the point, he distributes note cards from among the twenty he has brought. He asks his students to reflect on their future and who their role models will be. Marvin Winkelmann, who has received "a pink card in the format of a paperback book," hears an inner voice mandating that he outdo Herostratos by becoming a record-setting serial killer:

> I see the meaning of my life in entering the Guinness Book of Records as the man, who—outside of war and performing any function as dictator or general, in other words, with my own hands—has committed the most murders. I will thereby become famous, yes, immortal. I will reach one hundred murders, and Klenzke will be the first victim. My great role model is the Greek Herostratos, who in 356 BC set fire to the Temple of Artemis in Ephesus to become eternally famous. And he succeeded. But when I have completed my work, nobody will mention his name anymore. You can then forget Herostratos.

Without giving away "–ky"'s plot, it is fair to say that Winkelmann is soon off to a good start toward achieving his ambitions.[29]

In Philippe Arnaud's *La boîte à chagrins (Pandora's Box)* (2002), Léon Bertin, president of the French Republic who moonlights as a detective, hunts a serial killer who calls himself Herostratos. Bertin remembers the story of the ancient arson, but Raoul Solard, the Minister of the Interior, points out the continuing relevance of the crime in the modern age of sensational journalism: "[Herostratos] perpetrated his crime so as to remain in the memory of mankind. A little like those crazy people who kill simply to see their names in the papers."[30] Only a trap set by Bertin prevents the killer from spreading images of his gruesome murders on the Internet.

POETRY AND DRAMA

Poetry and drama portray Herostratos in many lights. Many Romantic or exoticist poets draw parallels between Herostratos and other criminals of antiquity or of the modern age, shifting emphasis from the ancient incendiary's thirst for fame to what these writers interpret as his pure joy in destruction or self-destruction. An exception to this pattern is a long nineteenth-century narrative poem written in French by a Polish writer, the pseudonymous Jean Polonius, which is closer to Herostratos fiction in its creation of sympathetic biographical details to account for the burning of the Artemision. Still it is more often on the stage than in narrative poetry that Herostratos steps forward as a strongly individualized protagonist. The richest tradition of Herostratos drama, much of it in verse, is found in Germany and Austria, where it has been continually reworked in many styles, including neo-Classicism, expressionism, and surrealist-absurdist conceptions. Although German-language playwrights have taken the lead, Herostratos's stage career has been worldwide; recently, a scholar has detected Herostratos's influence on Peter Shaffer's *Amadeus.*

Lord Byron, an ardent lover of Greece and its antiquities, bitterly denounced the removal of the Parthenon marbles in his poem, "The Curse of Minerva," which he first published privately in 1812.[31] Byron, in no mood for restrained discourse, indicted Lord Elgin as the perpetrator of a sacrilegious act of vandalism comparable to the burning of the Temple of Artemis. The poet imagines a moonlit encounter with the goddess Minerva (Pallas Athena), who is angered by Elgin's violation of her shrine. She lays her curse "on him and all his seed," and condemns him to the disdain of the most thoughtful among London's museum visitors:

> And last of all, amidst the gaping crew,
> Some calm spectator, as he takes his view,
> In silent indignation mix'd with grief,
> Admires the plunder, but abhors the thief.

As the goddess's ire gathers force, she brackets Elgin's name with the proscribed memory of Herostratos, and promises them both undying revenge:

> Link'd with the fool that fired the Ephesian dome,
> Shall vengeance follow far beyond the tomb,
> And Eratostratus [Herostratos] and Elgin shine
> In many branding page and burning line;
> Alike reserved for aye to stand accursed,
> Perchance the second blacker than the first.

It is with pardonable egocentricity that Athena has regarded the crime against her temple as "blacker" than the offense suffered by her sister Artemis.

Legends of the Roman Empire included a parallel to the crime of Herostratos—the slanderous tale that Nero took great pleasure in viewing the Great Fire at Rome in 64 AD, and might even have ordered the conflagration to be started. Herostratos and Nero are paired as destroyers in poems of Victor Hugo. In an ode of 1825, "Nero's Festive Song," the emperor, "master of the world and god of harmony," sings in the Ionian mode (the scale favored in

Herostratos's Ephesus) and accompanies himself on the lyre as he invites friends to a gala celebration of the burning of Rome.[32] By devastating the city he will triumph over divine oracles that promised immortality to his capital. "My friends," he asks in jest, "tell me how many more hours its eternity can last." Herostratos comes to Nero's mind as he exults in the blaze:

How beautiful is a fire when the night is black,
Herostratos himself would have envied my glory.

Not only the sheer pleasure of annihilation but competition with the gods motivates Nero. He begrudges Romans their worship of Jupiter and Christ when he would like to have a temple of his own.

The infamous fire lovers reappear toward the end of Victor Hugo's *The Contemplations*, a poetry collection published in 1856. In a long poem, "What the Ghost Says," a phantom encountered by a wanderer on a rocky summit delivers a frightening sermon about the postmortem metamorphoses of human evil into the elements of the universe, both animate and apparently inanimate.[33] For, as the specter proclaims, every evil human being, on his death, "gives birth to the monster of his life." The fires of Herostratos and Nero merge as the world's basest villainies transmigrate:

The soul of black Judas, after eighteen hundred years
Is dispersed and born again in men's spittle;
And the wind that long ago blew over Sodom
Mixes, in the abject hearth and beneath the crude cauldron,
Herostratos's smoke with Nero's flame.

In "Some Words to Another," also included in *The Contemplations*, Hugo proudly avows his leading role in revolutionizing French poetry, comparing himself figuratively to three men of violence, Louis-Auguste Papavoine, a random killer of two children; Herostratos; and Attila the Hun.[34]

Count Xavier Labensky, a Polish Romantic who wrote in French under the pseudonym Jean Polonius, published a book-length narrative poem, *Érostrate*, in 1840.[35] Critic Eugène Asse esteems him as a loner who shunned the literary clubs and journals of his era and became the first of the Romantics in France to write philosophical poetry borrowing its themes from pagan antiquity.[36] In his preface, Labensky cited Alessandro Verri's novel (which he claimed not to have read before composing his own work) as expressing "the idea that Herostratos, despite the barbarous insanity of his action, perhaps was in his heart of hearts better than what he had done and might have been animated by generous feelings." He also referred to Fontenelle's dialogues of Alexander and Herostratos, which had sought to establish that "the actions of the conqueror and the incendiary, as different as they were, had their point of departure in the same principle." Labensky found that the number of Herostratoses who embodied "suppressed ambition" was more significant than might appear at first glance "in a period like ours, when our unceasingly active democracy and our always-expanding education system inspire every day more ambitions than they can possibly satisfy."[37]

The Herostratos of Labensky's poem, in contrast to many other portraits of the arsonist, was neither lowly nor contemptible; rather, he was born in the wrong place and in the wrong time to achieve the success he craved. In his teens he carried off many athletic prizes in his native Ephesus, studied with Plato in Athens, and visited the famous temples of Egypt and India. When he returned home, he conceived an intense loathing for Ephesus, which had nothing to offer to his political dreams of a unified, independent Greece and to his aesthetic passions. Ephesus, he saw, was a city abandoned by the Greeks to Persian domination, where money ruled and artists had become effete.

Herostratos's disillusionment drives him into seclusion, until, at age thirty, he learns from his childhood sweetheart, Ithis, that a plutocrat named Thoas can claim her in marriage if he triumphs in an upcoming chariot race. Herostratos's jealousy is aroused. Trying to repeat a notable victory of his youth, Herostratos enters the race but his chariot is upset near the finish line when he is blinded by the aspect of a demonic statue that glowers over the hippodrome. His hated rival comes in first and is entitled to the hand of Ithis. Persuaded that he is forever the victim of fate, Herostratos sets fire to Artemis's temple and its trophies, including a memorial to his own long-past victory in athletic games. Although fame was his goal, the blaze has unintended consequences: it causes the death of Ithis (who had become a priestess to avoid marriage to the repellent Thoas) and unleashes widespread looting by Ephesian criminals. Pursued by a bloodthirsty mob, Herostratos plunges to his death in the sea, but only after predicting correctly that his name will come to symbolize fame-seeking destroyers:

And every time
That there's a blow struck against the laws,
Or a vast conflagration of a people or a realm,
Then—to designate the criminal—suddenly, like a ghost,

My name will appear to the mind of humanity.
I shall be the eternal symbol and type
Of every great destroyer, of everyone who prefers
To be cursed than for the public to forget him.[38]

Suicide is one of the last enticements offered by the Devil in part 7 of Gustave
Flaubert's prose poem *The Temptation of Saint Anthony,* the final version of
which was published in 1874.[39] The work summons up a kaleidoscopic se-
quence of visions with which Satan assails the faith and asceticism of St. Anthony (also known as Anthony Abbot), a fourth-century AD hermit saint of
the Egyptian desert. Throughout the poem Anthony's mind recalls obsessively the image of Ammonaria, "the child whom [he] used to meet every
evening at the cistern, when she took the oxen to drink." He continues in old
age to suffer from the blame that was meted out to him when his mystic voca-
tion caused him to leave home: his mother "sank to the ground, dying;" his
sister beckoned him to return; and little Ammonaria wept. In the concluding
scene 7 of *The Temptation,* the saint is overcome by remorse over his deser-
tion of his aged mother, who he fears has cursed him while tearing out her
white hair in grief. He imagines her corpse lying on the floor of her hut, "under the roof of reeds, between the crumbling walls," and about to be devoured
as carrion by a ravening hyena. "No," he consoles himself, "Ammonaria will
not have abandoned her!" As he wonders what has become of his childhood
playmate, his mind's eye sees her grown into a seductive woman whose trans-
parently clad beauty tortures him with sexual desire "even in the midst of
grief." He gazes over a cliff into an abyss and considers leaping to his death.
An aged woman, whom he mistakes for his mother but who later reveals herself to be Death, urges him to rival God by committing suicide:

> To do that which will make thee equal unto God—think! He created
> thee: thou wilt destroy his work—thou! and by thy courage,—of thy
> own free will! The enjoyment that Erostratus [Herostratos] knew was
> not greater than this. And moreover thy body has so long mocked thy
> soul that it is full time thou shouldst take vengeance upon it. Thou wilt
> not suffer. It will soon be over. Of what art thou afraid?—a wide, black
> hole. Perhaps it is a void![40]

An apparition of a young woman then comes forward to argue for life. After
taking her for Ammonaria, St. Anthony recognizes her to be the embodiment

of Lust. The two female specters together constitute "the Devil yet again, and under his twofold aspect: the spirit of fornication, and the spirit of destruction."

In this scene, Flaubert recognizes, as did Lucian in "The Passing of Peregrinus," that the suicidal impulse may be activated by a Herostratos-like wish for self-glorification. The self-destructive urge that is often inextricably bound to the Herostratic act is also noted in a striking aphorism of Friedrich Nietzsche: "*Extreme of Herostratism:* There could be Herostratuses who burned down their own temple where their images were venerated."[41]

The Herostratos theme may have influenced Peter Shaffer's reworking of his play, *Amadeus,* for American audiences. A probable source of *Amadeus* was Alexander Pushkin's short dramatic dialogue, *Mozart and Salieri.*[42] This verse play was conceived in 1826—only one year after Salieri's death, when rumors of his confession of Mozart's murder were still in the air—and was completed in 1830. In Pushkin's setting, Salieri pours poison into Mozart's glass both because his rival's superior gifts have introduced his soul to the bitterness of envy and because God has not justly rewarded his lifelong devotion to music. In an opening monologue, Salieri complains of his Creator's inequity:

> Where, where is justice, when the sacred gift,
> When deathless genius comes not to reward
> Perfervid love and utter self-denial,
> And toils and strivings and beseeching prayers,
> But puts her halo round a lack-wit's skull,
> A frivolous idler's brow? . . . O Mozart, Mozart![43]

After Mozart drinks the poison and falls asleep, his approaching death brings no relief to Salieri's torment. The murder is final confirmation of Salieri's inferiority, as he recalls Mozart's words spoken only moments before:

> But villainy and genius
> Are two things that can never go together.[44]

Shaffer claims not to have read Pushkin's drama before writing *Amadeus.* In the revision of the play for American productions, the elderly Salieri, contemplating suicide, asserts that he is innocent of murdering Mozart but has been falsely confessing the crime so as to be remembered in infamy:

> One moment's violence and it's done. You see, I cannot accept this. I did not live on earth to be His joke for eternity. I *will* be remembered! *I*

will be remembered!—if not in fame, then infamy. . . . All this month
I've been shouting about murder. . . . And now my last move. A false
confession—short and convincing! . . . *I am going to be immortal after
all!* And He is powerless to prevent it.[45]

God, however, is not powerless to prevent suicide, for Salieri's attempt to cut
his throat is ineffective.

In a scholarly paper, Professor Kerry Sabbag has pointed out that in the
American version of Shaffer's play, which Sabbag considers to reflect the author's final intentions, "Salieri's vindictive destructiveness combined with his
emphasis on fame suggests that in him the Cain myth [of violence motivated
by envy over God's preference of a rival's sacrifices] has become contaminated
and bears closer resemblance to that of Herostratus."[46] It should be noted, however, that even though the element of fame seeking has always been paramount
in the tradition of Herostratos, his crime, like Cain's fratricide, is a violation of
religious duty. Regarded in ancient times as an enemy of the gods, Herostratos
is presented in many of the literary works discussed in this chapter as incited to
the destruction of the Ephesus temple by the indifference of Artemis.

A Russian poet greatly admired by Pushkin, Nikolai M. Yazykov, calls on
the name of Herostratos in an 1823 poem decrying unrest and violence in his
country and abroad. Titling his work "To My Dressing Gown," Yazykov contrasts the peace and solitude of his ivory-tower existence as a university student in Tartu with the turmoil around him:

> The thinking student does not sleep:
> Wrapped in an author's dressing gown
> Disdaining blind society's noise,
> In ecstasies of thought, he mocks
> The Herostratus of our times.

The innuendo regarding a contemporary Herostratus may be aimed at Tsar
Alexander I, despised by the revolutionary literary circles to which the poet
belonged; the Decembrist uprising would be quelled two years later. Yazykov's
praise of the tranquil life, however, seems to rise above partisan fervor. The
narrator, garbed in a dressing gown, seeks to flee the world of political assassination, regardless of its ideological motivation:

> He does not fancy in his dreams
> The dirks of Sand or of Louvel. . . .

The killers he abhors are Karl Ludwig Sand, murderer of the writer and suspected Tsarist informer, August von Kotzebue, and Jean-Pierre Louvel, the assassin of the Duke de Berry, second in line to the French throne.[47] In his late teenage years, Pushkin also linked the figure of Herostratos and the murder of Kotzebue in an epigram targeting Alexandr Sturdza, an official in the Ministry of Education who was "known for his extreme obscurantist views":

> Slave of a crowned soldier,
> You deserve the fame of Herostratus
> Or the death of Kotzebue the Hun,
> And, incidentally, fuck you.[48]

The Russian literary interest in Herostratos continued into the Soviet era. The Ephesian ban on Herostratos's name is reflected in the title of *Forget Herostratus!* a satire written and staged by Grigory Ofshtein (1940–2000) under the pseudonym Grigory Gorin during the Brezhnev era. The work eluded the censors because the corrupt politicians it targets are dressed in ancient garb and the most obvious modern analogy drawn is to the rise of Adolf Hitler. The burning of the Artemision prefigures the Reichstag fire, and prison memoirs of Herostratos are probably intended to suggest *Mein Kampf.*[49]

A solo chorus, the Man of the Theatre, traveling back to Ephesus from the future, is able to bring to bear the terrible lessons of modern history. He instructs Cleon, the well-intentioned chief magistrate (*archon*) of the city, that Herostratus will be reborn many times as a bane of mankind:

> But from time to time *he* will appear on earth again—a reincarnation of Herostratus. Once more he will proclaim: "Do what you will, fearing neither the gods nor mankind!" And all over the planet fires will rage, blood will flow and the innocent will perish. And people will ask in bewilderment: "Where has this scourge come from?" Yet it has an ancestry going back over two thousand years! And it began here—in Ephesus.[50]

Because the history of evil, unless understood, will be repeated, the Man of the Theatre believes that the Ephesian policy of suppressing the memory of criminals is misguided. Crime must be remembered and detested: "That is why I have come to you, Archon. That is why I say to you: 'Do not try to lull your memory asleep by consigning this man to oblivion. Arm it instead with anger, for memory is man's best weapon against evil.'"[51]

Herostratos is portrayed by Gorin as a cunning swindler. A "free citizen of Ephesus" who went bankrupt as a dishonest trader in fish, vegetables, and wool, he faces trial in Cleon's court for the temple arson. The Persian satrap, Tissafernes, postpones the trial pending receipt of instructions from the Delphic oracle. In the meantime, Tissafernes's vain wife, Clementina, secretly visits Herostratos in the hope that he will publicly announce before the expected execution that the actual motive for his crime was not desire for fame but an unrequited passion for her. Herostratos agrees but, as his price, demands that during the play's intermission she make love with him.

When Tissafernes learns of his wife's betrayal, Herostratos offers a new deal for his silence. He will preserve Clementina's reputation for virtue if the satrap will appoint him as "overseer" of a thousand Ephesians whom he has secretly been bribing with drinks financed by the publication of his memoirs:

> By now I can call on a good thousand faithful supporters who will go through fire and water for me. We will dissolve the People's Assembly, abolish the election of judges and trial by jury. You will establish the kind of order that *you* want in Ephesus, and I will see to it that you are obeyed. People will start to respect and fear Herostratus—after all, the gods themselves will have forgiven his act of effrontery. They may even start thinking that Herostratus is one of the gods himself.[52]

Unable to stand by as an idle witness of the threatened rise of this proto-Fascist, the Man of the Theatre hands a knife to Cleon. Although the magistrate is ordinarily devoted to the maintenance of law and order, he stabs Herostratos to death. To the Man of the Theatre, he murmurs, "I have killed a man for the first time in my life." The sounds of the reconstruction of the temple are heard offstage, and the Man of the Theatre demands to learn who the builders are: "What are their names? Tell me at least one of their names. . . . It's important for us to know."[53] Once again, as the curtain descends, Gorin has emphasized the indispensability of historical memory.

The name of Herostratos is embedded in the German language as the common noun *Herostrat,* the German form of the original Greek. The word *Herostrat* is defined by a German dictionary as "a criminal motivated by a craving for fame" and a related adjective, *herostratisch,* and the abstract term, "Herostratentum," are also in use.[54] Perhaps the familiarity of these words in German literary discourse has contributed to the frequent appearances of the ancient Herostratos in the plays and poems of Germany and Austria.

In *Herostrat*, an 1898 five-act verse tragedy by a German Jewish dramatist, Ludwig Fulda, born Ludwig Anton Salomon (1862–1939), the destruction of the Artemision is due to rivalry in art and love.[55] Fulda's Herostratos is a gifted Ephesian sculptor who wastes his talents on the production of souvenirs—miniature clay reproductions of Artemis's cult statue. His employer values his profitable work but regards him as "phlegmatic, moody, stubborn and crazy." It is small wonder that there is darkness in his soul, for he secretly nurses dreams of a greatness to match the heroism of his father, who died in defense of the city. The appearance of a deep crack in the head of the archaic wooden statue of the goddess gives the young sculptor the opportunity that he has been waiting for. He persuades civil and temple authorities to permit him to carve a new image in marble. His euphoria over the commission is, however, shaken when the city fathers summon the renowned Praxiteles from Athens to sculpt a competing figure of Artemis. The arrival of Praxiteles precipitates unanticipated turmoil. The Athenian offends the pious Ephesians by publicly greeting Herostratos's betrothed, Clytia, as the mortal embodiment of Artemis and makes matters worse by choosing the young woman as the model for his statue. Enraged that Clytia is to pose for his rival, with whom she is falling in love, Herostratos attempts to stab Praxiteles but the attack is foiled.

Herostratos is now easy prey to the suggestion of the conservative temple priest that he smash Praxiteles's statue. When he draws the curtain protecting the work from public view, a shudder of awe runs through his body; he cannot raise his hammer against an immortal masterpiece that will keep Clytia's beauty forever young; instead, he shatters his own inferior work. When Clytia confesses her love for Praxiteles, Herostratos's sense of Artemis's injustice is complete:

> O wonderful world. Everything, everything for one man,
> Nothing for me, not even crumbs from his table,
> Not a speck of blossom from his full bouquet!
> Is this how the great, powerful goddess
> Divides her gifts? And I, a stupid fool
> Trusted her righteousness, and
> With hundredfold deeper ardor
> Loved her than he![56]

Herostratos takes vengeance on the goddess by burning her temple, happy to achieve through crime the fame he sought in art. He tells his judges that their ban on the memory of his name is doomed to fail:

Fruitless effort!
More easily could you shackle the winds, bind the sea's waves
And extend your law from Scythia
To the Pillars of Hercules!
You can kill me, but not my name.
On indestructible tablets I engraved it
In letters of flame . . . [57]

Herostratos awaits his executioners after rejecting Clytia's plan for him to flee with her and Praxiteles to Athens. Her scheme would have been illusory, for the faithless Praxiteles has taken ship without her.

Utopian playwright and poet Hugo Sonnenschein (1889–1953), who also wrote as "Sonka," emphasized the pure joy in destruction that overmasters the Herostratic soul. Born near the Czech city of Brno, Sonnenschein survived Auschwitz only to die in a postwar Communist prison. His early one-act play *The Utopia of Herostratos* (1910) is a parable of nihilism set at a Viennese farewell party.[58] Ruben Seethal, an aimless young man, is about to leave for Italy with his teenage girl friend Hanna, whose love he believes has given him the will to find meaningful work and ultimately to establish a utopian community. His fellow lodger, Arnold Mahlberg, prefers to study the ideal society imagined by Plato's *Republic*. Into the midst of Seethal's wellwishers comes Camillo Dambra, who opposes to his friends' dreams of the future his own obsession with death and ruin: "We are at our very core life-deniers. We must be so: from envy, because there are also life-affirmers. From the joy of destruction. . . . There was once a generation that said: *après nous le déluge!* But I say: we want the deluge now!"[59] What Dambra does not want is that anyone "will ever again be happy." With this end in view, he empties a vial into Seethal's drink but an observant guest smashes the glass. A second opportunity comes to the nihilist when Seethal leans out of the window, thinking of a lost love. Dambra pushes the yearning Seethal to his death and, at the curtain, triumphs in the act of murder: "Nobody is going to Italy!"

In a brief dramatic scene, *Der Wahnsinn des Herostrat* (*The Insanity of Herostratos*), by German Expressionist poet Georg Heym (1887–1912), Herostratos bares his riven soul as he awaits execution.[60] The criminal's interior monologue in a prison cell reveals that he is a goldsmith consumed with resentment against other artisans; street urchins who stick out their tongues at him; prostitutes who charge him double; and the soothsayers, priests, lawyers, and officials of Ephesus. He despises "unknown men" who, unlike himself, "have not wept hot tears over fame, who have not beat both fists against [their] beds at night because of pathological ambition." Another source of his feeling of superiority is his sense of unrivaled devotion to the goddess Diana of Ephesus, whom others weary with "so many requests, such complaints." It is Diana, he claims, who called him up into the mountains to inspire the idea of burning her temple that had been desecrated by the unworthy:

> Oh, Diana of Ephesus, who must put up with insults, avenge my name, as I avenged yours. Nobody respects you anymore. Only I and a few others still believe in you, when lovingly your sad face gazes out at me from my art works. Yes, it was time that in the hundred-breasted temple I extinguished the names of the goddess's profaners and melted them down in the gigantic flames. It was your work, Goddess, that like a ray sent the message to me through my mind's night. I acted as if I were drunk and staggered like a blind man; I hardly could think out what I was doing.

When the fire broke out, horrified onlookers quickly identified the arsonist, and Herostratos exults in the certainty of his worldwide celebrity:

> Then I heard my name roaring like a wave among the people. Famous so far and wide, like a flood that was now growing. Today Ephesus's million knows it, and tomorrow Asia. In another day it swells up through Greece, Thrace, Istria, Scythia and Parthia, Bactria, Babylon and Arabia. . . . And there are people who live on the other side of the ocean who will hear it like the strokes of bells resounding in their ears. "This is a man who threw away for fame his little morsel of life so that he could live forever."

When the scene ends, the gates of Herostratos's prison open and light falls on the inmate, "a tiny man, with the wild eyes of a lunatic."

Austria's absurd-surrealist playwright Wolfgang Bauer (born 1941) included a play in miniature, "Herostratos," in his first published work, *Microdramas* (1964).[61] Bauer reflects the international character of the Herostratic impulse to violence, but the gaze of his play is retrospective. The titular hero makes his entrance in an Alaskan tavern, snowflakes in his hair and blood from his lower lip streaming down his toga onto the floor. Announcing his arrival to the barmaid Madeleine, he tears off his toga and stands before her "stark naked but dead earnest." To hear and see no evil, she stops her little ears and blinks. After stage directions describe the settings of Madeleine's bedroom and the tavern's cellar, Herostratos, garbed in a brand new toga, with price tag still attached, reappears in ancient Ephesus. He removes a newspaper sheet from his garment and sings of a false report that he has cooked up for the world. As he hawks his street ballad, he tries unsuccessfully to set fire to the temple by striking matches against a marble column. When his box is used up, the theater's prompter comes to his aid by hurling a hydrogen bomb into the shrine. The Greeks may have had a superior culture, Bauer concedes, but when it comes to destruction, nothing surpasses the modern age.

In his stage career Herostratos has not always taken a villain's role. Leipzig-born Carl Ceiss's *Herostratos,* a chamber play in Classical Greek form developed in four versions between 1982 and 1986, turns the affair at Ephesus topsy-turvy.[62] Ceiss presents the title character as a lowly hod carrier victimized by a deep-dyed plot of Deinokrates, an ambitious architect. The positions of the two men at the base and peak of the construction trades symbolize the playwright's theme of the exploitation of the common people by their power-mad leaders. At the same time, the building process in which both Herostratos and Deinokrates are engaged is the source of the play's dominant image of fire. The clay that Herostratos carries to workmen is hardened by fire into bricks embodying the architect's pitiless resolve. Deinokrates himself drives home the lesson:

Our life is as easily shaped as moist clay.
We hold ourselves in our own hands.
If you do not harden it in a fiery kiln
The clay runs off like water in the passing hours.
Fired bricks durably survive
Hundreds of years. The choice is everybody's—clay or stone.

Deinokrates schemes with his mistress, a priestess of Artemis, to destroy the temple so that he can build an even greater structure in its place. He incites Herostratos's rage against Artemis by arranging the murder of his wife and newborn child who had been entrusted to the goddess's protection. A complication arises after the double killing, for the priestess turns out to be the hod carrier's sister-in-law and repents her role in the conspiracy. Deinokrates enters the temple, persuaded that he will have to torch the shrine on his own, but Herostratos pursues him, crying: "The fire is mine." On the next day, historian Theopompus arrives in Ephesus and establishes Deinokrates's guilt by disclosing that the architect had been quarrying limestone for the new temple even before the conflagration. Theopompus bribes an Ephesian to reveal the name of Herostratos so that, as the real-life Theopompus had done, he can include that detail in his historical work despite the ban on the arsonist's memory.

Mark David Chapman's murder of John Lennon fuses with Herostratos's arson in Lutz Hübner's play *The Orifice of the Heart: The Ballad of Herostratos Chapman* (1998).[63] Scenes of Chapman's increasingly unhinged emotional responses to his obscurity and alienation are framed by choral interludes lamenting Herostratos's rejection by the "silent" Artemis and by the great mass of humanity that does not know his name.

By the end of the fourth act, Chapman has learned through his reading that he is the reincarnation of many outcasts: "I have read and researched a lot, and I've found my story everywhere in the great books of mankind. I've been here on earth a thousand times and I will eternally return. There are novels about me, films, plays, and I knew nothing about it, I wasn't aware of it."[64] Three of his predecessors in suffering appear before him: Holden Caulfield, who recognizes him as one of his readers who has vainly sought something that the world does not offer; Jesus, who asks whether Chapman is ready to take up His Cross; and finally, Herostratos. Still bitter in his afterlife, Herostratos advises that Mark continues to face the task of shooting "the crow," a bird of ill omen that he had spared in childhood. To Chapman, the crow represents the fame of John Lennon, which has cast a "dark, evil shadow over [his life]."

In the fifth-act dénouement, the assassination of Lennon and the Ephesus fire proceed simultaneously: Mark becomes united with his victim (visualized as a double whom he will embrace, lying in a pool of blood at his feet) and with his ancient forerunner, Herostratos. The Chorus intones the merger of the two crimes:

> I am your death, we are a pair, here; the flame throws itself upon you and the fire breaks through the roof. Now a thousand eyes open, a thousand mouths want to cry out, a thousand fingers point at me; I was once Nobody, but now I make an entrance into my own history. And so I burn myself into the world's memory. I open my heart to you, my heart opens up. Look in the orifice of my heart, see my name written in gold, and lower down is your name, Herostratos, a flame.[65]

Herostratos is spared the death penalty in a German-language chamber play by Jean-François de Guise, *Der Fall Herostratos* (*The Herostratos Case*) (2003).[66] A composer born in Lorraine in 1970 and raised in France, Switzerland, England, and Germany, de Guise conceives his play's protagonist as a reluctant terrorist. Neither the gods nor the self-seeking Ephesians smile upon him. His humble career as a hod carrier ends when the architect Demitrios and the contractor Paionios favor more modern building materials. His subsequent business as a tavern keeper is dealt successive blows. The goddess Artemis gives his pregnant wife a son instead of the daughter on whom he had counted to lure customers. Then the entire enterprise is destroyed when Demitrios and Paionios, planning to build a new Temple of Artemis on the site of the tavern, manage to have it expropriated by the city council. Shunted to a remote market district, the luckless Herostratos tries his hand at manufacturing religious objects for the temple's visitors but goes bankrupt just when he is on the eve of perfecting a trendy incense burner.

In the midst of his troubles Herostratos resists the blandishments of Fanaticos, who has invited him to join the "Union against Idolatry." He tells the recruiter that he "will have nothing to do with terrorism," but Fanaticos prefers a more legalistic definition, "strategic, planned, and politically motivated violent criminality with the goal of destabilizing the ruling system through the spreading of anxiety and fear." Fanaticos's words turn out to be more violent than his group's actions, for the worst outrage that they can perpetrate is to daub the Artemision with red graffiti. The wrongdoers are rounded up and within a little time the public, which was at first impressed by their audacity, had forgotten their names.

The lesson that minor nuisances do not win durable fame inspires Herostratos to burn down the temple. After he confesses his crime and motive in court, the arsonist is sentenced with surprising mildness: the chief judge Syndicos imposes as the sole penalty a ban, under penalty of death, for any Ephesian to mention or record his name. From now on the criminal will be known exclusively as "the madman of Ephesus." Set at liberty, Herostratos dictates to Theopompus (whom de Guise transforms from a historian into a sports and war reporter) the news article on the case's outcome:

> For Herostratos's crime the death penalty would have been the only justifiable retribution. But it is plain that what has happened could not be extinguished or atoned for by death. It is doubtful, though, that keeping the criminal's name silent will lead to the success desired by Ephesus. On the contrary, it is assumed that the concept of a proverbial "Herostratic act" will burn itself like a wild fire into the vocabulary of humanity.

Appropriately, dramatic adaptations of the Herostratos story include a work by Nazli Eray, a major figure in the literature of Turkey, the modern homeland of Ephesus. Eray was inspired to write her early comedy, *Herostratus* (1979),[67] by a deep interest in history that also causes her to introduce many historical figures in her novels.[68]

The first scene of Eray's play is set in Ephesus. Three policemen, who are to form the chorus in a modernist reenactment of the catastrophe of 356 BC, exchange views on the principal characters. Herostratus's "mind was disturbed"; the "guy has one anxiety fit after the other and is constantly popping tranquilizers." His best friend is the goat-footed god Pan, a jazz musician who is an "old junkie . . . on record with the Narcotics Bureau." Pan went on dope because of his hopeless love for Daphne, a nurse in the intensive care unit of the American Hospital. Daphne hates Pan's jazz and is spellbound by the rock music of the weak-voiced pop star Üzeyir, who relies on mighty amplification at a concert in the Temple of Artemis.

At the American Hospital, sensations arrive in pairs. Icarus is an emergency case, having drowned after melting his waxen wings by flying too close to the sun, and Alexander the Great is born in the maternity ward, inspiring his proud father to exclaim, "I'll do my best to ensure his success in life. I'll see to it that he receives the very best education. He'll attend only the best schools. My son will be a great man." The glory of the royal birth contrasts sharply with the sorrows of Pan and Herostratus. In the intermission of Üzeyir's successful rock concert at the temple, Daphne laughs at Pan's marriage proposal. Herostratus seeks out his downcast friend to confide his plan to set the Temple of Artemis on fire to immortalize his name. Pan fails in his attempt to discourage the wild project:

Pan: Why do you want to immortalize your name, Herostratus? After you die, why is it so important for you to have your name live on?

Herostratus: *(In an offended tone)* See, even you don't understand me. You're immortal anyway, a bloody god. Besides, you have your music. Even if you are forgotten, your music will one day be understood and live on. So of course you can't see why I want my name immortalized.

Pan: *(Laughs)* Is it really that important? But how will you immortalize your name by burning down the Temple?

Herostratus: Just think a bit. The Temple of Artemis is the largest temple in the city. Furthermore, it's known as one of the Seven Wonders of the World. By setting it in flames, I'll pass into the annals of history as the man who burnt down the Temple of Artemis.

Pan: Do you think it's so easy to set a huge temple like that on fire? What if you fail?

Herostratus: Why should I? The rags are all ready. *(Takes out a bundle of rags from under his toga.)* Here they are.

Pan: *(With interest)* A Molotov cocktail?

Herostratus: No, no. It's my own discovery. Much more effective.

Pan: Herostratus, don't be in a rush. Put this business off until another night.

Rejecting Pan's advice, Herostratus destroys the temple and is seized by the trio of policemen. They will not believe him when he swears that the fire was a "deliberate arson" that he had planned to confess. To substantiate his oath, he leads his captors to his friend Pan, to whom he had told everything. Herostratus, however, is in for a shock: Pan has turned into an ancient statue of a sad-faced god with goat's feet. Herostratus speculates that, "unable to stand the suffering [of Daphne's rejection] any longer, he's gone and turned himself to stone."

Acts 2 and 3 of the play briefly depict reflections of Herostratus's germinative violence in the twentieth century. In act 2 the American Sixth Fleet drops anchor in the harbor of Ephesus, inspiring protesting students to chant: "Down with Imperialism!" In the final act, the Cultural Center in Istanbul's Taksim Square is set ablaze, and the samba associated throughout the comedy with Herostratus is heard playing softly. Pan and Herostratus are seen sitting together at the foot of a tree.

Eray based this scene on an actual event that occurred in the 1970s; the persons responsible for the fire were never found.[69] In rooting the play's catastrophic finale in reality, Eray became one of the first writers of imaginative literature to link the Herostratos tradition with terrorism of the modern era.

NONFICTION

Spanish vocabulary, like German, includes an abstract term drawn from the name of Herostratos—*erostratismo* (Herostratism), which is defined in the *Pequeño Larousse* as "mania that impels the commission of crimes to obtain celebrity." The same dictionary provides a biography of Herostratos that is spiced with Hispanic elements: "A shepherd of Ephesus who, desiring, like the conquerors [*conquistadores*], to make himself famous by means of some memorable destruction, burned the temple of Diana. . . . His name has passed into literature to characterize those who commit crimes to merit fame."[70] The traces of Spanish literature and history in this summary are readily noted. Don Quixote—not ancient tradition—identifies Herostratos as a "shepherd," because the Don's mental landscape is peopled largely by knights and shepherds. Moreover, what European people would be more likely than the Spanish, long mesmerized by their Age of Conquest, to conceive that Herostratos was inspired to seek fame by the example of "the conquerors"?

The aspiration of Herostratos for immortality figures significantly in *Tragic Sense of Life* by Miguel de Unamuno, the eminent Spanish novelist, poet, philosopher, and author of a celebrated book-length essay on *Don Quixote*.[71] The tragic sense to which the work's title refers arises from the combat of reason with the will and vital feeling in coming to terms with human longing for the immortality of the soul. In chapter 3 of *Tragic Sense,* Unamuno pauses to consider what he calls humanity's "hunger of immortality," a yearning that he believes to be the "very substance of [humanity's] soul." He observes, however, that since the medieval faith in the immortal soul has receded, we have been impelled to find solace in the perpetuation of fame:

> When doubts invade us and cloud our faith in the immortality of the soul, a vigorous and painful impulse is given to the anxiety to perpetuate our name and fame, to grasp at least a shadow of immortality. And hence the tremendous struggle to singularize ourselves, to survive in some way in the memory of others and of posterity.[72]

At the root of the eagerness for lasting fame, Unamuno argues, is vanity. The vain man, like the avaricious one, substitutes the means for the end, and pursues the means for its own sake. In the modern intellectual world, Unamuno cites a "rabid mania" for originality at the expense of truth, a competitiveness that extends "the violent struggle for the perpetuation of our name . . . backwards into the past, just as it aspires to conquer the future." We are "jealous of the geniuses of former times, whose names, standing out like the landmarks of history, rescue the ages from oblivion."[73] Unamuno sees a "tremendous passion" in "this longing that our memory may be rescued, if it is possible, from the oblivion which overtakes others." This powerful emotion, he points out, gives rise to envy, the cause of Cain's fratricide:

> From it [the longing for perennial fame] springs envy, the cause, according to the biblical narrative, of the crime with which human history opened: the murder of Abel by his brother Cain. It was not a struggle for bread—it was a struggle to survive in God, in the divine memory. Envy is a thousand times more terrible than hunger, for it is spiritual hunger.[74]

Tragic Sense of Life does not address the question of whether Cain, like Herostratos, intended to suffer for his crime. However, as a general proposition, Unamuno is persuaded that "for the sake of a name man is ready to sacrifice not only life but happiness." As a professor of Greek at the University of Salamanca as well as a Cervantes scholar, Unamuno readily turned to Classical literature to document his argument that even negative fame can serve to satisfy a hunger for eternal remembrance: "And there are some who covet even the gallows for the sake of acquiring fame, even though it be an infamous fame: *avidus malae famae* (hungry for infamy), as Tacitus says."[75]

To conclude his reflections on the desire for eternal celebrity as an end in itself, Unamuno makes reference to another source from Classical antiquity, the example and tradition of Herostratos. "Erostratism [Herostratism]," he asks rhetorically, "what is it at bottom but the longing for immortality, if not for substantial and concrete immortality, at any rate for the shadowy immortality of the name?" It is wrong, he suggests, to blame on pride the wish to leave behind an "ineffaceable name" because the Herostratic impulse arises instead from the "terror of extinction."[76]

Early in his career, Portuguese poet Fernando Pessoa anticipated that he would soon win literary eminence. His editor and English-language translator Richard Zenith cites Pessoa's letter to his mother dated June 5, 1914, in which he predicted that within five or ten years he would be recognized as "one of the greatest contemporary poets."[77] Only modest critical approval, however, greeted his publications; he therefore came to rely, with well-founded assurance, on recognition by future generations that would grant him the fame likely to elude him during his lifetime. To explore the ramifications of the hope that remained to him, he began around 1930 to write (in English, his second language) *Erostratus and the Search for Immortality.*

What brought Herostratos to his mind? Zenith believes that he may have recalled an allusion in *Sartor Resartus,* a classic work by Thomas Carlyle, one of his favorite English authors from childhood: "By what strange chances do we live in History? Erostratus by a torch. . . ."[78] Or perhaps the more famous reference to the arsonist in Sir Thomas Browne's *Urn Burial* had suggested Pessoa's title and theme. Still, the choice seems ironic because Pessoa bore no resemblance to the scourge of Ephesus. He was (to borrow his own words) no mere "crasher into fame" as the apparent mediocrity Herostratos became by torching a beloved temple; to the contrary, the poet transformed himself through decades of achievement into a wonder of the modern literary world.

The posthumous edition of Pessoa's *Erostratus* consists of a series of seventy disconnected observations—many left only in fragments at his death— on immortal fame and its shorter-lived counterfeits, but literary fame is the author's real preoccupation. Even his discussion of the crime of Herostratos (in excerpt 17) recreates the destruction of the temple as an act driven by an aesthetic motive. Pessoa visualized the incendiary as a Greek having "that delicate perception and calm delirium of beauty which distinguishes still the memory of his giant clan." In the poet's imagination, Herostratos had burned the Artemision "in an ecstasy of sorrow, part of him being burnt in the fury of his wrong endeavour." Pessoa's invention of Herostratos's self-inflicted injury is eerily predictive of the willingness of the modern terrorist to commit suicide in pursuit of an often elusive goal. Pessoa's terrorist leaves no room even for a possible change of heart: we can properly think of him as "having overcome the toils of a remorse of the future, and facing a horror within himself for the stalwartness of fame."

Herostratos's impious destruction of the Temple of Artemis, a deed that caused the ancients to rank him among the enemies of the gods, reminds Pessoa of "that terrible element of the initiation of the Templars, who, being first proven absolute believers in Christ . . . had to spit upon the Crucifix. . . . The God they spat upon was the holy substance of Redemption. They looked into hell when their mouths watered with the necessary blasphemy." It was a "love of beauty," though, that Pessoa believed to have moved Herostratos's Greek soul to crime, and if he is conceived in this manner, "we may justify the remembrance." If Herostratos acted under the spell of beauty, "he comes at once into the company of all men who have become great by the power of their individuality. He makes that sacrifice of feeling, of passion, . . . which distinguishes the path to immortality."[79]

In a brief philosophical meditation, "Destroying and Building" (included in his 1923 collection *Potestas Clavium*), Lev Shestov, a Russian Existentialist, tests the common belief that "the final goal of man is to build and that destruction is in itself a terrible thing that can be justified only if it is a temporary step leading to new building."[80] Common sense "declares with assurance" that "one of the most monstrous of crimes is the crime of Herostatus. Without any reason this man destroyed the Temple of Diana, one of the great marvels of art. People like Herostratus must be put into chains in order not to be able to destroy."

Yet Shestov notes the carelessness and ease with which nature "deforms or destroys the most beautiful works, its own as well as those of man." He cites troubling examples of nature's disposition to annihilate what it has created:

Did Mount Vesuvius take pity on Herculaneum and Pompeii? Was the fire afraid to destroy the library of Alexandria? Far more: nature systematically destroys everything that it creates. Alexander the Great and

Plato, Pushkin and Gogol, and so many others who could have built so many beautiful temples—all these it has pitilessly annihilated. Did it make [the dueling adversary] d'Anthès' hand tremble when he coldly directed his pistol against Pushkin in the duel? Why did it not then intervene? Why does it systematically destroy everything that it creates and everything that men create? Why must it send men old age, which transforms the most wondrous beauty into ugliness, weakens the minds of the most intelligent, and ruins the most active will? Why death, which puts an end to the most daring enterprises? Destruction, death—this is the inevitable end of all nature's works. The moralist and sociologist can forget this. But the philosopher does not forget it. He can not and, if you wish, must not forget it.

Even the "divine Plato," Shestov argues, is a destroyer, because in his dialogue *Phaedo* he defines his own craft, philosophy, as "a preparation for death and a gradual dying."

In the years preceding the World Trade Center attack, a number of essayists and journalists have related the tradition of Herostratos to modern issues. One of the most provocative comments is a 2001 speech delivered by James Bowman, media critic of *The New Criterion*.[81] Bowman argues that our media culture has fostered a new era of Herostratos by trivializing the standards for acquiring reputation. He notes that in heroic ages reflected in Homer and in medieval epics such as *The Song of Roland*, reputation was equated with "honor," the respect accorded by contemporaries and future generations for military strength and bravery. Roland feared that "to blow his horn and summon the help of the main army" at a moment when his motive might be construed as a fear for his life "might mean that someone would 'sing a bad song about me in France.'"

In Bowman's view, the times of heroism and honor have given way to a "Herostratian age" ruled by a media-fueled obsession with celebrity, whether for good or ill:

But what in the age of Herostratus has happened to honor, that familiar daily concern of military and governing élites from pre-historic times up until the day before yesterday? . . . I'd like to turn briefly to what we of the dominant culture today have instead of honor. Nature (as the scientists assure us) abhors a vacuum, and into the moral vacuum created by the disappearance of the idea of honor from our public life has rushed a horrible mutant substitute that goes under the name of "fame" or "celebrity."

The new celebrity culture substitutes "authenticity for bravery, virtue or strength." Authenticity, according to Bowman, is validated by public suffering, such as the travails of Elizabeth Taylor and Princess Diana or of participants in television's survivor shows, or sometimes even by involvement in scandals. Bowman concludes by applauding Attorney General John Ashcroft's appeal to the media to deny the Oklahoma City bomber, Timothy McVeigh, "access to the podium of America with the blood of America."

In a 1999 article, "Names That Live in Infamy," science fiction writer David Brin had anticipated Bowman's position by advocating, perhaps in less than full earnest, the enactment of a Herostratos law that would embody the spirit of the Ephesian ban on memory.[82] Brin quoted the comment of Marvin Hier about the motives of hate crime perpetrators: "The reason they are doing this is for their moment of glory, when they feel the whole world is stopping to take notice of them." The trend, Brin suggested, was by no means limited to hate crimes:

> It's an all-too-familiar pattern. The Oklahoma City terrorists, Unabomber Theodore Kaczynski, . . . and killer Mark David Chapman all showed a yearning for attention, both in the headline-grabbing nature of their crimes and in their polemics after capture. Whatever their diverse rationalizations for wreaking harm, it also surely had a lot to do with getting noticed in an era that reveres fame.
>
> Society appears to be trapped, obliged to pay madmen the attention they crave, in direct proportion to the hurt they do.
>
> This is not a new problem. Two millennia ago, in the Hellenistic era, a young man torched one of the seven wonders of the ancient world— the Temple of Diana at Ephesus. When caught and asked why, he replied first with grievances against individuals and his city state, then admitted that he really wanted to make a mark, to be remembered. Since he wasn't a great warrior, or creative person, his best chance was to gain infamy by destroying something.

Conditions had become ripe for a repetition of such crimes; fame itself had been "made sacred" and films and novels had exalted "the image of romantic loners."

Are there solutions? Brin asks. One possibility is suggested to him by the Ephesian prohibition on Herostratos's memory. Brin concedes that "coerced forgetfulness is out of the question in a free society" but asserts that "courts already do have some authority to order name-changes." Suppose, he continues in revery, that power were widened, so that any criminal sentenced for a truly heinous crime could be renamed as part of his punishment, with a moniker that invokes disdain. New history books might state: "Robert F. Kennedy was slain in 1968 by Doofus 25*." The asterisk is there to let anyone find the assassin's former name in a footnote, if they are truly interested, so no one is actually suppressing knowledge.

The meaning of Herostratos has been analyzed by Professor Eric Gans, whose principles of "Generative Anthropology" espouse, with modifications, the theories of René Girard. These theories derive the history of social order from the resolution of crises provoked by imitative and rivalrous desire of human beings for the same objects (*mimetic desire*). Professor Gans applies his anthropological hypotheses in a 1997 article, "Herostratus Forever"—an entry in his online series, *Chronicles of Love and Resentment*—where he suggests that the fame of the ancient criminal arises not from his deed but from "the impotent interdiction to which it gave rise" when Ephesian authorities forbade the mention of his name under penalty of death.[83] Herostratos is in fact remembered "as the one society wants to forget." While speculating that "perhaps Herostratus never existed," Gans makes many assumptions about his character and motives. To understand his relevance to our times he should be imagined as "in no way oppressed or victimized." If his resentment may have been due in part to rivalry, Gans speculates, it cannot have been as titanic as the competitiveness that inspired the wrath of Achilles. It is no accident that history tells us nothing of Herostratos's rivals for he knew that he would have no biographers and would be remembered only for one act of destruction. "From the anonymity of the respectable middle class, he rises in one stroke above the human condition."

Without knowledge of the World Trade Center disaster that lay four years in the future, Professor Gans underestimates the extent to which the world's economy could be devastated by a Herostratic crime against a symbol of American economic power:

> Is it not remarkable that no one in history has equaled, let alone improved on, Herostratus' example? We have had assassinations of kings and presidents, terrorist attacks on buildings and airplanes, massacres of millions; but he alone is remembered for destroying the central sacred locus of his society. The world of the marketplace is no longer guaranteed by a temple. Burning down the New York Stock Exchange would scarcely register on the seismograph of the global economy.

Yet Gans seems correct in defining the existential issue faced by the Herostratos figure as a "market problem." The more a Herostratos, ancient or modern, "realizes how justly the 'rational' social order evaluates him, the greater his resentment against humanity and the cosmos in which it operates." According to Gans, the world's notion of Herostratos's "true" market value brought home to the arsonist the general perception of his mediocrity.

In 1999 Gans felt compelled to revisit the Herostratos theme in the light of the Columbine massacre and other mass murders. Faced by the difficulty of explaining the strange tendency of the general public to identify with the mass murderer, or as Gans puts it, their "curious mimetic relationship," he leaves aside "the unbalanced few who would follow the killer's example." Instead, he suggests, "Our 'mourning' for his victims, whom we come to know only after their death, relieves our own aggression. This relief may be psychologized in a number of ways: as the fulfillment of unconscious impulses, the projection of hostilities, or as I prefer to put it, the deferment of resentment." Herostratos, closely related to multiple killers in motivation, "sacrifices his life, in principle at least, to the pleasure of being recognized." Gans finds that the remedies against the Herostratos syndrome have an ethical dimension:

> Since the classic supply curve suggests that the publicitary attractiveness of acts of mass murder would grow with their increasing rarity, stamping them out altogether would require the eradication of the Herostratus syndrome from the entire population—hardly a realistic assumption. This does not make any less clear the ethical imperative we as individuals and collectivities should follow to prevent them: *act as to defer resentment.*[84]

Afterword

THE STUDY OF the Herostratos syndrome can heighten our sense of realism when we appraise the odds in the struggle against terror. The impulse to commit terrorist acts in quest of fame is deeply imbedded in the human personality and has spread chaos for more than two millennia. There is no more room for hope that these crimes can ever be totally eliminated than that we can some day eradicate serial killings, which, like terrorist atrocities, are aimed at headlines as well as victims.

Accepting these limitations on our prospects for total victory, we do well to focus our counterterrorism campaigns on disruption of identifiable terrorist organizations and on the control of weapons of mass destruction. The fame-driven terrorist, whether acting alone, like the Unabomber, or in a group, will remain a more elusive foe. The origins of his compulsion for glory may be difficult to probe and impossible for detectives to profile. Throughout the centuries, however, our forebears have believed that the hunter of negative fame may act out of a desire to compensate for past humiliations, which society ignores at its peril. A second lesson is offered by many commentators cited in these pages: although we cannot obliterate the name of the glory seeker, as the Ephesians unsuccessfully sought to do, we should resist the temptation to convert him into a media star.

Appendix: Herostratos in Art and Film

ART

1. Künstlergruppe Teilbereich Kunst (a group of artists called Section Group Art), consisting of Rudolf Herz, Stephan Huber, and Thomas Lehnerer. Exhibition: "Herostratos," or, "The Man Who Set Fire to the Temple to Become Immortal," Akademie der Bildenden Künste, Munich 1980, http://www.rudolf herz.de/DER_MANN/HTML (accessed May 18, 2004).

The exhibition Web site states: "The renewed publication of [Herostratos's] name by 'Teilbereich Kunst' . . . represents an explicit breach of the old sanction and is thus a direct reference to his motive. This symbolizes the conditions of existence for the artist, which are decisively determined by alienation."

2. Tomas Nittner, *Herostratos or the Vanity of Terror*, red watercolor on Fabriano paper (1992), http://netzraum.de/auge/nittner/raum_3_z.html (accessed May 18, 2004). The central image appears to be cruciform and is reinforced by small cross-like shapes in the background.

3. Lisa Ruyter, *Herostratus* (1997), acrylic on canvas, 60 x 72 inches. Exhibited Kent Gallery, "A Delicate Condition"; curator, Jerry Kearns; New York City, February 1998. A young woman in a sun hat sits on a giant translucent horse in front of a cityscape. In April 2003 the painter advised by e-mail: "I title all my paintings after movies. I have a list of movie titles that could also be place names that I use to select a title after a painting is made. I have not always seen the movie, as is the case with 'Herostratus.'"

4. Samuel Sevada, *Herostratus*, photograph by a Russian artist of the head of a bearded man near a flaming column, posted June 15, 2001, http://www. photoforum.ru/rate/photo.php?photo_id=5030.

FILM

1. *Herostratus,* dir. Don Levy (United Kingdom, 1967). A well-meaning person tries to persuade a failed poet not to leap from a rooftop and falls to his death in a struggle. Helen Mirren made her first screen appearance in a minor role.

2. *Herostratus,* dir. Rouben Kochar (USA/Armenia, 2001). The satrap Tissafernes insists that, despite the inclination of the Ephesian population to be merciful, Herostratos shall not go unpunished for the arson.

Notes

Hard copies of all online publications cited in this book are in the archives of the Department of Special Collections, Kent State University Libraries, Kent, Ohio.

INTRODUCTION

1. "Der Alte vom Berge u. A. Terrorismus—ein uraltes Phänomen: Woher kommt der Terrorismus?" ("The Old Man of the Mountain and Others. Terrorism, an Age-Old Phenomenon: Where Does Terrorism Come From?" *Ego-Net,* Nov. 2001, http://www.berlinx.de/ego/1101/art3.htm (accessed Jan. 14, 2003).

2. Walter Laqueur, "Left, Right, and Beyond: The Changing Face of Terror," in *How Did This Happen? Terrorism and the New War,* ed. James F. Hoge Jr. and Gideon Rose (New York: PublicAffairs, 2001), 71.

3. Walter Laqueur, *The New Terrorism: Fanaticism and the Arms of Mass Destruction* (New York: Oxford Univ. Press, 1999), 265.

4. Maxwell Taylor and Ethel Quayle, *Terrorist Lives* (London: Brassey's, 1994), 8.

5. Ibid., 35.

6. Ibid., 7, 16.

7. Ibid., 149–50. The attraction of fame was also emphasized by a terrorist trainer interviewed in Pakistan in 2002 under the supervision of Professor Jessica Stern: "One becomes important due to his work. Successful operations make a militant famous and glamorous among his fellow men." Jessica Stern, *Terror in the Name of God: Why Religious Militants Kill* (New York: HarperCollins, 2003), 217.

8. Avishai Margalit, "The Suicide Bombers," *New York Review of Books* 50, no. 1 (2003): 38.

9. "Mind of the Suicide Bomber," *CBSNews.com,* May 25, 2003, a summary of a report in *60 Minutes,* http://www.cbsnews.com/stories/2003/05/23/60minutes/main555344.shtml (accessed May 12, 2004).

10. Taylor and Quayle, *Terrorist Lives*, 13, 57.

11. Laqueur, *The New Terrorism*, 265. Other criminals Laqueur brackets with Herostratos as deranged are John Hinckley Jr., who shot President Reagan, and the would-be assassins of Presidents Theodore Roosevelt and Franklin D. Roosevelt.

12. The federal definition of "international terrorism" includes violent acts that appear to be intended "(i) to intimidate or coerce a civilian population; (ii) to influence the policy of a government by intimidation or coercion; or (iii) to affect the conduct of a government by mass destruction, assassination, or kidnapping." 18 U.S.C. § 2331. A typical state statute, Code of Virginia § 18.2, under which the first of the Washington sniper cases was prosecuted, defines "act of terrorism" as a felony committed with the intent to "(i) intimidate or coerce a civilian population; or (ii) influence the policy, conduct or activities of the government of the United States, a state or locality through intimidation or coercion." See Donna Lyons, "States Enact New Terrorism Crimes and Penalties," *National Conference of State Legislatures, State Legislative Report* 27, no. 19 (Nov. 2002): 1–4.

13. Ricardo J. Quinones, *The Changes of Cain* (Princeton, N.J.: Princeton Univ. Press, 1991), 3.

14. See chapter 4 for a discussion of the case of Samuel Byck. *Assassins* was successfully revived on Broadway in 2004.

1. The Birth of the Herostratos Tradition

1. The alternative translations of "Herostratos" have been respectively suggested to me by two Classics professors, David Lupher of the University of Puget Sound and Thomas Martin of the College of the Holy Cross. I am grateful for their advice.

2. *Oxford Classical Dictionary*, 3d ed., ed. Simon Hornblower and Antony Spawforth, s.v. "names, personal, Greek" (Oxford, U.K.: Oxford Univ. Press, 1996), 1022–24.

3. *Paulys Real-Encyclopädie der Classischen Altertumswissenschaft (Neue Bearbeitung)*, ed. Wilhelm Kroll (Stuttgart, Ger.: J. B. Metzler, 1913), 8:1145; Plutarch, "Life of Marcus Brutus," in *The Lives of the Noble Grecians and Romans*, trans. John Dryden and rev. Arthur Hugh Clough (New York: Modern Library, n.d.), 1200.

4. The noncitizen residents included mercenary soldiers, skilled workers, and traders, who "formed at best a transient element in city populations" and "stood low in the scale of respectability and integration in the community." Paul McKechnie, *Outsiders in the Greek Cities in the Fourth Century* BC (London: Routledge, 1989), 178.

5. Alessandro Verri, *La Vita di Erostrato* (1815), discussed in chapter 6.

6. Robert Graves, *The Greek Myths* (Baltimore, Md.: Penguin, 1961), 1:84.

7. "Hymn 27: To Artemis," *The Homeric Hymns*, trans. Michael Crudden (Oxford, U.K.: Oxford Univ. Press, 2002), 87.

8. *Oxford Classical Dictionary*, s.v. "Artemis," 182–84. For a discussion of the archetypal "Lady of the Beasts," see Erich Neumann, *The Great Mother: An Analysis of the Archetype*, trans. Ralph Manheim (Princeton, N.J.: Princeton Univ. Press, 1974), 268—80. A feminist meditation on Artemis responds to the goddess's immanence in modern issues relating to preservation of the natural environment, chastity and solitude, the shyness of female adolescence, and Amazonian athleticism. Ginette Paris,

Pagan Meditations: The Worlds of Aphrodite, Artemis, and Hestia (Woodstock, Conn.: Spring, 1997). The goddess is embodied in Gwendolen Harleth, the skittish archer in George Eliot's last novel, *Daniel Deronda;* Sir Hugo Mallinger refers to Gwendolen as "a perfect Diana." George Eliot, *Daniel Deronda,* intro. A .S. Byatt (London: Everyman's Library, 1999), 174.

9. Selahattin Erdemgil, *Ephesus Ruins and Museum* (Istanbul, Turk.: Net Turistik Yayinlar, 1989), 26–28.

10. John Romer and Elizabeth Romer, *The Seven Wonders of the World: A History of the Modern Imagination* (New York: Holt), 233.

11. Selahattin Erdemgil, *Ephesus Ruins and Museum,* 30–31; Pliny, *Natural History* 36.21.95–97, trans. D. E. Eichholz, Loeb Classical Library (Cambridge, Mass.: Harvard Univ. Press, 1962); Anton Bammer and Ulrike Muss, *Das Artemision von Ephesos* (Mainz am Rhein: Verlag Philipp von Zabern, 1996), 43–45 (Croesus's political motives). Bammer and Muss, successive directors of the Artemision Project of the Austrian Archeological Institute, estimate the dimensions of the Archaic Temple at 338 feet long and 197 feet wide and the Hellenistic Temple at 410 feet long and 236 feet wide. The latter calculations approximate those of Pliny the Elder, who, on the basis of his visit to the latter temple, stated its dimensions to be 425 feet long and 225 feet wide.

12. W. R. Lethaby, *Diana's Temple at Ephesus* (London: B. T. Batsford, 1908).

13. Peter Green, *Alexander of Macedon 356–323 BC: A Historical Biography* (Berkeley: Univ. of California Press, 1992), xxxiii.

14. Bammer and Muss, *Das Artemision von Ephesos,* 54.

15. Romer and Romer, *The Seven Wonders of the World,* 150. Michael Grant observes that the Archaic Artemision "was believed to be the first monumental edifice ever made entirely of marble—except for the ceiling and roof beams, which were of cedarwood." Michael Grant, *The Rise of the Greeks* (New York: Scribner's, 1988), 169.

16. Cicero, *De Natura Deorum* 2.27, trans. H. Rackham, Loeb Classical Library (Cambridge, Mass.: Harvard Univ. Press, 1967).

17. Cicero, *De Divinatione* 1.23.47 (publ. with *De Senectute* and *De Amicitia*), trans. William Armistead Falconer, Loeb Classical Library (Cambridge, Mass.: Harvard Univ. Press, 1971).

18. Plutarch, "Life of Alexander," *The Lives of the Noble Grecians and Romans,* 802. Peter Green attributes the prediction of disaster to "Persian propaganda, put out when the [Macedonian] invasion had already taken place." Green, *Alexander of Macedon,* 36–37.

19. Strabo, *The Geography of Strabo* 14.1.22, trans. Horace Leonard Jones, Loeb Classical Library (Cambridge, Mass.: Harvard Univ. Press, 1960).

20. Valerius Maximus, *Memorable Doings and Sayings* 8.14, ed. and trans. D. R. Shackleton-Bailey, Loeb Classical Library (Cambridge, Mass.: Harvard Univ. Press, 2000). In the course of a discussion of word usage in Virgil's poetry, Aulus Gellius (123–ca. 169 AD), like Valerius Maximus, refers to the ban on Herostratos's remembrance without mentioning his name: "in days gone by the common council of Asia decreed that no one should ever mention the name of the man who had burned the temple of Diana at Ephesus." *The Attic Nights of Aulus Gellius* 2.6.13–18, trans. John C. Rolfe, Loeb Classical Library (Cambridge, Mass.: Harvard Univ. Press, 1961). The refer-

ence to the "common council of Asia" as the entity that ordered the damnation of Herostratos's name is unique in the ancient sources and may be a hyperbolic means of asserting that other Ionian cities honored the Ephesian decree. During the Roman Empire, under which Aulus Gellius lived, Asia (i.e., Asia Minor) was a province; each province had a "council" charged with celebration of the imperial cult. *Oxford Classical Dictionary*, s.vv. "Asia, Roman province," "Asia Minor," and "concilium," 189–91, 375.

21. Aelian [Claudius Aelianus], *On the Characteristics of Animals* 6.40, trans. A. F. Scholfield, Loeb Classical Library (Cambridge, Mass.: Harvard Univ. Press, 1959).

22. Caius [or Gaius] Julius Solinus, *The Excellent and Pleasant Worke* (*Collectanea Rerum Memorabilium*), trans. Arthur Golding (1587); facsimile reproduction intro. George Kish (Gainesville: Scholars' Facsimiles and Reprints, 1955), chap. 52. I have modernized the spelling of the Golding translation.

23. Lucian, *The Passing of Peregrinus*, in *Lucian [Works]*, trans. A. M. Harmon, Loeb Classical Library (Cambridge, Mass.: Harvard Univ. Press, 1936), 5:26–27. Professor Barry Baldwin, having observed that "there is no warrant for dogmatising on other people's religious sincerity," expresses his reservation about the objectivity of *The Passing of Peregrinus*: "For all we can tell, the Lucian picture of Peregrinus may be a total caricature." Barry Baldwin, *Studies in Lucian* (Toronto, Can.: Hakkert, 1973), 104–5.

24. C. M. Bowra, *The Greek Experience* (New York: Mentor, 1963), 33.

25. Ibid., 51.

26. Ibid.,137.

27. Gregory L. Ulmer, *The Legend of Herostratus: Existential Envy in Rousseau and Unamuno*, University of Florida Monographs, Humanities, no. 45 (Gainesville: Univ. Presses of Florida, 1977), 18.

28. Hermann Bengtson, *The Greeks and the Persians from the Sixth to the Fourth Centuries*, trans. John Conway (New York: Delacorte, 1968), 305.

29. Sigmund Freud, "Anxiety and Instinctual Life," in *New Introductory Lectures on Psycho-Analysis [1933]*, trans. W. J. H. Sprott (New York: Norton, n.d.), 140.

30. Sigmund Freud, "The Acquisition and Control of Fire," in *The Standard Edition of the Complete Psychological Works of Sigmund Freud*, trans. and ed. James Strachey (London: Hogarth), 22 (1932–36):187.

31. Norman N. Holland, *The I* (New Haven, Conn.: Yale Univ. Press, 1985), 208.

32. Scott Dowling, M.D., e-mail to Donald K. Freedheim, Ph.D., Feb. 2, 2003. Dr. Dowling's communication was made in response to my inquiry.

33. Victor-Pierre Stirnimann, "The Terror and the Temple," in *Jungian Reflections on September 11: A Global Nightmare*, ed. Luigi Zoja and Donald Williams (Einsiedeln, Switz.: Daimon Verlag, 2002), 99; Strabo, *The Geography of Strabo*, 14.1.22.

34. Victor-Pierre Stirnimann, "The Terror and the Temple," 100.

35. Page duBois, *Torture and Truth*, (New York: Routledge, 1991), 35.

36. Antiphon, "On the Murder of Herodes," in *Minor Attic Orators I: Antiphon, Andocides*, trans. K. J. Maidment, Loeb Classical Library (Cambridge, Mass.: Harvard Univ. Press, 1968), 183. In another court speech, Antiphon argued that the defendant's refusal to let slaves be questioned under torture amounted to strong evidence in the plaintiff's favor. Michael Gagarin, *Antiphon the Athenian: Oratory, Law, and Justice in the Age of the Sophists* (Austin: Univ. of Texas Press, 2002), 146.

37. Antiphon, "On the Murder of Herodes," 189nb. Fourth-century BC Athenian sources examined by Professor Danielle S. Allen reveal "three cases where a citizen or freeman was subjected to torture or threatened with torture, despite the law against torturing citizens. Two of the three victims tortured had started life as slaves. The third man had always been free but was also a naturalized and not a native citizen." Allen, *The World of Prometheus: The Politics of Punishing in Democratic Athens* (Princeton, N.J.: Princeton Univ. Press, 2000), 215.

38. duBois, *Torture and Truth,* 63.

39. See note 37 above, regarding three fourth-century BC Athenian cases in which Professor Allen notes that freedmen or a naturalized citizen were subjected to torture.

40. duBois, *Torture and Truth,* 42.

41. Theodore Mommsen, *Römisches Staatsrecht* (Graz, Aus.: Akademische Druck-und Verlagsanstalt, 1953), 2:1129–32, 3:1190–91; *Römisches Strafrecht* (Graz, Aus.: Akademische Druck-und Verlagsanstalt, 1955), 987–90.

42. Allen, *The World of Prometheus,* 202–13.

43. Katariina Mustakallio, *Death and Disgrace: Capital Penalties with Post Mortem Sanctions in Early Roman Historiography* (Helsinki, Fin.: Suomalainen Tiedeakatemia, 1994).

44. Mustakallio, *Death and Disgrace,* 55; Livy, *Rome and Italy* (bks. 6–9 of *The History of Rome from Its Foundation*), trans. Betty Radice (London: Penguin, 1982), 64.

45. Tacitus, *The Annals* 2.32 and 3.17–18, in *The Complete Works of Tacitus,* trans. Alfred John Church and William Jackson Brodribb, ed. Moses Hadas (New York: Modern Library, n.d.), 69–70, 110–11.

46. Marianne Bergmann and Paul Zanker, "'Damnatio Memoriae,' Umgearbeitete Nero-und Domitiansporträts: Zur Ikonographie der flavischen Kaiser und des Nerva," *Jahrbuch des Deutschen Archäologischen Instituts* 96 (1981): 317–412.

47. See note 20 above.

48. *Herodotus* 1.148, trans. A. D. Godley, Loeb Classical Library (Cambridge, Mass.: Harvard Univ. Press, 1966).

49. Lucian, *The Passing of Peregrinus,* 26–27nl.

50. Aeschines, "Against Ctesiphon," in *Aeschines,* trans. Chris Carey (Austin: Univ. of Texas Press, 2000), 200–201.

2. The Globalization of Herostratos

1. Gilbert Highet, *The Classical Tradition: Greek and Roman Influences on Western Literature* (New York: Oxford Univ. Press/Galaxy, 1957), 11–14; *Lucian [Works],* vol. 1, trans. A. M. Harmon, Loeb Classical Library (Cambridge, Mass.: Harvard Univ. Press, 1961), xiii–xiv; W. Martin Bloomer, *Valerius Maximus and the Rhetoric of the New Nobility* (Chapel Hill: Univ. of North Carolina Press, 1992), 2; Valerius Maximus, *Memorable Doings and Sayings,* vol. 1, ed. and trans. D. R. Shackleton Bailey, Loeb Classical Library (Cambridge, Mass.: Harvard Univ. Press, 2000), 5–6.

2. In 1170 John of Salisbury witnessed the assassination of Thomas Becket, who had succeeded Theobald as Archbishop of Canterbury.

3. John of Salisbury, *Policraticus: Of the Frivolities of Courtiers and the Footprints of Philosophers,* ed. and trans. Cary J. Nederman (Cambridge, U.K.: Cambridge Univ. Press, 1990), intro. and bk. 7, chap. 1, xx, 148–50.

4. Joseph B. Pike, *Frivolities of Courtiers and Footprints of Philosophers: Being a Translation of the First, Second, and Third Books and Selections from the Seventh and Eighth Books of the* Policraticus *of John of Salisbury* (Minneapolis: Univ. of Minnesota Press, 1938), bk. 8, chap. 5, 313.

Christian treatises in later centuries cite references to Herostratos by other Classical authors, including Solinus and Cicero. The Aristotelian John Case, in his discussion of the respect due sacred buildings of the past and present, remarks: "I shall say nothing of the men of our times like Herostratus and Julian, yet I shall say this one thing: if God employed lightning to obliterate Xerxes' troops sent to despoil Apollo's temple, a conspicuously superstitious work, just because of their evil intention, what punishment, good God, are they destined to undergo who suffer, not Apollo's temples, but those of the divinity, to be wasted and trampled underfoot?" John Case, *Sphaera Civitatis* (*The Sphere of the Commonwealth*) (1588), bk. 7, chap. 12, hypertext ed. Dana F. Sutton (Irvine, University of California, posted Mar. 13, 2002), http://eee.uci.edu/~papyri/sphaera/7.2eng.html/ (accessed May 14, 2004).

In his *Exposition of the New Testament*, John Gill (1690–1771) refers to several Classical authors in recounting the history of Artemis's temple at Ephesus, including its destruction by Herostratos. John Gill, *An Exposition of the Old and New Testaments* [1809–1810] (Paris, Ark.: Baptist Standard Bearer, 1989), Acts 19:27.

5. Edgar Finley Shannon, *Chaucer and the Roman Poets* (Cambridge, Mass.: Harvard Univ. Press, 1929), 338–39.

6. It has been argued, however, that Chaucer's acquaintance with Valerius may have been limited to a thirteenth-century compendium of quotations. Richard L. Hoffman, "The Influence of the Classics on Chaucer," in *Companion to Chaucer Studies*, ed. Beryl Rowland (Toronto, Can.: Oxford Univ. Press, 1968), 172.

7. Geoffrey Chaucer, *The House of Fame*, in *The Modern Reader's Chaucer*, ed. John S. P. Tatlock and Percy MacKaye (New York: Free Press, 1912), 540–41; Anne Worthington Prescott, *Imagining Fame: An Introduction to Geoffrey Chaucer's The House of Fame* (Santa Barbara: Fithian, 2003), 90. Prescott notes that "Professor B. J. Whiting of Harvard said, in the 1950s, 'If you would understand Chaucer, read the daily newspapers.'" Prescott, *Imagining Fame*, 101. Professor B. G. Koonce comments that Chaucer's reference to the "world's end" is "a punning allusion to the Last Judgment" that "gives even more poignancy to John of Salisbury's warning that a far greater madness than destroying the temple of Diana is that of destroying the temple of the Holy Spirit." B. G. Koonce, *Chaucer and the Tradition of Fame: Symbolism in* The House of Fame (Princeton, N.J.: Princeton Univ. Press, 1966), 243.

8. Sheila Delany, *Chaucer's House of Fame: The Poetics of Skeptical Fideism* (Chicago: Univ. of Chicago Press, 1972), 23, 81.

9. Jacob Burckhardt, *The Civilization of the Renaissance in Italy: An Essay*, 3d rev. ed. (London: Phaidon, 1950), 93.

10. Michel de Montaigne, "De la Gloire," in *Essais 2*, ed. Pierre Michel (Paris: Livre de Poche, 1972), bk. 2, chap. 16.

11. J. M. Cohen, introduction to his translation of Montaigne, *Essays* (Harmondsworth, U.K.: Penguin, 1958), 21.

12. William Shakespeare, *The Tragedy of Coriolanus*, ed. R. B. Parker, Oxford World's Classics (New York: Oxford Univ. Press, 1998), 321n to lines 11–15.

13. Geoffrey Ribbans, "Herostratus: Notes on the Cult of Fame in Cervantes," in *Cervantes for the 21st Century/Cervantes para el siglo XXI: Studies in Honor of Edward Dudley*, ed. Francisco La Rubia Prado, Documentación cervantina, no. 18 (Newark, Del.: Juan de la Cuesta, 2000), 185–98; the quotation concerning Renaissance and Baroque texts is on 194. Professor Leo Braudy has observed: "Throughout the seventeenth century moralists cite the figure of Herostratus (as had Chaucer) as an example of the wickedness that was done for fame." Leo Braudy, *The Frenzy of Renown: Fame and its History* (New York: Oxford Univ. Press, 1986), 350.

14. Miguel de Cervantes, *Don Quixote*, trans. J. M. Cohen (Harmondsworth, U.K.: Penguin, 1950), pt. 2, chap. 8, 514–20.

15. Juan Ruiz de Alarcón y Mendoza, *La Verdad Sospechosa*, Collección Austral (published with *Los Pechos Privilegiados*) (Madrid, Spain: Espasa-Calpe, 1969), act 1, scene 8, 31–32.

16. Luís Vaz de Camões, *The Lusíads*, Oxford World's Classics (New York: Oxford Univ. Press, 1997), 47.

17. Sebastián de Covarrubias Orozco, *Emblemas Morales 1610*, Centuria 2, Emblem 55 (Menston, U.K.: Scolar, 1973).

18. Qtd. by Duncan Moir in introductory note to Covarrubias Orozco, *Emblemas Morales*.

19. Sir Thomas Browne, *Hydrotaphia (Urn Burial); and The Garden of Cyrus* (1658), ed. Frank L. Huntley (New York: Appleton-Century-Crofts, 1966), 39–48; Frank Livingstone Huntley, *Sir Thomas Browne: A Biographical and Critical Study* (Ann Arbor: Univ. of Michigan Press, 1962). Browne's ironic contrast of Herostratos's fame and the temple architect's anonymity appears to echo lines from sec. 68 of "An Inquisition upon Fame and Honour" by Sir Fulke Greville, first Baron Brooke (1554–1628):

Herostratus shall prove, Vice governes Fame;
Who built that Church, he burnt, hath lost his name.

"An Inquisition upon Fame and Honour," in *Poems and Dramas of Fulke Greville, First Lord Brooke*, ed. Geoffrey Bullough (New York: Oxford Univ. Press, 1945), 1:209.

Simplicius Simplicissimus encounters Herostratos as an infernal gatekeeper when he pays an unintended visit to Hell in Johann Jakob Christoffel von Grimmelshausen's 1672 satire, *Die Verkehrte Welt (The Topsy-Turvy World)*.

20. Bernard Le Bovier de Fontenelle, *Nouveaux Dialogues des Morts*, ed. Donald Schier (Chapel Hill: Univ. of North Carolina Press, 1965), 108–11.

21. *Dialogues of Fontenelle*, trans. Ezra Pound (London: Egoist, 1917), 9–11.

22. Colley Cibber, *The Tragical History of King Richard III As It is Acted at the Theatre Royal*, an adaptation of Shakespeare's play (London: B. Lintott, ca. 1700), a facsimile produced in 1978 by UMI, Ann Arbor, Mich.; Leonard R. N. Ashley, *Colley Cibber*, rev. ed. (New York: Twayne, 1965), 47–52.

23. [John Lemprière], *Lemprière's Classical Dictionary of Proper Names Mentioned in Ancient Authors Writ Large* [1788], 3d ed., intro. R. Willets (London: Routledge and Kegan Paul, 1984), s.v. "Eratostratus," 228; William King, *An Historical Account of the Heathen Gods and Heroes Necessary for the Understanding of the Ancient Poets* (1710), intro. Hugh Ross Williamson (Carbondale: Southern Illinois Univ. Press, 1965), 128.

24. [Gabriel Harvey], *Foure Letters, and certaine Sonnets: Especially touching Robert Greene, and other parties, by him abused; But incidently of divers excellent persons, and some matters of note* (London: John Wolfe, 1592), facsimile ed. (Menston, U.K.: Scolar, 1969), 1, 37. The latter page is erroneously numbered 29 in this facsimile of the first edition.

In 1753 Paul Sandby caricatured artist William Hogarth in an etching as Herostratos, the "Vile Ephesian," burning the Temple of Diana. David Bindman, *Hogarth and His Times: Serious Comedy* (Berkeley: Univ. of California Press, 1997), 108.

25. Allen Johnson, *Jefferson and his Colleagues: A Chronicle of the Virginia Dynasty* (New Haven, Conn.: Yale Univ. Press, 1921), 76–80.

26. See chapter 6 for a discussion of Unamuno's *Tragic Sense of Life.*

27. [Judith Sargent Murray], "The Reaper," no. 5 in the *Federal Orrery,* Boston, Nov. 20, 1794, http://www.hurdsmith.com/judith/reaper5.htm (accessed April 20, 2004). Murray discontinued the series after this essay, angered that Paine edited her work with a heavy hand and had suggested that her husband John Murray, pastor of the first Universalist church in America, had collaborated in her writings. Bonnie Hurd Smith, "'I Am Jealous for the Honor of Our Sex': Introducing Judith Sargent Murray," http://www.hurdsmith.com/judith/introduction.htm (accessed May 14, 2004).

3. THE DESTROYERS

1. Yuri Tarnopolsky, Essay 34, "On Loss," http://users.ids.net/~yuri/Essay34.html (accessed May 14, 2004).

2. Qtd. in John Quail, *The Slow Burning Fuse: The Lost History of the British Anarchists* (St. Albans, U.K.: Granada/Paladin, 1978), 152. Ernest Vizetelly notes the coincidence that the third act of *William Tell* "figured curiously enough, in the programme at the Paris Opera House on the night when [Felice] Orsini and his confederates attempted the lives of Napoleon III and the Empress Eugénie." Ernest Alfred Vizetelly, *The Anarchists: Their Faith and Their Record* (London: John Lane, 1911), 137–38.

3. H. B. Irving, *Studies of French Criminals of the Nineteenth Century* (London: William Heinemann, 1901), 337.

4. David Nicoll, *The Greenwich Mystery* (1897), included as app. D in Norman Sherry, *Conrad's Western World* (Cambridge, U.K.: Cambridge Univ. Press, 1971), 379; Hermia Oliver, *The International Anarchist Movement in Late Victorian London* (London: Croom Helm, 1983), 103.

5. Sherry, *Conrad's Western World,* 230. A contemporary drawing of the crime scene (see page 39) is preserved in England's National Archives, ref: HO144/257/A55660.

6. Qtd. in Nicoll, *The Greenwich Mystery,* app. D to Sherry, *Conrad's Western World,* 387.

7. Ibid., 379.

8. Oliver, *The International Anarchist Movement,* 101–3.

9. Ibid.,103; *London Times,* February 27, 1894.

10. Quail, *The Slow Burning Fuse,* 150.

11. *Morning Leader,* Feb. 19, 1894, qtd. in Sherry, *Conrad's Western World,* 238.

12. Nicoll, *The Greenwich Mystery,* app. D to Sherry, *Conrad's Western World,* 381.

13. Ibid., 382.

14. Sir Robert Anderson, *The Lighter Side of My Official Life* (London: Hodder and Stoughton, 1900), 176.

15. Nicoll, *The Greenwich Mystery,* 383.

16. Ibid., 391.

17. Oliver, *The International Anarchist Movement,* 103–4.

18. Nicoll, *The Greenwich Mystery,* 391, 381.

19. Ibid., 393.

20. Quail, *The Slow Burning Fuse,* 162, 167–68. David Muley states: "There were few who were willing to condone Samuels' actions in the Bourdin affair (especially for the fact that he earned three guineas for a newspaper interview in which he recounted his close connection with Bourdin." David Muley, "Popular Accounts of the Greenwich Bombing and Conrad's *The Secret Agent," Rocky Mountain Review* (Fall 2000): 52.

21. "Propaganda by Deed—The Greenwich Bomb of 1894," http://www.nmm. ac.uk/site/request/setTemplate:singlecontent/contentTypeA/co.../00500300f00 (accessed May 15, 2004). The article was provided by Margaret Pension of the Royal Greenwich Observatory from *Open Space,* a newsletter formerly published by the Particle Physics and Astronomy Research Council.

22. Joseph Conrad, *The Secret Agent: A Simple Tale,* ed. Martin Seymour-Smith (New York: Penguin, 1986), 39.

23. Bernard Potter, "Dangerous Foreigners in Britain: The Historical Background," National Europe Centre Paper no. 45 (Nov. 4, 2002), http://www.anu.edu.au/NEC/porter.pdf (accessed on June 2, 2003; site now discontinued). Assistant Commissioner Anderson's memoirs reflect police hostility to the lack of enthusiasm for anti-anarchist measures shown by British participants in the Rome Conference. Anderson, *The Lighter Side of My Official Life,* 176–77.

24. Conrad, *The Secret Agent,* 64.

25. Ibid., 65–68.

26. Ibid., 102.

27. Ibid., 111.

28. Ibid., 207. Luckier than Verloc, Samuels lived to a ripe old age. Far from becoming a target for revenge on the part of Martial Bourdin's family, he remained on close terms with Martial's brother Henri. Oliver, *The International Anarchist Movement,* 107.

29. Conrad, *The Secret Agent,* 81, 221–22.

30. Ibid., 82.

31. Tamura Masahiro, "Heisei Restoration," *Look Japan* (Oct. 2000), http://www.look japan.com/LBsc/00OctCult.html (accessed May 16, 2004). In this book names of Japanese persons generally are stated in the order followed in the Japanese language, i.e., surname first. An exception is made for names customarily rendered in English with the surname last, e.g., Yukio Mishima. Long-vowel accents are omitted except in bibliographical references.

32. *Kyoto Shinbun,* July 3, 1950. This news report, unless otherwise indicated, is the source of my descriptions of the fire and the first investigations.

33. Nancy Wilson Ross, intro. to Yukio Mishima, *The Temple of the Golden Pavilion,* trans. Ivan Morris (New York: Knopf, 1959), vii. Page citations are made to this first American edition.

34. Donald Keene, intro. to Yukio Mishima, *The Temple of the Golden Pavilion* (London: Everyman's Library, 1994), ix.

35. Mizukami Tsutomo, *Kinkaku Enjō* (Tokyo: Shinchō Bunko, 1979), 10, 287.

36. Ibid., 18.

37. Ibid., 243.

38. The dating of the arsonous impulse as "two or three weeks ago" cannot be accepted literally, since the fire was set on July 2, 1950, more than four weeks before the interrogation. Hayashi should be understood as indicating that he had irrevocably decided on the crime only shortly before its commission.

39. Mizukami Tsutomo, *Kinkaku Enjō*, 277–80.

40. Ibid., 280–81.

41. Ibid., 281.

42. Ibid., 267–68.

43. Ibid., 282.

44. Fujii Hidetada, "Ore ga aitsu de . . . *Kinkaku Enjō* ni okeru kousei ishiki?" ("How Consciously Did Mizukami Tsutomo Construct His *Kinkaku Enjō?*"), *Bungaku* 56, no. 8 (1988): 40–58.

45. Mishima told Donald Keene that his visit to Hayashi in his cell "added nothing to what he had previously known." Keene, introduction to Mishima, *The Temple of the Golden Pavilion*, ix.

46. Mishima, *The Temple of the Golden Pavilion* (New York: Knopf, 1959), 6.

47. Ibid., 63.

48. Ibid., 142.

49. Ibid., 135.

50. Ibid., 191.

51. Ibid., 194–95.

52. Ibid., 262.

53. *Kyoto Shinbun*, Sept. 12, 1955.

54. Kabuki Glossary (U~Z), http://www.kabuki21.com/glossaire_8.htm (accessed May 24, 2003).

55. Mishima, *The Temple of the Golden Pavilion*, 206.

56. Sawaki Kodo, *The Dharma of "Homeless Kodo,"* with commentaries by Uchiyama Kosho [1972], http://terebess.hu/english/sawaki.html; 4 (accessed May 15, 2003).

57. Mishima, *The Temple of the Golden Pavilion*, 184.

58. Nose Masayo, "Masterpieces of Japan on Stage," *Kyoto Shinbun*, July 22, 2002.

59. Marguerite Yourcenar. *Mishima: A Vision of the Void*, trans. Alberto Manguel (Chicago: Univ. of Chicago Press, 2001), 34.

60. Mishima, *The Temple of the Golden Pavilion*, 231.

61. Yourcenar, *Mishima*, 38.

62. Nose, "Masterpieces of Japan on Stage"; *Mainichi Shinbun*, July 2, 1999. The latter article notes the forty-ninth anniversary of the fire.

63. Arima Raitei, article contributed to the column "Watashi no Rirekisho" ("My Résumé"), *Nihon Keizai Shinbun* (*Japanese Financial Times*), March 3, 2003.

64. Ibid.

65. Keene, introduction to Mishima, *The Temple of the Golden Pavilion*, xii.

66. Amir Pasic, "Mostar in Bosnia and Hercegovina," http://w3.tyenet.com/kozlich/tarsom.htm (accessed June 19, 2003).

67. Rebecca West, *Black Lamb and Grey Falcon: A Journey through Yugoslavia* (New York: Viking, 1943), 288.

68. Sarah Jane Meharg, "Identicide and Cultural Cannibalism," *Peace Research Journal* 33 (Nov. 3, 2001): 89–98.

69. "Croatians Destroy Historic Ottoman Bridge in Bosnia," http://w3.tyenet.com/kozlich/kiss.htm (accessed June 19, 2003).

70. Suha Özkan, "The Destruction of Stari Most," *Development Network* 14 (Spring 1994): 5–7. The Aga Khan Award for Architecture was conferred in 1986 on nongovernmental efforts to restore and preserve the historic center of Mostar.

71. "Croatians Destroy Historic Ottoman Bridge in Bosnia."

72. Qtd. in Amir Pastic, "Mostar in Bosnia and Hercegovina."

73. Suha Özkan, "The Destruction of Stari Most."

74. "The Two Big Statues in Bamiyan," http://www.photogrammetry.ethz.ch/research/bamiyan/buddha/statue.html (accessed May 17, 2004).

75. "Destructive Frenzy in Afghanistan: Comments by the Taliban," March 2, 2001, http://www.archaeology.org/magazine.php?/page=online/news/afghanistan/taliban (accessed May 17, 2004).

76. "Destructive Frenzy in Afghanistan: Comments from the United Nations," March 2, 2001, http://www.archaeology.org/online/news/afghanistan/UN (accessed May 17, 2004).

77. Alex Spillius, "Taliban Ignore All Appeals to Save Buddhas," May 3, 2001, http://www.telegraph.co.uk/news/main.jhtml?xml=/news/2001/03/05/wtal05.xml (accessed June 12, 2003; site discontinued).

78. "Adamant Taleban Rejects Iran's Offer," March 4, 2001, http://newsarchives.indiainfo.com/spotlight/taleban/04-mar-taleban1.html (accessed June 12, 2003; site discontinued).

79. "NY Museum Offers to Buy Relics from Afghan [*sic*]," March 2, 2001, http://newsarchives.indianinfo.com/spotlight/taleban/02-mar-museum.html (accessed June 12, 2003).

80. "U.S. Museums to Join Forces to Save Ancient Art," March 3, 2001, http://newsarchives.indiainfo.com/spotlight/taleban/03-mar-usaf.html (accessed May 17, 2004).

81. "Photos Document Destruction of Afghan Buddhas, *CNN.com/WORLD*, March 12, 2001, http://www.cnn.com/2001/WORLD/asiapcf/central/03/12/afghan.buddha.02 (accessed May 17, 2004).

82. Meharg, "Identicide and Cultural Cannibalism."

83. Stirnimann, "The Terror and The Temple," in *Jungian Reflections on September 11*, ed. Zoja and Williams, 88–90.

4. THE KILLERS

1. Raymond Hesse, *Les Criminels peints par eux-mêmes* (Paris: Bernard Grasset, 1912), 2.

2. Qtd. in Brigitte Hamann, *Elisabeth: Kaiserin wider Willen* (Munich, Ger.: Piper, 1989), 589. Hamann's work has been translated into English (with some omissions) as *The Reluctant Empress* (New York: Knopf, 1986).

3. Qtd. in Hamann, *Elisabeth*, 598.

4. Maria Matray and Answald Krüger, *Der Tod der Kaiserin Elisabeth, oder Die Tat des Anarchisten Lucheni* (Munich, Ger.: Verlag Kurt Desch, 1970), 209, 299.

5. Luigi Lucheni, *Mémoires de l'Assassin de Sissi, Histoire d'un Enfant Abandonné à la Fin du XIXe Siècle Racontée par Lui-même,* preceded and followed by Santo Cappon, *L'Histoire de l'Assassin d'Elisabeth, dite Sissi, impératrice d'Autriche et reine de Hongrie* (Paris: cherche midi, 1998), 31–33.

6. Cappon, *L'Histoire de l'Assassin,* 38.

7. Ibid., 16–17.

8. Matray and Krüger, *Der Tod der Kaiserin Elisabeth,* 311–12. Attorney General Georges Navazza would refer to the picture postcard in his argument at Lucheni's trial. *Procès Lucheni: Réquisitoire de M. le Procureur-Général G. Navazza à l'Audience de la Cour d'assises de Genève du 10 novembre 1898* (Geneva, Switz.: W. Kündig, 1899), 10.

9. Cappon, *L'Histoire de l'Assassin,* 37.

10. Ibid., 53.

11. Ibid., 55–58; *Procès Lucheni: Réquisitoire de M. le Procureur-Général G. Navazza,* 21–22.

12. Ibid., 47.

13. Ibid., 60.

14. Mark Twain, "The Memorable Assassination," in *What Is Man? and Other Essays,* ed. Albert Bigelow Paine (New York: Harper, 1917), 167–81.

15. Hamann, *Elisabeth,* 601.

16. Lucheni's memoirs are in Cappon, *L'Histoire de l'Assassin.*

17. Lucheni, *Mémoires de l'Assassin,* 173.

18. Jack Jones, *Let Me Take You Down: Inside the Mind of Mark David Chapman, the Man Who Killed John Lennon* (New York: Villard, 1992), 250.

19. Ibid., 190.

20. Ibid., 124.

21. Ibid., 132.

22. Fenton Bresler, *Who Killed John Lennon?* (New York: St. Martin's, 1989), 125.

23. Jones, *Let Me Take You Down,* 137.

24. Ibid., 177.

25. Ibid., 195.

26. Ibid., 19.

27. Ibid., 31.

28. Ibid., 78, 75.

29. Ibid., 79–82.

30. Bresler, *Who Killed John Lennon?,* 278.

31. James W. Clarke, *American Assassins: The Darker Side of Politics* (Princeton, N.J.: Princeton Univ. Press, 1982); Clarke, *On Being Mad or Merely Angry: John W. Hinckley, Jr. and Other Dangerous People* (Princeton, N.J.: Princeton Univ. Press, 1990).

32. Clarke, *American Assassins,* 14, 16.

33. Ibid., 14–16.

34. Ibid., 267.

35. Ibid., 126.

36. Gerald Posner, *Case Closed: Lee Harvey Oswald and the Assassination of JFK* (New York: Random House, 1993), 33.

37. Rudolf Augstein, "Herostratus in Dallas," *Der Spiegel* (1993), http://www.geo cities.com/mdmorrissey/augstein.htm (accessed Nov. 9, 2002).

38. Clarke, *American Assassins,* 176.

39. "George Wallace: Settin' the Woods on Fire," *American Experience* (2000), program transcript, pt. 2, http://www.pbs.org/wgbh/amex/wallace/filmmore/transcript/transcriptl.html (accessed Aug. 16, 2003).

40. Ibid.

41. Clarke, *American Assassins,* 177.

42. Ibid., 181–82.

43. A portrait of Bremer on a Web site of *The American Experience* reports that the first half of his diary was "unearthed in 1980 from its burial place in an excavated landfill." http://www.pbs.org/wgbh/amex/wallace/sfeature/assasin.html (accessed Aug. 16, 2003). Note the misspelling "assasin" in the URL.

44. Arthur H. Bremer, *An Assassin's Diary,* intro. Harding Lemay (New York: Harper's Magazine Press, 1973), 10.

45. Bremer, *Assassin's Diary,* 93.

46. Ibid., 98.

47. Ibid., 26.

48. Ibid., 77.

49. Ibid., 104.

50. Ibid., 105.

51. Ibid., 118.

52. Ibid., 119.

53. Clarke, *American Assassins,* 191.

54. Ibid., 131.

55. *Washington Post,* Feb. 23, 1974.

56. Ibid.

57. Ibid.

58. Clarke, *American Assassins,* 134.

59. *Washington Post,* Feb. 24, 1974.

60. Transcription of Samuel Byck's last tapes, qtd. in Clarke, *American Assassins,* 136, 140.

61. Stephen Sondheim (music and lyrics) and John Weidman (book), *Assassins* (New York: Theatre Communications Group, 1991), 55–56.

62. Clarke, *On Being Mad or Merely Angry,* 3.

63. Ibid.

64. Ibid., 29.

65. Peter W. Low, John Calvin Jeffries Jr., and Richard J. Bonnie, *The Trial of John W. Hinckley, Jr.: A Case Study in the Insanity Defense* (Mineola, N.Y.: Foundation, 1986), 25.

66. Ibid.

67. Ibid., 98.

68. "John Hinckley's Letter to Jodie Foster Written Immediately before Assassination," http://www.law.umkc.edu/faculty/projects/ftrials/hinckley/LETTER.HTM (accessed May 18, 2004).

69. Low, Jeffries, and Bonnie, *The Trial of John W. Hinckley, Jr.,* 45–46.

70. Ibid., 46–47.

71. Alston Chase, *Harvard and the Unabomber: The Education of an American Terrorist*, (New York: Norton, 2003), 62–63.

72. Albert Borowitz, *Blood and Ink: An International Guide to Fact-Based Crime Literature* (Kent, Ohio: Kent State Univ. Press, 2002), 281–82.

73. Chase, *Harvard and the Unabomber*, 89.

74. Theodore Kaczynski, "The Unabomber Manifesto," in John Douglas and Mark Olshaker, *Unabomber: On the Trail of America's Most-Wanted Serial Killer* (New York: Pocket Books, 1996), 191, 206.

75. Ibid., 221.

76. Ibid., 270.

77. Ibid., 197.

78. Ibid., 241–48.

79. Chase, *Harvard and the Unabomber*, 229.

80. Ibid., 304.

81. Ibid., 291.

82. Ibid., 337–38.

83. Ibid., 342.

84. Ibid., 342.

85. Ibid., 41.

86. Ibid., 352. In Chase's endnotes, the coded diary is identified as the source of the quoted entry. Ibid., 415.

87. Ibid., 329.

88. Ibid., 356.

89. Brooks Brown and Rob Merritt, *No Easy Answers: The Truth behind Death at Columbine* (New York: Lantern, 2002), 1–96.

90. *RockyMountainNews.com*, Oct. 4, 2002. http://www.rockymountainnews.com/drmn/columbine/article/O,1299,DRMN_106_1460306... (accessed Aug. 28, 2003; site discontinued).

91. Brown and Merritt, *No Easy Answers*, 4.

92. Jefferson County Colorado Sheriff, "The Columbine High School Shootings: Narrative Time Line of Events 11:10 A.M. to 11:59 A.M." http://denver.rockymountain news.com/shooting/report/columbinereport/pages/narrative_time.htm (accessed Aug. 28, 2003; site discontinued).

93. Jefferson County Colorado Sheriff, "The Columbine High School Shootings: Bomb Summary," http://denver.rockymountainnews.com/shooting/report/columbine report/pages/bombs_text.htm (accessed Aug. 28, 2003; site discontinued).

94. Brown and Merritt, *No Easy Answers*, 39.

95. Ibid., 20.

96. Ibid., 51, 121.

97. Ibid., 50–51.

98. Nancy Gibbs and Timothy Roche, "The Columbine Tapes," *Time* 154, no. 25 (Dec. 20, 1999): 42.

99. Ibid., 41–42.

100. Ibid., 42.

101. Ibid., 42.

102. David J. Krajicek, "Nobody Loves a Crime Reporter," http://www.cmsu.edu/cjinst/journal_articles_i2/5_Krajicek.pdf (accessed May 18, 2004).

5. Herostratos at the World Trade Center

1. André Glucksmann, *Dostoïevski à Manhattan* (Paris: Robert Laffont, 2002); Victor-Pierre Stirnimann, "The Terror and the Temple," in *Jungian Reflections on September 11: A Global Nightmare,* ed. Luigi Zoja and Donald Williams (Einsiedeln, Switz.: Daimon Verlag, 2002).

2. Peter Patti, "Chi?" ("Who?"), *Binario 1,* http://it.geocities.com/marilyn_3d/grattacieli2.htm (accessed May 17, 2004).

3. Open letter, posted Sept. 11, 2001, on "Have Theology Will Argue" bulletin board of www.ezboard.com (accessed Oct. 6, 2003).

4. Carlos Freymann, "It Is Best Not to Kick a Sleeping Giant," *San Antonio Business Journal,* October 22, 2001, http://sanantonio.bizjournals.com/sanantonio/stories/2001/10/22/editorial1.html (accessed Oct. 6, 2003).

5. "Da Antiguidade à Era Moderna, atentados refletem intolerância," *GloboNews .com,* September 20, 2001, http://globonews.globo.com/GloboNews/article/0,6993, A117090–915,00.html (accessed Oct. 6, 2003; site discontinued).

6. "Hildegarde," entry posted September 27, 2001, in "Attentats: quels changements en Suisse," bulletin board of *Largeur.com,* http://www.largeur.com/expDebat.asp?pagePos=2&debID=2366 (accessed May 20, 2004).

7. The two quotations I excerpted are from Natalia Starichkova, "Remedies against Terrorists, or How Will You Take It?" *Rosbalt News Agency,* November 1, 2001, http://www.rosbaltnews.com/2002/01/11/23901.html (accessed Oct. 20, 2003). I have made minor stylistic changes in the online English version.

8. Torsten Kleinz, "Wieviel Osama darf's sein?" *Telepolis,* December 21, 2001, http://www.heise.de/tp/deutsch/inhalt/co/11405/1.html (accessed Jan. 13, 2003).

9. Jean Daniel, "Leur Dieu a Soif" ("Their God Is Thirsty"), *Le Nouvel Observateur,* 1925, September 26, 2001, http://www.nouvelobs.com/evenement/daniel1.html (accessed May 20, 2004).

10. Pascal Ory, "Erostrate," *France Culture,* April 4, 2002, http://www.radiofrance.fr/chaines/france-culture2/premiere_.../fichebillet.php?diffusion_id=637 (accessed Oct. 6, 2003; site discontinued).

11. "Eróstrato, el avión de la Luna, a un año de su colisión" ("Herostratos, the Airplane of the Moon, One Year after Its Collision"), *Nexos,* student periodical of EAFIT University, http://www.eafit.edu.co/old_Edicion/107/erostrato.htm (accessed Apr. 19, 2003; site discontinued).

12. Jean Daniel, "Ce qui a changé dans la pensée" ("What Has Changed in Our Thinking"), *Le Nouvel Observateur* 2027, September 11, 2003, http://www.nouvelobs .com/dossiers/p2027/a214600.html (accessed Oct. 6, 2003).

13. Professor David Lupher and Alvar Minaya, e-mail messages posted March 7, 1999, under the caption "toppling towers & burning temples" in a mailing list maintained by the Ohio State University Classics Department, http://omega.cohums.ohio-state.edu/mailing_lists/CLA1999/03/0270.php (accessed May 20, 2004).

14. Professor David Lupher, e-mail message posted October 26, 2001, under the caption "Herostratos," in a mailing list maintained by the Ohio State University Classics Department, http://omega.cohums.ohio-state.edu/mailing_lists/CLA-L/2001/10/0523.php (accessed May 20, 2004).

15. Joe McCleskey, Web log entry, posted June 12, 2002, http://home.pacbell.net/jmcclesk/2002_06_09-archive.html (accessed Jan. 10, 2003; site discontinued). Qtd. by permission of Mr. McCleskey.

16. Fyodor Dostoevsky, *Demons,* trans. Richard Pevear and Larissa Volokhonsky, intro. Joseph Frank (New York: Everyman's Library, 2000).

17. Glucksmann, *Dostoïevski à Manhattan,* 14.

18. Ibid., 23–24.

19. Ibid., 31.

20. Ibid., 24.

21. Ibid., 111–12.

22. Ibid., 121.

23. Ibid., 121, 26. In his later book, *Ouest contre Ouest (West against West)* (Paris, Plon: 2003), Glucksmann argues passionately that since the end of the Cold War, Europe's enemy is not the United States but nihilism. He notes that well before the "human bombs," the "possessed of Sade and Dostoyevsky made it a point of honor not to distinguish between the joy of destruction and the joy of being destroyed." Ibid., 106.

24. Glucksmann, *Dostoïevski à Manhattan,* 43, 91.

25. Ibid., 245–46.

26. Ibid., 259.

27. Ibid., 126.

28. John Fraim, "A New Extraversion in Analytical Psychology?" http://www.cgjungpage.org/content/view/439/28/ (accessed May 20, 2004).

29. Robert Hinshaw, preface to *Jungian Reflections on September 11,* ed. Zoja and Williams, 10.

30. Stirnimann, "The Terror and the Temple," in *Jungian Reflections on September 11,* ed. Zoja and Williams, 87, 90.

31. Ibid., 91.

32. Ibid.

33. Ibid., 91–92.

34. Ibid., 92.

35. Ibid., 92–93.

36. Ibid., 93–94.

37. Ibid., 96–101.

38. Ibid., 103.

39. Ibid., 103, 105.

6. The Literature of Herostratos Since the Early Nineteenth Century

1. Alessandro Verri, *La Vita di Erostrato,* 2d ed. (Milan, Ital.: La Vita Felice, 2000).

2. Gianfranco Dioguardi, *Attualità dell'Illuminismo milanese: Pietro Verri e Cesare Beccaria* (Palermo, Ital.: Sellerio, 1998), 28.

3. Verri, *La Vita di Erostrato*, 14.

4. Ibid., 134.

5. Ibid., 78–79.

6. Ibid., 92–93.

7. Ibid., 120.

8. Ibid., 121.

9. Ibid., 131–32.

10. Marcel Schwob, *Vies imaginaires* (Paris: Gallimard, 1957), 11.

11. Ibid., 31–32.

12. Ibid., 33. Like Schwob, the Italian jurist Bruno Cassinelli, in an imagined defense speech for Herostratus, couples him with the Ephesian philosopher Heraclitus:

> Unknowingly Herostratos reaffirms and confirms Heraclitus: everything changes, it is true, and from the glory of a dead and desiccated temple the soul of a new kind of hero takes pride. . . . I ask you, what difference do you draw between Herostratos, destroyer of marble and mosaics, and a philosopher who completely destroys a moral and spiritual world.

Bruno Cassinelli, *Io Defendo* (Milan, Ital.: "Corbaccio" dall'Oglio, 1951), 17–18.

13. Jean-Paul Sartre, "Erostratus," in *The Wall and Other Stories*, trans. Lloyd Alexander (New York: New Directions, 1948), 81–104.

14. Ibid., 91–92.

15. André Billy, *L'Assassinat d'Alain Guyader* (Paris: Flammarion, 1951), 9.

16. Alain Nadaud, *La Mémoire d'Érostrate* (Paris: Éditions du Seuil, 1992).

17. Ibid., 22.

18. Ibid., 16.

19. Ibid., 209–12. In positing the influence of Heraclitus on Herostratos's crime, Nadaud appears to echo Marcel Schwob's "imaginary life" of the incendiary.

20. Jerzy Limon, "Der Herostrat von der Bierutstrasse," in *Ansichten: Jahrbuch des Deutschen Polen-Instituts* 12 (2001): 130–45.

21. Ibid., 139.

22. Ibid., 141.

23. Umberto Eco, *Foucault's Pendulum*, trans. William Weaver (San Diego, Calif.: Harcourt Brace Jovanovich, 1989), 618–19.

24. Stephen Lemons, "Remembering Dec. 8, 1980," http://dir.salon.com/people/feature/2000/12/08/lennon_remembered/index.html (accessed May 20, 2004). Joan Tewkesbury's early drafts of the *Nashville* screenplay borrowed heavily from the 1973 murders of a Grand Ole Opry banjo player, David "Stringbean" Akeman, and his wife by intruders seeking cash hidden in their home. Jan Stuart, *The Nashville Chronicles: The Making of Robert Altman's Masterpiece* (New York: Limelight, 2003), 20–21, 59, 78; Warren B. Causey, *The Stringbean Murders* (Nashville, Tenn.: Quest, 1975).

25. Eco, *Foucault's Pendulum*, 619.

26. Terenci Moix, *Chulas y famosas, o bien, La venganza de Eróstrato* (Barcelona, Spain: Círculo de Lectores, 1999).

27. Ibid., 405.

28. Ibid., 410.

29. "-ky" (pseudonym of Horst Bosetzky), "Herostratos kannst du dann vergessen," in school crimes short-story anthology, *Der Mörder Schwänzt den Unterricht* (*The Murderer Plays Hooky*), ed. Leo P. Ard (pseudonym of Jürgen Pomorin) (Dortmund, Ger.: Grafit Verlag, 1994), 31–35.

30. Philippe Arnaud, *La boîte à chagrins: Une enquête du Président Bertin* (Marseilles, France: L'Écailler du Sud, 2002), 22.

Brief allusions are made to Herostratos in short stories by Anton Chekhov and Hans Christian Andersen. In Chekhov's "Fat and Thin" (1883), two middle-aged men who were schoolmates in their youth meet by chance at a railroad station. The thin man reminds his comrade, now grown quite fat, how he was teased in class with the nickname Herostratos "because you burned a hole in a schoolbook with a cigarette." *Early Stories, 1883–1886,* trans. Constance Garnett (New York: Modern Library, 1999), 15. The Councillor in Andersen's tale "The Shoes of Fortune" heaps abuse on the "rascally English" because their attack on the Danish fleet off Copenhagen during the Napoleonic Wars "still floated vividly" before his eyes as "the Herostratic event of 1801." Hans Christian Andersen, "The Shoes of Fortune," http://www.classicbook shelf.com/library/hans_christian_andersen/andersen_s_fairy_tales/3/.

Herostratos even turns up unexpectedly in children's fiction. In *Der Geist der Llano estakata* (*The Spirit of the Stockaded Plain*), a novel of the American West by Karl May for an illustrated German boys' periodical in 1888, Hobble-Frank, a master of hilarious malapropisms, confuses Herostratos with King Herod's wife, Herodias. The circumstances of Herostratos's crime also emerge in bizarre distortions from Frank's unstable memory:

> Herodias was that Mexican scoundrel who in the famous port city of Ephorus burned the summer villa of the goddess Diana, to be precise, only on the valid ground that his name should be whispered by sounding brass to posterity.

http://www.karl-may-stiftung.de/kamerad/geist/llano18.html (accessed May 28, 2004).

31. George Gordon, Lord Byron, "The Curse of Minerva," in *The Poetical Works of Lord Byron* (London: Oxford Univ. Press, 1945), 142–45. For an account of Byron's antipathy to Lord Elgin, see Theodore Vrettos, *The Elgin Affair: The Abduction of Antiquity's Greatest Treasures and the Passions It Aroused* (New York: Arcade, 1997).

32. Victor Hugo, "Un Chant de fête de Néron," *Odes,* bk. 4, ode 15, in *Odes et ballades; les orientales* (Paris: Garnier/Flammarion, 1968), 181–83.

33. Hugo, "Ce que Dit la Bouche d'Ombre," *Les Contemplations,* bk. 6, no. 26 (Paris: Livre de Poche, 1965), 462–87. The reference to Herostratos and Nero is on 472.

34. Hugo, "Quelques Mots à un Autre," *Les Contemplations,* bk. 1, no. 26, 73–77. The allusion to Herostratos and his rivals in violence is on 75.

35. [Xavier] Labensky, *Érostrate (1840),* in facsimile ed., *Poésies; Empédocle; Érostrate* (Geneva, Switz.: Slatkine Reprints, 1973).

36. Eugène Asse, *Les Petits Romantiques* [1900], facsimile ed. (Geneva, Switz.: Slatkine Reprints, 1968), 45–56.

37. Labensky, *Érostrate,* v–xii.

38. Ibid., 196.

39. Gustave Flaubert, *The Temptation of St. Anthony,* trans. Lafcadio Hearn (Garden City, N.Y.: Halcyon House, n.d.).

40. Ibid., 167–68.

41. Friedrich Nietzsche, *Human, All Too Human,* trans. R. J. Hollingdale (Cambridge, U.K.: Cambridge Univ. Press, 1996), 228 (vol. 2, pt. 1, no. 66).

A contemporary Belgian poet has eroticized the Herostratic act. Willem M. Roggeman, "Érostrate," trans. Evelyn Wilwerth into French from Flemish (Marseilles, France: Autres Temps, 2000). A lover addresses his mistress:

> Between the columns
> of your temple
> I bring tender ravages.
> I nibble gently
> at your lower lip
> and find the word Ephesus
> on your tongue.

Herostratos performs a thematic function in a collection of Finnish poems. Ulf-Erik Qvickström, *Herostratos* (Porvoo, Fin.: Werner Söderstrom Osakeyhtiö, 1975). The epigraph invokes the figure of the eponymous destroyer:

> Awake Herostratos,
> the candelabra have been lit!
> The splendid flight of blue flames!
> Sweet bonfires of heretics!
> The unique harmony of smoking villages!
> To our time, to our time!

Herostratos puts the poet in mind of two famous American criminals. In "Machinegun-Kelly," (included in a section entitled "Terror"), a wounded man climbs up to an attic and observes his pursuers, commenting enigmatically, "Don't look back. It's easy. You are there already." A poem called "Harry Longbaugh (Sundance Kid)" is a prisoner's reminiscence of the day when at age twelve he stole a horse and began his criminal career: "That day in Sundance," he muses, "I realized my type; me and Wyoming, / one desolate land." I thank Markku Salmela for the translations of the quoted passages.

42. Alexander Pushkin, "Mozart and Salieri," in *The Poems, Prose, and Plays of Alexander Pushkin,* ed. Avrahm Yarmolinsky (New York: Modern Library, 1936), 428–37.

43. Ibid., 430.

44. Ibid., 435–36.

45. Peter Shaffer, *Amadeus,* 1st American ed. (New York: Harper and Row, 1981), 94.

46. Kerry Sabbag, "Cain and Herostratus: Reappropriation of Mozart Myths," paper read in program of American Association of Teachers of Slavic and Eastern European Languages, New York City, Dec. 30, 2002.

47. N. M. Yazykov, "K Khalatu/To My Dressing Gown," bilingual text of the poem, http://max.mmlc.northwestern.edu/~mdenner/Demo/ . . . /dressing_gown.htm (ac-

cessed Jan. 9, 2003; site discontinued). Pushkin refers to "inspired Yazykov" in *Eugene Onegin,* chap. 4, stanza 31.

48. T. J. Binyon, *Pushkin: A Biography* (New York: Knopf, 2003), 56.

49. Grigory Gorin, *Forget Herostratus!* in *Stars in the Morning Sky: Five New Plays From the Soviet Union,* intro. Michael Glenny (London: Nick Hern, 1989). A Hungarian-born film director, Géza von Cziffra, has purported to identify a historical link between Herostratic influence and the burning of the Reichstag. Cziffra claims that a clairvoyant, Erik Jan Hanussen, tried to ingratiate himself with the Nazis by issuing hypnotic commands to the Reichstag arsonist, Dutch communist Marinus van der Lubbe. According to Cziffra's highly fictionalized biography of Hanussen (first published in 1978), the psychic's scheme was inspired by a tragicomedy about Herostratos that he read in his youth. Géza von Cziffra, *Hanussen, Hellseher des Teufels* (*The Devil's Clairvoyant*) (Munich, Ger.: Knaur, n.d.), 26–29.

50. Gorin, *Forget Herostratus!* 219.

51. Ibid.

52. Ibid., 242.

53. Ibid., 247.

54. *Der Grosse Duden Fremdwörterbuch,* vol. 5 (Mannheim, Ger.: Bibliographisches Institut, 1996), 271.

55. Ludwig Fulda, *Herostrat* (Stuttgart, Ger.: J. G. Cotta'sche Buchhandlung Nachfolger, 1899).

56. Ibid., 133.

57. Ibid., 150–51.

58. Hugo Sonnenschein, *Ichgott, Massenrausch und Ohnmacht* (poems); and *Die Utopie des Herostrat* (one-act play) (Vienna, Aus.: Genossenschaftsverlag, 1910).

59. Sonnenschein, *Die Utopie des Herostrat,* 106.

60. Georg Heym, "Der Wahnsinn des Herostrat," http://gutenberg.spiegel.de/heym/gedichte/Druckversion_herostra.htm (accessed May 28, 2004).

61. Wolfgang Bauer, "Herostratos," in *Die Sumpftänzer: Dramen, Prosa, Lyrik aus zwei Jahrzehnten* (Cologne, Ger.: Kiepenheuer and Witsch, 1978).

62. Carl Ceiss, *Herostratos: Kammerspiel* (1982–1986), unpublished typescript furnished by the author; performance rights controlled by Virtueller Dramen Verlag, Berlin.

63. Lutz Hübner, *Herzmündung: Die Ballade von Herostratos Chapman,* typescript (Cologne, Ger.: Hartmann and Stauffacher, 1998).

64. Ibid., 70.

65. Ibid., 75. Two nineteenth-century French opera composers have set libretti based on variants of the Herostratos theme. A two-act opera, *Érostrate,* by Ernest Reyer (born Louis Étienne Ernest Rey) was performed at Baden-Baden in the summer of 1862 and at the Paris Opera ten years later. "[Jules] Méry, who wrote Reyer's book, makes Erostrate commit arson to win the courtesan Athenaïs who, content with what he has done for her sake, leaps with him into the flames." Frederick H. Martens, *A Thousand and One Nights of Opera* (New York: Appleton, 1926), 68. Jacques-François-Fromental-Élie Halévy (born Levy), composer of *La Juive,* left an incomplete score for an opera *Érostrate* (which dates from around 1825).

66. Jean François de Guise, *Der Fall Herostratos* (Aken/Elbe, Ger.: Lothringer Verlag für Bühne und Musik, 2003).

67. Nazli Eray, *Herostratus* (1979), trans. Sebnem Bahadir. I thank Ms. Eray and Dr. Suha Oguzertem for procuring a revised 2004 version of the English translation.

68. Nazli Eray, e-mail, dated January 25, 2004. Eray also advises that "no other Turkish writer has written about Herostratus."

69. Nazli Eray, e-mail, dated January 25, 2004.

70. *Pequeño Larousse Ilustrado* (Buenos Aires, Arg.: Editorial BABEL, 1943), 374, 1188.

71. Miguel de Unamuno, *Tragic Sense of Life* (1913), trans. J. E. Crawford Flitch (New York: Dover, 1954); Miguel de Unamuno, *Vida de Don Quijote y Sancho* (1905), 3d ed., ed. Alberto Navarro (Madrid, Spain: Ediciones Cátedra, 1998).

72. Unamuno, *Tragic Sense of Life,* 52. Film director Martin Scorsese espoused a similar theory in an interview conducted by his collaborator on *Taxi Driver,* screenwriter Paul Schrader, on January 29, 1982, for *Cahiers du Cinéma:* "The thing about being remembered is that it replaces fate and the salvation of the soul. How could you replace that? You can't." Paul Schrader, *Taxi Driver,* introduction (London: Faber and Faber, 1990), xiii.

73. Unamuno, *Tragic Sense of Life,* 53–54.

74. Ibid., 55.

75. Ibid., 55–56.

76. Ibid., 56–57.

77. Qtd. by Richard Zenith in his introduction to Fernando Pessoa, *Heróstrato e A Busca da Imortalidade (Erostratus and the Search for Immortality)*, trans. Manuela Rocha from English into Portuguese and including original English text (Lisbon, Spain: Assírio and Alvim, 2000), 25.

78. Thomas Carlyle, *Sartor Resartus*, Oxford World's Classics (New York: Oxford Univ. Press, 1987), bk. 1, chap. 7.

79. Pessoa, *Heróstrato,* 142–43.

80. Lev Shestov, "Destroying and Building," in *Potestas Clavium,* trans. and intro. Bernard Martin (Athens: Ohio Univ. Press, 1968), 39–42.

81. James Bowman, "From Heroes to Herostratus," an address to the Friends of *The New Criterion,* New York, Apr. 18, 2001, http://jamesbowman.net/articleDetail. asp?pubID=456 (accessed May 18, 2004).

82. David Brin, "Names That Live in Infamy," *salon.com Media* (Aug. 13, 1999), http://www.salon.com/media/feature/1999/08/13/nameless/print.html (accessed May 18, 2004).

83. Eric Gans, "Herostratus Forever," in *Chronicles of Love and Resentment,* no. 87 (Apr. 5, 1997), http://www.anthropoetics.ucla.edu/views/view87.htm (accessed May 18, 2004).

84. Gans, "Herostratus Revisited," in *Chronicles of Love and Resentment* no. 177 (Aug. 7, 1999), http://www.anthropoetics.ucla.edu/views/vw177.htm (accessed May 18, 2004).

In Europe it is a centuries-old fashion in political journalism to invoke Herostratos as an apt parallel to writers and opposition figures who irresponsibly attack governmental leaders regardless of the harm that may ensue to their country. A polemical journalist, Maximilian Harden, after charging that Kaiser Wilhelm II was surrounded by a kitchen cabinet of homosexuals, was denounced as a "disciple of Herostratos," who was willing to bring Germany to ruin in the interest of personal notoriety. Maximilian Jacta, *Accusé levez-vous: Procès Célèbres d'Allemagne,* trans. Denis Simon (Verviers, Bel.: Editions Gerard, 1967), 53. References to Herostratos have been made in connection with political controversies in Ukraine and Poland. Mykola Neseniuk, "The Herostratos Effect," from the archives of Ukrainian newspaper, *The Day,* http://day.kiev.ua/DIGEST/2001/01/1-page/1p4.htm (accessed Apr. 19, 2003); Slawomir Majman, "Remembering Herostratos," *Warsaw Voice,* Aug. 6, 2000, http://www.warsaw voice.pl/old/v615/Viewpoint00.html (accessed Apr. 19, 2003).

Index

Aelian (Claudius Aelianus): *On the Char-
    acteristics of Animals,* 7, 10
afterlife. *See* immortality: quest for
Agitatore, 74
Akeman, David "Stringbean," 178n24
Alexander I (tsar of Russia), 142
Alexander the Great: ambition of, 6–7, 23,
    31, 69, 121–22; birth of, simultaneous
    with Herostratos's crime, 4–5, 8, 11–14,
    124; in literature, 23–24, 150, 154–55
al-Qaeda, xvii, 111
Allen, Danielle S., 16–17
Altman, Robert, 133, 178n24
anarchists and anarchism, 37–49, 72–76,
    100, 129, 169n2, 170n23
Andersen, Hans Christian: "The Shoes of
    Fortune," 179n30
Anderson, Jack, 92–93
Anderson, Robert, 42
Annan, Kofi, 67
Apollo, 2, 19
Arima Raitei, 63
Arnaud, Philippe: *La boîte à chagrins,* 135
arson and arsonists, 62–63, 116, 118, 121,
    123, 128, 132–33, 146; and bed-wetting
    and ambition, 12–13; in Istanbul,
    Taksim Square, 151. *See also* Hayashi;
    Herostratos, burning the Artemision;
    Reichstag fire, the

Artemis, the goddess, 1, 4, 11, 115, 121, 136,
    163n8; as Diana, 2, 5, 18, 146; in litera-
    ture, 127, 131–32, 144, 146–48, 163–64n8.
    See also Temple of Artemis
    (Artemision)
Artemision. *See* Temple of Artemis
    (Artemision)
Ashikaga Yoshimitsu, 51–52
Ashcroft, John, 156
assassins and assassinations, 19, 71–84, 133,
    142, 148, 166n2, 169n2; American politi-
    cal, 84–99; Pausanius, 7, 33
Assassins, musical, xix, 93
Asse, Eugène, 137
Associated Press, 68, 105. *See also* media
Athena Pronaia, 19
Athens, 15–16, 22, 30–31
Atlanta Constitution, 90
Atta, Mohamed, 118
Aubrey's *Brief Lives,* 126–27
Augstein, Rudolf: "Herostratus in Dallas," 85
Aulus Gellius, 18, 164n20
autobiographical records by criminals, 71;
    bin Laden video, xvii, 116; Bremer di-
    ary, 87–90, 99, 174n43; Byck tapes, 92–
    93, 99; Columbine and videos, 108–9;
    Hinckley letter to Jodie Foster, 96–97,
    99; Lucheni memoir and postcard, 75,
    78–79, 173n8; *Mein Kampf,* and

Herostratos prison memoirs, 142;
Unabomber writings, 101–5
Autonomie Club, 40, 42

Baltimore-Washington Airport, 90–93
Bamiyan statues. *See* Giant Buddhas
Bammer, Anton, 5
ban on memory, 4, 6–7, 16–19, 128, 131, 142.
See also damnatio memoriae
Bartlett, John: *Familiar Quotations,* 31, 32
Bauer, Wolfgang: "Herostatos," 146–47
Becket, Thomas, 21, 166n2
Bengston, Hermann, 11
Bernstein, Leonard, 92–94
Berry, Duke of, 142
Bevington, Louis Sarah, 44–45
Billy, André, 130
bin Laden, Osama, xvii, 69, 114–16
Blankenship, Jessica, 80–81
Bloom, Richard, 84
bombs and bombings, 37–49, 100–105, 118
Bosetzky, Horst ("-ky"): "You Can Then
Forget Herostratos," 134–35
Bourdin, Martial, 38–43, 45, 170n20
Bowman, James: "From Heroes to
Herostratus," 155–56
Bowra, C. M., 9
Bremer, Arthur Herman, 85–90, 99, 174n43
Brin, David: "Names That Live in Infamy,"
156–57
Brown, Brooks, 105–8
Browne, Thomas: *Urn Burial,* 29–30, 32,
153, 168n19
Bucqueroux, Bonnie, 110
Buddhas. *See* Giant Buddhas
bullying, 56, 61–62, 79, 107
Burckhardt, Jacob, 23
Byck, Samuel, 85–86, 90–94, 99
Byron, Lord: "The Curse of Minerva," 136

Caesar, Julius, 1, 22–24
Caffè, Il, 123
Caligula, 116
Camões, Luís Vaz de, 27
Cappon, Santo, 78–79
Carlyle, Thomas, 123; *Sartor Resartus,* 153
Carneal, Michael, 108
Carter, Dan T., 87
Carter, President Jimmy, 96, 99

Case, John, 167n4
Cassinelli, Bruno, 178n12
Catcher in the Rye (J. D. Salinger), 80, 81,
83, 84, 148
Ceiss, Carl: *Herostratos,* 147–48
Cervantes, Miguel de, 25–26
Chapman, Gloria, 79, 81, 82
Chapman, Mark David, 79–84, 99, 133, 148,
156
Chase, Alston: *Harvard and the
Unabomber,* 100–105
Chaucer, Geoffrey, 22, 167nn6–7
Chekhov, Anton: "Fat and Thin," 179n30
Chersiphron, 4, 32
Cibber, Colley, 31–32
Cicero: *On the Nature of the Gods,* 5–6, 11,
19, 21, 24, 167n4
Clarke, James W., 84–86, 89–90, 94–95, 99
Clausewitz: dictum of, 117–18
Cloots, Anacharsis, 119
Columbine High School, 99, 105–10, 158
Commonweal, 38, 40, 41, 42, 44
Communist Manifesto, the, 119
Conrad, Joseph: *The Secret Agent,* 37, 45–49,
100
Cook, Alex, 53
copycat crimes, 60–61, 133
Cotta, Aurelius, 18
Covarrubias Orozco, Sebastián de:
Emblemas Morales, 27–29
crime journalism, 109–10, 135
cultural cannibalism, 68–69
curses, religious, 18, 19
Cybele, 3
Cziffra, Géza von, 181n49

Dalai Lama, the, 67
damnatio memoriae, 16–19, 62–63, 142, 156–
57, 164n20. *See also* ban on memory
Daniel, Jean, 115–16
de Guise, Jean-François: *Der Fall
Herostratos,* 148–49
De Montebello, Philippe, 67
Decamps, Henri-Louis-Charles, 37
Delany, Sheila, 23
Delphi, temple at, 19
Demetrius of Phalerum, 30, 31
destruction, 116, 177n23; by nature, 154–55
Diagoras, 7

Diderot, Denis: *Encyclopedia,* 124
Dietz, Park Elliott, 97–98
Dionysius of Halicarnassus, 17
Don Marzio, 73–74
Don Quixote, 25–26, 151, 152
Dostoyevsky, Fyodor Mikhailovich, 117–20
Dowling, Scott, 13
Drakulic, Slacvenka, 65–66
duBois, Page, 14–15
Dwyer, Jean, 92

Eco, Umberto: *Foucault's Pendulum,* 133–34
Egami Taizan, 61, 63
Ehrlichman, John D., 90
Ekenberg, Martin, 101, 103
Elgin, Lord, 136
Eliot, Georges: *Daniel Deronda,* 164n8
Elisabeth of Austria, Empress, 72–79
emblem books, 27
Enlightenment, the, 123
Enryaku Temple, 60
envy, as motive for terrorism, 10, 25, 152
Ephesus, 2, 111, 121; inhabitants of, 114, 120;
     in literature, 131–32, 138, 146–50,
     180n41; museum, 3–4
Epstein, Charles J., 104
Eray, Nazli: *Herostratus,* 149–51
Erdemgil, Selahattin, 3–4
existentialism, 128, 130
expressionism, 136, 145–46

fame, 4, 16, 32, 34–35, 84–86, 143, 151, 155–56;
     crime in pursuit of, 41, 69, 82, 88–89, 92–
     93, 96–98, 100, 105, 108–9, 159, 168n13;
     desire for, 6–11, 71–72, 77, 117, 126; in lit-
     erature, 20–27, 29, 131, 152–53. *See also*
     ban on memory; *damnatio memoriae*
Fawcett, Anthony: *John Lennon: One Day
     at a Time,* 81, 83
Federal Bureau of Investigation, 104–5,
     108–9, 156
Fielding, Henry: *Joseph Andrews,* 31
Figaro, Le, 73
Flaubert, Gustave: *The Temptation of
     Saint Anthony,* 139–40
Fontenelle, Bernard Le Bovier de, 30, 138
Forel, Auguste, 76
Foster, Jodie, 85, 95–97
Fraim, John, 120
France Culture, 115

Franch, Santiago Salvador, 37
Freud, Sigmund, 11–12
Freymann, Carlos, 113
Fujii Hidetada, 57
Fulda, Ludwig: *Herostrat,* 144–45

Gans, Eric: "Herostratus Forever," 157–58
Garesh, Paul, 83
Garrick, David, 32
Gautier, Alfred, 76
Gelernter, David, 104
Giant Buddhas, Bamiyan, Afghanistan, 37,
     66–70, 121
Gibbs, Nancy, 108
Gill, John, 167n4
Girard, René, 157
Giuliani, Rudy, 114
Globe, the, 44
Glucksmann, André, 111, 117–20, 177n23
Golden Pavilion. *See* Temple of the
     Golden Pavilion (Kinkakuji), Kyoto
Goldstein, Renée, 92
Goldstein, Naomi, 83
Gorin, Grigory. *See* Ofshtein, Grigory
Gorish, Paul. 83
Goupil, Romain, 117
Goutrat, Maître, 130
Greene, Robert, 33
Greenwich Observatory, London, 37–49
Greville, Fulke, 168n19
Grimmelshausen, Jakob Christoffel von,
     168n19
Grozny, Chechen capital, 118
Guyader family, 130

Hajruddin, Mimar, 64
Haldeman, H. R., 90
Halévy, Jacques-François-Fromental-Élie:
     Érostrate, 181n65
Hamann, Brigitte, 78
Hanussen, Erik Jan, 181n49
Harden, Maximilian, 182n84
Harmon, A. M., 18
Harris, Eric, 105–9
Harvey, Gabriel, 33
hate-crime perpetrators, 156
"Have Theology Will Argue" (Web bulle-
     tin board), 112–13
Hayashi Yoken, 49–63, 99, 171n38
Hearst, Patricia, 90, 93

Henry, Émile, 38
Henry II of England, King, 21
Heraclitus, 127–28, 132, 178n12
Hermocles, 7
"heroic outlook" of ancient Greeks, 9
Herodes, 15
Herostratos, 12, 18, 36, 72, 99, 123–24, 141;
    ban on memory of, 18, 24, 114; burning
    the Artemision, 4–5, 8, 11–14, 17, 113;
    confession of, 7, 14–16; and fame, 34,
    70, 77–78, 120–21; in Greek and Roman
    literature, 5–19; in literature from
    Middle Ages to eighteenth century,
    20–35, 151; motives, 9–11, 16, 100, 115,
    122; name, 1–2, 20, 32, 143, 151, 182n84;
    and World Trade Center, 118–19; on
    World Wide Web, 112–14, 116–17
Herostratos in post–eighteenth century:
    art, 160; fiction, 14, 123–35; film, 86, 95,
    96, 133, 161, 178n24; nonfiction, 151–58;
    poetry and drama, 135–51
Herostratos syndrome, xii–xiv, 71, 84–85,
    108–9, 113–14, 133–34, 136, 158
Herz, Rudolf, 160
Hesse, Raymond, 71–72
Heya Teruko, 56, 62
Heym, Georg: Der Wahnsinn des
    Herostrat, 145–46
Hier, Marvin, 156
Higginbotham, James, 113
Hinckley, Jack, 94, 95
Hinckley, Jo Ann (Jodie), 94
Hinckley, John, Jr., 85–86, 94–99
Hitler, Adolf, 108, 114, 142
Hogarth, William, 169n24
Hokusai prints, 126–27
Holland, Norman N., 12–13
Holstlaw, Mark, 108, 109
Homeric hymn in honor of Artemis, 2, 155
Horyuji Temple, 50, 60, 61
Huber, Stephan, 160
Hübner, Lutz: The Orifice of the Heart: The
    Ballad of Herostratos Chapman, 148
Hugo, Victor, 136–37

iconic buildings and structures attacked.
    See Giant Buddhas, Bamiyan, Afghani-
    stan; Greenwich Observatory, London;
    Reichstag, the; Stari Most (Old Bridge),
    Mostar, Bosnia-Herzegovina; Temple of

Artemis (Artemision); Temple of the
    Golden Pavilion (Kinkakuji), Kyoto;
    World Trade Center, the
identicide, 68–69
ideology, 111, 119
immortality: quest for, 13, 115, 119, 122, 126,
    152–54
Ionia, 4, 18
Irving, H. B., 38
Irving, Henry, 32
Islam, 64, 66, 68–70, 119, 122

Jacobin Club, France, 119
Jamal, Qudratullah, 68
Jefferson, Thomas, 33–34
Jews, Sephardic, 64
John of Salisbury, 20–22, 166n2, 167n7
Johnson, Sally, 102
Jones, Jack, 79–82, 84
Journal de Genève, 73
Jungian analysis of terrorism, 120–22
Jupiter, temple of, 17
"just world" phenomenon, xv

Kabuki Glossary, 60
Kaczynski, Ted (Unabomber), 99–105, 109,
    156
Karimov, A., 69–70
Kean, Edmund, 32
Keene, Donald, 53, 63
Kemble, John Philip, 32
Kennedy, Edward, 94
Kennedy, Robert F., 88
King, William, 33
Kinkakuji. See Temple of the Golden Pa-
    vilion (Kinkakuji), Kyoto
Kinkel, Kip, 108
Klebold, Dylan, 105–9
Kleinz, Torsten, 114
Kochar, Rouben, 161
Kotzebue, August von, 142
Krajicek, David J., 109–10
Krüger, Answald, 75
"-ky." See Bosetzky, Horst ("-ky")
Kyoto Shinbun, 59, 61

Labensky, Count Xavier (Polonius):
    Érostrate, 135–39
Lafrance, Pierre, 67
Laqueur, Walter, xiv–xv, xviii

Largeur.com, 113–14
Lehnerer, Thomas, 160
Lemay, Harding, 88
Lemprière, John, 32–33
Lennon, John, 79–84, 95–96, 133, 148
Lennon, Sean, 82–83
Leto, the Titaness, 2
Levy, Don, 161
Libo Drusus, 17–18
Liceo Theatre, Barcelona, 37, 40
Limon, Jerzy: "The Herostratos of Bierut Street," 132–33
Lindbergh, Charles, 129
Livy, 17
Lombroso, Cesare, 76
London Times, 37, 38
Louvel, Jean-Pierre, 142
Lubbe, Marinus van der, 181n49
Luccheni, Louise, 74
Luce, Henry, 114
Lucheni, Luigi, 73–79, 99, 173n8
Lucian: *The Passing of Peregrinus,* 8–10, 20, 30
Lupher, David, 116

Machiavelli, Niccolò, 23
Macready, William Charles, 32
Maidment, K. J., 15
Majendie, Vivian, 40, 43–44
Manlius, Marcus, 17
Margalit, Avishai: "The Suicide Bombers," xvii
Marprelate, Martin, 33
Marshall, Arthur, 89, 90
martyrs, xvii, 109, 122
Matray, Maria, 75
Matsuura, Koichiro, 67
May, Karl: *Der Geist der Llano estakata,* 179n30
McCleskey, Joe, 117
McFarland, Michael, 79–80
McVeigh, Timothy, 104, 109, 156
media, the, 85, 98–99, 109–10, 114, 159; coverage of terrorism, xvi–xvii, 114–15
Meharg, Sarah Jane, 64–65, 68
Melville, Chief Inspector, 42
Merritt, Rob, 106
Midas of Lydia, King, 4
Minaya, Alvar, 116
Minerva (Pallas Athena), 136

Mishima, Yukio, 57–58, 60–62, 171n45
Miura Momoshige, 54–57
Mizukami Tsutomo, 53–56, 63
Mizushima Keiji, 63
Moix, Terenci: *Chulas y famosas, o bien, La venganza de Eróstrato,* 134
Monde, Le, 117
Montaigne, Michel de, 23–24
Moriaud, Pierre, 76
Morning Leader, 41
Morris, Ivan, 63
Mozart. *See* Salieri and Mozart
Murakami Jikai, 52, 55, 57
Murphy, Reg., 90
Murray, Judith Sargent, 34–35
Murray, Gilbert, 104, 105
Murray, Henry A., 102
Muslims, 29, 64–65
Muss, Ulrike, 5
Mustakallio, Katariina, 17
Mutawakil, Wakil Ahmad, 67

Nadaud, Alain: *La Mémoire d'Érostrate,* 130–32
naming, in Greece, 1–2
Napoleon, 124, 126, 169n2
Napolean III, 169n2
narcissistic personality disorder, 84, 97–98
Nashville (Altman), 133, 178n24
National Enquirer, 114–15
Navazza, Georges, 76, 79, 173n8
neo-Classicism, 136
Nero, 116, 136
New York Herald, 73
New York Times, 87, 104
Nexos, 115
Nicoll, David, 40, 42–45
nihilism, 117, 119–20, 145, 177n23
Nittner, Tomas, 160
Nixon, President, 88, 90–91, 93, 99
Nose Masayo, 62–63
Nouvel Observateur, Le, 115–16

Ofshtein, Grigory: *Forget Herostratus!* 142–43
Okakura, Tenshin, 49
Oklahoma City bombing, 104, 122
Oliver, Hermia, 40, 43–44
Omar, Mullah Mohammed, 66–67, 69
Ono, Yoko, 83

Orrery, the, 34–35
Ory, Pascal, 115
Osborne, Mack, 85
Oshichi, 60
Oswald, Lee Harvey, 85
Özkan, Suha, 65–66

Pallas Athena, 136
Pan, 150–51
Paris (France), 37–38, 169n2
Pasic, Amir, 64
Parker, R. B., 24
Parthenon, the, 4
Patti, Peter: *Binario 1,* 111–12
Pausanius, 7, 33
Peloponnesian War, 6, 15–16
Pentagon, the, 111
Penthouse, 104
Peregrinus, 8, 165n23
Pessoa, Fernando: *Erostratus and the
    Search for Immortality,* 153–54
Philip of Macedon, King, 6–7, 21, 33, 92
Philo of Byzantium, 3
Plato, 155
Playwrights Horizon, New York City, 93
Pliny the Elder, 4
Plutarch: "Life of Alexander," 6, 11, 16, 19,
    24, 32
Polonius, Jean. *See* Labensky, Count Xavier
Pompeius Trogus, 24
Pope, Alexander: *The Dunciad,* 31
Poseidon, 18
Posner, Gerald, 85
Pound, Ezra, 31
Prescott, Anne Worthington, 22
Presley, Elvis, 114
Prometheus myth, 12
Pushkin, Alexander, 140, 142, 155

Quail, John, 37, 41, 44
Qvickström, Erik: *Herostratos,* 180n41

Rabin, Yitzhak, 114
Ravachol (François-Claudius
    Koeningstein), 37
Reagan, Ronald, 94, 96, 99
Reichstag fire, the, 142, 181n49
Renaissance, the, 23, 33
resentment, 157–58
revenge, 102–3, 105, 108, 114

Reyer, Ernest: *Érostrate,* 181n65
Ribbans, Geoffrey, 25–26
Roche, Timothy, 108
Roggeman, Willem M.: "Érostrate," 180n41
Romer, John and Elizabeth, 5
Rosbalt News Agency, Russia, 114
Ross, Nancy Wilson, 53, 63
Rothschild, Baroness Julia, 72
Rudolf, Crown Prince, 72
Ruiz de Alarcón y Mendoza, Juan, 26–27
Rushdie, Salman, 19
Ruyter, Lisa, 160

sacrilege, 9, 10, 123
Sade, Marquis de, 119
Salieri and Mozart, 140–41
Salisbury. *See* John of Salisbury
Salisbury, Lord, 44
Samuels, H. B., 38, 40–46, 48, 170n20
San Antonio Business Journal, 113
Sand, Karl Ludwig, 142
Sandby, Paul, 169n24
San Francisco Chronicle, 105
Sartoris, Giacomo, 75
Sartre, Jean-Paul: "Erostratus," 128–29, 130
Sarvastivadin school of Buddhism, 69
Sawaki (Zen master), 61
schizophrenia, 56, 84, 98
Schrader, Paul, 182n72
Schwartz, Daniel, 84
Schwob, Marcel: *Vies imaginaires* (1896), 126
Scorsese, Martin, 86, 95, 96, 182n72
Scribonius family. *See* Libo Drusus
Secolo, Il (Milan), 72
Sevada, Samuel, 160
Shaffer, Peter: *Amadeus,* 136, 140–41
Shakespeare, William, 24, 31–32, 124
Shannon, Edgar, 22
Sheffield Daily Times, 42
Shestov, Lev: "Destroying and Building,"
    154–55
Solinus, Gaius Julius, 7, 9, 167n4
Sondheim, Stephen, 93
Song of Roland, The, 155
Sonnenschein, Hugo: *The Utopia of
    Herostratos,* 145
Spiegel, Der, 85
Spielberg, Stephen, 109
Stari Most (Old Bridge), Mostar, Bosnia-
    Herzegovina, 37, 64–66, 118

Starichkova, Natalia, 114
Stirnimann, Victor-Pierre, 13–14, 69–70, 111, 120–22
Strabo, 6, 13
Sturdza, Alexandr, 142
suicide, 18, 78, 81, 89, 101, 139, 154; and Columbine, 106, 109; and destruction, 48, 112–14, 118, 121–22; Hayashi and, 55, 57, 62; of Peregrinus, 8–9, 165n23; of Salieri, 140–41
Suleiman the Magnificent, 64
Sullivan, Allen, 84
surrealist-absurd drama, 136
Sztáray, Countess Irma, 72–73

Tacitus, 17
Taliban regime, 66–69
Tarantino, Quentin, 109
Tarnopolsky, Yuri: "On Loss," 36
Taxi Driver (Scorsese), 86, 95, 96
Taylor, Maxwell, and Ethel Quayle (Terrorist Lives), xv–xviii
Taylor, Philip, 45
Telepolis, 114
Temple of Artemis (Artemision), 3–5, 13, 142, 164n11, 164n15; destruction of, 9, 16, 36, 66, 78, 113, 115, 121, 123, 156; in literature, 25, 117, 138, 144, 149–51, 154; as temple of Diana, 7–8, 18. See also Artemis, the goddess
Temple of the Golden Pavilion (Kinkaku-ji), Kyoto, 37, 49–63, 116, 171n38
temples, 3–4, 17, 19, 60–61, 111, 122
terrorism, 36, 47, 49, 104, 112, 120–22, 159; definition of international, 163n12; modern, 116, 151, 154
Thebes, 31, 125
Theobold, Archbishop of Canterbury, 21
Theopompus of Chios, 6–7, 19, 147–49
Thornley, Kerry, 85
Timaeus, 5
Time, 108–9, 114
Times of India, 67

torture, 4, 14–19, 165n36, 166n37
Twain, Mark: "The Memorable Assassination," 76–78
Twin Towers. See World Trade Center

Ulmer, Gregory L., 10
Unabomber. See Kaczynski, Ted (Unabomber)
Unamuno, Miguel de, 10, 34; Tragic Sense of Life, 152–53
urbicide terror, 118
urethral erotism: Freud and, 11–13

Vaillant, Auguste, 37
Valerius Maximus: Memorable Doings and Sayings, 6–7, 9–10, 14, 20–22, 32, 164n20
vanity as a motive, 49, 76
Vatanparvar (Patriot), 69
Vera d'Aragona, Prince Ramiero de, 74
Verri, Alessandro: La Vita di Erostrato, 2, 123–26, 128, 137–38
Vetsera, Baroness Mary, 72
video games, 106–7

Wallace, Governor George, 86–89
Washington Post, 92, 104, 133
Watergate, 90
Weidman, John, 93
West, Rebecca, 64
Wilkof, Lee, 93
Williams, Donald, 120
Wood, John Turtle, 4
World Trade Center, the, 111–22

Xerxes, wars of, 7–8, 126

Yamada (Kyoto policeman), 52–53
Yazykov, Nikolai M.: "To My Dressing Gown," 141–42
Yourcenar, Marguerite, 61–63

Zenith, Richard, 153–54
Zoja, Luigi, 120